# A STUDENT'S GUIDE
# TO CREATIVE WRITING

Part One
SHORT FICTION

# Naomi Long Madgett

Eastern Michigan University

Penway Books
Detroit

Library of Congress Catalog Number: 79-93055
ISBN: 0-916418-24-3

PENWAY BOOKS
*(The instructional division of Lotus Press)*

Post Office Box 21607
Detroit, Michigan 48221

# Contents

# Preface

While a number of helpful books on the writing of fiction or poetry have been published within recent years, I have found few to be even partially satisfactory for my own classroom needs. In fact, they are usually not designed to be textbooks in the first place. Many of these books concentrate on one genre or the other, not both. Most are also written for the beginning or more experienced writer who is working toward a goal of commercial success or seeking to sharpen already mastered skills. This is the person who frequents writers' conferences, subscribes to at least one writers' magazine, and in other ways has demonstrated an interest in learning or perfecting his literary skills.

Most college textbook publishers do not publish any book which is concerned primarily with the writing techniques commonly called "creative". Those few books which are so designed usually include more general kinds of information as well, and are not as detailed as they might be on the writing of short stories and poetry, in particular. Books which concentrate on these genres are usually not as writer-oriented as they are reader-oriented, many being anthologies which present and sometimes help the student to analyze a collection of professionally written material. While much can be learned from them, they just do not go far enough.

In my years of conducting classes in imaginative or creative writing on the university level, I have found a need for the kind of book that this one intends to be. It is designed with my own students in mind and attempts to satisfy many of the needs of my own classes. Students who elect to take this course may be highly motivated and creative persons who enjoy writing, do it well, and wish to explore the possibilities of pursuing a writing career, either full-time or on a free-lance basis. The majority of them, however, do not fall into this category. They may be English majors or minors, upperclassmen who are required to take one of several writing classes, and this one, according to the catalogue description, sounds the least tedious. Or they may be majors in other departments who simply enjoy the challenge of such a class. They may be only fair writers, sometimes quite marginal ones, who have simply come along for the ride. Perhaps I have taught them in another class and they are paying me the compliment of wishing to continue their study with me. They might easily be intimidated by the reading of professionally written stories which they cannot hope to duplicate, but they are willing to try something at which they can hope to attain some degree of success. The results each semester may run the gamut from several publishable stories to many bumbling efforts which have some strong points but are generally unimpressive. Nevertheless, I have been encouraged semester after semester by the consistent improvement — sometimes quite dramatic — observable within just one term. Critical comments of first drafts, offered by instructor and other students, often contribute to vast improvement in the final draft.

It is the intention of this book, therefore, to provide enough guidance for the capable and highly-motivated student to improve his skills, and at the same time to encourage the less talented student to work toward success within the scope of his limitations. For this purpose, appendices have been included to present the work of college students rather than established authors. Here are models which are more reasonable and accessible to the average student than the literature they are accustomed to reading in textbooks. It is my hope that the instructor who uses this book will not only assign it as reading but will also discuss each example of writing and analyze with the students its strengths and weaknesses. Suggested activities are also provided as an indication of what might be done to stimulate an interest in the techniques discussed throughout the book.

The observations, guidelines, and suggestions which I have included have come from such a wealth of sources — including my own experiences and observations as a writer and teacher — that it is impossible to credit the sources. They have become such an integral part of my consciousness that I would be at a complete loss to tell where and from whom I first learned that one method works better than another, or that a particular skill can be learned best by following this or that procedure. A half century of writing and publication, the ingestion of hundreds, perhaps even thousands, of articles offering helpful suggestions to writers, my attendance at and participation in numerous writers' conferences, and the many writers' workshops of which I have been a part have left me with some lasting impressions, whose sources (often duplicated and reinforced) I have forgotten, but whose substance has lingered with me through the years.

In this time of increased awareness of the rights of women, the use of the generic "he" bothers me. Why should the pronoun denoting the male be accepted as the standard, with females being relegated to a secondary position? Certainly the long acceptance of the pronoun *he* to denote both male and female members of society is discriminatory and unjust. In writing this book, I had to consider how I would handle this matter. Would I use the cumbersome "he or she" combination in every sentence? Could I shorten this by writing "(s)he" whenever the sex was not specified, and risk getting involved in the reflexive "him/herself" construction? After much deliberation, I came to the conclusion that such efforts to rebel against the long-accepted pronoun would distract unnecessarily from the content of the material and would be so awkward as to become ludicrous at times. I have elected, then, for want of a solution, to go along with tradition until such time as some less awkward and cumbersome alternative becomes available, at the same time emphasizing that I do not for a moment overlook the individuality of womankind or minimize her contributions to the cultural growth and development of modern civilization.

I wish to ackowledge the help which I have received on this book. I am indebted to the English Department at Eastern Michigan University and those individuals or committees which agreed to grant me leave time for this project. I am also grateful to my students in English 335 (Imaginative Writing) for the clarity of their vision and their general helpfulness and cooperation. I owe a special word of thanks to those students who generously granted me permission to include their work: Craig Hamann for his story, "Passing Through"; Linda Decker for her story, "Rites of Passage"; "Parth Galen" (a pen-name) for his story, "Wasted"; Kimberly Liedel for her photograph; Dan McClory for his story, "Pickin' Apples"; Ann Michelle Morgan for her story, "To Look the Other Way"; Lori Schaefer for three untitled poems; Renée Walton Schwall for four untitled poems and her story, "Early Winter," Kathleen Slayden for her story, "Acceptance," Saulte Declercq for her poems, "Touch-Clear — The Shaking Off," "Touch-Clear — The Taking Hold," "Our Children," "Pocket Girl," "Boa," and "Moon-Child," and John Reinhard for his poems, "Spying on a Woman Swimming Nude in Lake Superior," "Before the Snow," "Dark Martha Works in a Greasy Spoon," "Oh, Could Cheryl Ferguson Dangle," and "Walking the River." Three additional students permitted me to use their work. They are Hilton Neale, a student at University of Detroit, whose story, "Cast the First Stone" appears here, Cynthia L. Robinson, a student at Hampton Institute, whose story, "Come the Moon," is also a part of the appendices, and Cornelia Withers, a student at Michigan State University, whose poem, "Dawn," is included. I am equally grateful to other students whose in-class exercises in poetry are included.

Grateful acknowledgment is made to the following professional poets for permission to reprint their poems: James A. Emanuel for "The Negro" from *The Treehouse and Other Poems* (Detroit: Broadside Press, 1968); May Miller for "June Has Gone" and "The Scream" from *Dust of Uncertain Journey* (Detroit: Lotus Press, 1975); and Dudley Randall for "Ballad of Birmingham" from *Cities Burning* (Detroit: Broadside Press, 1968). Poems by Naomi Long Madgett are from the following sources: "When I Was Young" from *Songs to a Phantom Nightingale* (New York: Fortuny Press, 1941); "Tree of Heaven" from *Star by Star* (Detroit: Harlo Press, 1965); "Offspring" and "Grand Circus Park" from *Pink Ladies in the Afternoon* (Detroit: Lotus Press, 1972); and "Conquest" and "Washerwoman" from *Exits and Entrances* (Detroit: Lotus Press, 1978). The excerpt concerning the revision of "Grand Circus Park" is from "By Fools Like Me" by Naomi Long Madgett in *Goal-Making for English Teachers* edited by Henry B. Maloney (Champaign, Ill.: National Council of Teachers of English, 1973).

I also wish to thank Professor John Schmittroth for his example in the guidance of students in Creative Writing classes and the members of Detroit Women Writers for the sharing of their knowledge and experience over the years.

March, 1980

Naomi Long Madgett
Professor
Department of English Language
    and Literature
Eastern Michigan University
Ypsilanti, Michigan

Part One
SHORT FICTION

## Chapter 1

## Developing a Character

Of the various elements which make up a piece of fiction, characterization is probably the single most important one. It is therefore recommended that the development of the main character come before any other consideration.

A common mistake in writing is to begin with a plot and then attempt to create a character who will fit into it. A number of stories are conceived in just that way, but their value as literature is often questionable. Plot and character should be seen as inseparable considerations since serious readers are interested in characters performing actions rather than in the actions alone. While action-centered fiction satisfies the tastes of many who read on a superficial level, it is the purpose of this book to guide students toward a more complex and ultimately satisfying kind of writing than can be achieved by letting the tail wag the dog. If the story is important enough to tell, it is important enough to require a fully thought out and credible character. Such a character can then determine what direction the plot will take.

In order to help you create a three-dimensional main character, a list of questions is provided as the basis of a literary case study. You may think of other questions to add. Certainly the short story in which this emerging character may appear will not describe him in all the details covered here; in fact, only a small fraction of this information will become a *direct* part of your narrative. But if you are tempted to ask, "Why should I do all this work, then, if I'm not going to use it in my story?" keep in mind that, unless a character really lives in *your* mind, you will never make him come alive in the minds of your readers. Although you will not make direct references to all the details of this complex personality, simply knowing what those details are will permit you to write about your protagonist with depth, understanding, and authority. If your knowledge of him is superficial, your portrayal of him on paper will also be superficial, unconvincing, and even sometimes contradictory. If you want your audience to believe in the existence of this person, you will need to have a thorough knowledge of him and a full understanding of what makes him tick.

### IDENTIFICATION

The first advice, then, is to decide who the main character, the protagonist, is. (He is the one who faces a seemingly insurmountable problem and will take some significant action to try to solve it.) Is this character male or female? How old? What is his ethnic or racial background? With what religion, if any, does he identify? What is his socio-economic level?

Where will you find him? He could be yourself, a family member, or an acquaintance. There is no need to be afraid to write about yourself, assuming that everyone will recognize you and know that the story is really about your own life. Many stories are highly autobiographical, and there is no reason to avoid including your own experiences in your writing. But if you keep in mind that you are creating fiction and not writing an autobiographical sketch, it will soon become apparent that the true story is only a beginning point for the fictional one that will develop as you become more and more involved in the writing process. A living person — yourself or anyone else who serves as your model — is far too complex a personality in real life to be reduced to the comparative simplicity which a short story demands. As you write, you will begin to refine your real-life model, eliminating all the irrelevant personality traits that have no bearing on the particular problem with which the story deals. You will then find yourself embellishing, reinforcing, and adding to the traits that *are* relevant, creating new scenes from your imagination rather than your experience. Soon you will discover that the character really isn't *you* any more — or your neighbor, spouse, sister, roommate, or best friend — but someone *like* that model, now moving in his own fictional world completely independent of the way things really were or are in *your* world.

Of course, if your model *is* someone you know, you will certainly wish to be cautious in choosing his name so as to avoid any possible identification by others who may know him.

A word of caution is in order regarding the use of real-life models; it is very difficult to be objective about those to whom we are very close. It is not always possible to see the truth about them, especially unpleasant aspects of it, and it is therefore advisable for some writers to confine their characters to persons who are only casually known or completely made up persons who have no recognizable connection with anyone real. Wherever your character begins, be prepared to give him a life independent of real life.

## ENVIRONMENT

Once you have selected your character, create a present environment for him. Where does he live and with whom? Spouse, lover, family members, or alone? In what kind of city, neighborhood, and street does he live? What kind of house or apartment? How many rooms does he occupy? How are they furnished? What kinds of reading material, wall hangings, music, or recreational material would be apparent to a visitor? Are his living quarters clean, orderly, well cared for? Overly so? If not, to what degree of order are they kept? Are any areas outstanding in their appearance — junkier than others, better kept, showing more traffic? What do his bedroom and bathroom, in particular, look like? What about the kitchen?

## HISTORY

Now give your character a past life. When and where was he born? How many other children were in the family? What sex were they? What was his position of birth — eldest child, middle or youngest? Where did he live during childhood? What kind of neighborhood was it? Did his parents live together throughout his developmental years? How did they get along with each other and with their children? What was the family's socio-economic status? Its religious preference? To what extent was the character exposed to and influenced by early religious training? What kind of schools did he attend? How successful was he in his learning experiences? What were his parents' educational backgrounds? What expectations did they have for him regarding education and career? In what vocations or professions were his parents engaged? Did they enjoy their work? What expectations did the parents have for the character's eventual marriage? Was he in contact with his grandparents? How far away did they live? How close was their relationship? What individuals in the protagonist's past life exerted the greatest influence over him? In what ways? Who were his models? As a child, what were his ambitions for his adult years?

## RELATIONSHIPS

How many friends of the same sex does the protagonist have? Of the opposite sex? What is the balance between his real friends and casual acquaintances? What is the quality of those friendships? How does he feel about his closest friends? How does he treat them? (For example, does he feel altruistic toward them, or does he exploit them?) How do his friends feel about him? Have any incidents occurred in the past to test a friendship? How does he react in a group when someone makes a derogatory remark about a person whose friendship he values?

How does he get along with each member of his family now? How did he get along with each one during his childhood and adolescence? How well does he get along with his peers, his colleagues, his neighbors, those with whom he has romantic alliances? Is he considered by others to be generally friendly and reasonably outgoing? Does he really enjoy being among people, or does he prefer to be alone? Do those who love him like him as well? Is his regard for and treatment of others consistent?

How does he feel about himself? Does he enjoy his own company? Does he approve of the kind of person he is? The answers to these questions are extremely important.

## BELIEFS AND VALUES

What does the protagonist believe and believe in? What is important to him? What are his individual truths? How does he view the nature of his world and his relationship to it? What does he believe to be the purpose and value of life? What is he living for? What are his immediate and ultimate goals and ambitions? Who are his models? Why? How does he feel about death? If he has lost someone close in death, how does he explain the experience and the meaning of it all? Who or what does he see as the supreme influence on his life? God? Astrology? Hard work? Luck? The ability to outwit others? Does he believe in an afterlife? If so, what does he think it will be like? What does he see as "the good life" and the ideal way to live? What are his biases and prejudices? What does he like and dislike? When is he happiest? Most relaxed? Most uncomfortable?

## APPEARANCE

What does this character look like? Does he classify himself as attractive, average, homely, or something else? How do others classify him on the scale of physical attractiveness? What features of face and physique distinguish him from others? What is the color and texture of his hair? How does he wear it? Is it worn in the latest style, perhaps, or one that is strictly his own? Is he fairly average in build or somewhat (or very) tall, short, slim, or heavy? Is he satisfied with his general appearance — facial features, hair, build? If not, how would he like to change them? Does he have some distinguishing mark, such as a mole, an unruly eyebrow, eyes that always squint, a one-sided smile, a tendency to blush easily, a foot that turns slightly inward, stubby fingers, a mouth that turns down at one corner, a lock of hair that never is in place? (It is just such individual traits which will help a fictional character to come alive. Don't overlook them.)

How does your character walk? (A person's walk is a highly individual characteristic which may suggest something quite significant about his personality.) How does he talk? What is the pitch and tone of his voice? What is the tempo of speech? Does he speak with a regional accent? Is there anything unusual about his vocabulary? Does he use standard English most of the time? Does he use some words or expressions that are typically his own?

What particular mannerisms or visible habits set him apart from others? Does he always lick his lips, for example, whenever he is getting ready to tell a lie? Does he always tell funny jokes with a straight face? Does he tap nervously with a pencil or pen when he is in deep thought, or unconsciously pull the joints of his fingers to make them pop? Does he mumble under his breath when he is trying to figure something out? Here again, such individual habits are extremely helpful in creating a character who is unlike any other.

How does he dress? While clothes do not *make* the man or woman, they certainly do proclaim a great deal about the person who wears them. The clothing itself, as well as the way it is worn, is another important detail to explore.

## PERSONALITY CATCH-ALL

What descriptive words are most appropriate for your protagonist? How would you sum him up in just a few words? Are there any other things you can think of to indicate who he is, what he is like, and why he is the way he is? Unless you now have a complete mental image of him, unless he really exists for you and is as close as your closest friend, you will need to give him a great deal more thought before going on with your story idea. It may be that the character you have chosen just will not work for you and, painful as the task may be, perhaps you should discard him entirely and look for another subject.

## WHAT'S IN A NAME?

As you are thinking about your character, a name may come to mind. Consider whether that name fits that personality as well as it should. An appropriate name is an additional way of creating the kind of character that you have in mind. It is not — at least, it should not be — simply a handle. Without being too obvious, it is possible to select last names, as well as given names, that suggest certain personality traits. (The name of Cyrus Steele is particularly suitable for the main character in "Cast the First Stone" in the appendix. It suggests a coldness and rigidity which mark the man.) Suggestive names, however, should not be so obvious as to be ludicrous, unless that is the effect intended.

## EXERCISES

1. (Written) Using the foregoing questions as a guide, write an analysis or case study of a character who you feel would make an interesting protagonist of a short story. Be sure to include some information under each of the categories discussed: identification, environment, history, relationships, beliefs and values, and appearance. Also provide a name. It is not necessary to write this information in complete sentences; an outline or notes will do.
2. (Written) In an exchange of papers, read the character analysis written by one of your classmates. On a separate sheet of paper, answer the following questions: (1) How well do you feel you know the character from what has been written? (2) What do you feel was omitted that you would like to know? (3) Is the character real and believable to you? If so, what information was particularly helpful? If not, what can you suggest to make the character come more alive? (4) In just one sentence, what problem(s) can you

foresee that this character might face?

3. (Oral) In the class as a whole, or in groups of about four students, read aloud one or several of the written character analyses and describe this character's reactions in the following situations: (1) He is killing time before a job interview by entering a strange coffee shop. (Describe his manner of entering the shop. Tell where he chooses to sit if there are booths and tables available. Describe what goes on in his mind as he waits to be served or drinks his coffee.) (2) He is being considered for a promotion on his job, along with a co-worker with whom he is on friendly terms. They meet in the supervisor's office prior to the final interviews before the selection is made and are left alone for about fifteen minutes as they wait to be called. (Describe the conversation that takes place between the protagonist and his competitor. Relate his thoughts.) (3) If the protagonist is male, assume that he is at a disco with his girlfriend and a strange man comes to their table and makes an insulting remark about his date. Or assume that the protagonist is the female in the same situation and her male escort simply ignores the remark. What happens next? (4) Create your own situation and discuss the probable reactions of the protagonist.

## METHODS OF CHARACTERIZATION

The best advice that can be given about the portrayal of characters is: "Don't tell; show." That sounds simple, but it is not always easy to do. Our natural tendency is to describe someone through our own vision and expect our listener or reader to take our word for it. But if the character is to become lifelike and vivid to the reader, then the reader must be able to see him for himself and make his own judgment. The writer must go beyond straight narration, beyond the mere telling, to the showing. Through dramatization — permitting the character to act out the way he is, or letting other characters demonstrate his traits — rather than narration alone, the reader becomes an eye-witness. Of course, some telling must be done in the story for the sake of economy, if for no other reason, but it should be in conjunction with more indirect methods of revealing character.

Let us take some examples of direct (telling, narration) and indirect (showing, dramatization) characterization from a short story by Crawford Weeks entitled, "All That Glitters". These excerpts do not represent the entire story and are not in sequence, so the plot cannot be pieced together from them, but they will demonstrate the point.

### Direct Method: Describing the Character

*Rod was the smartest and most handsome member of his class at Maynard College. His excellence showed in everything he undertook, including academic achievement, sports, and success with girls. Most of his female peers considered him equal at least to Apollo because of his masculine build, his golden, naturally curly hair, and his incomparable and somehow suggestive smile. But while many admired him in an objective way, vying with each other for an opportunity to be seen with him, even in the most casual conversation, few, if they ever thought about it, would admit that they really liked him. It was obvious that he was more interested in himself than in anyone else and spent a considerable part of his time preparing his face and form for public display and admiration.*

*They would have been less likely to seek his favor if they had known in what detail he described his female conquests to other men on campus, embellishing truth with his own inventiveness. Among other males he had the reputation of a show-off, a cad, and a phony.*

### Indirect Methods

### 1. *REVEALING THE CHARACTER THROUGH HIS SURROUNDINGS*

*The bathroom was unusually spacious and bright. On one wall was a large leaded glass window. A colorful stained glass design occupied the middle sections, permitting the bright sunshine to burst through in many-hued rays. In addition to this abundance of natural light, bright fluorescent lamps blazed on either size of a great spotlessly-gleaming sliding mirror.*

*A sense of golden brilliance dominated the room. The yellow tiles reflected it. The thick gold and white bath towels bore testimony. No matter that several of these lay in sodden heaps in the middle of the floor. No matter that the dressing table and toilet top were littered with a profusion of empty beer cans, spilled lotion bottles, and capless toothpaste tubes with part of their contents oozing out, or that a stench of half-smoked cigarettes rose from the soap dish where they had been mashed out. It was still somehow a room in which a golden splendor triumphed over an impression of benign and forgivable decay.*

## 2. SHOWING THE CHARACTER IN ACTION

*Rod emerged fully dressed from his bedroom, took one backward glance at the unmade bed and clothing scattered wherever it had fallen, and quickly slammed the door behind him. He paused in front of a full-length mirror and stared at himself. He turned to check his left profile, patting his hair for the third time, and then turned again to view his frontal image. Then he thrust his right hand into his trouser pocket, but thinking better of it, removed it. Giving himself an approving smile, he turned away reluctantly and started toward the door.*

*As he passed the table just inside the front door, he flicked a speck of dust from the large portrait of himself in cap and gown. It was arranged in such a way that the lamplight fell directly upon the curly golden hair, a large mass of which protruded from the confinements of the cap. Turning the switch, he opened the door and stepped casually into the carpeted hallway.*

## 3. LETTING THE CHARACTER TALK

*"So jus' don't bug me about it, man, okay? When I get some bread I'll get the damn' thing fixed. But I don't know what you're so uptight about; that thing's just a heap o' junk anyways. If ya gotta be so damn' fussy about other people drivin' your car, ya shouldn't leave the car keys layin' aroun' while you're tryin' to make out with some broad. Man, as much as I've done for you, I don't see what you got to complain about."*

## 4. REVEALING THE CHARACTER'S THOUGHTS

*He remembered the incident and felt suddenly ashamed and old. He knew--had really always known, he supposed--what was behind it all. Again he saw his father's face, angry and disapproving, rejecting him, marvelling at his unworthiness. Why was it, he wondered, that he could never seem to please the man? Again he heard the intonations of his father's voice ridiculing him, snarling the "Junior" as if it were a curse. "Gerald Burnett, Jr.," he said aloud, emphasizing the last word. What if the girls knew who he really was--not the dashing, handsome Rod they chased after, but his father's despised son? Angrily he swept his hand across the desk sending everything flying to the floor.*

## 5. LISTENING TO WHAT OTHERS SAY TO THE CHARACTER

*"Sure, Rod, you're right, I really do want to go. I've been dreaming about it for weeks. But it suddenly came to me the other night--when you said what you did about doing favors--that I didn't want to go with you. Yeah, sure, I enjoy your company--to a point. And yes, I know you can probably get any girl you want--well, almost. So maybe I should feel lucky you chose me--but somehow, I don't. See, I don't like to be the recipient of favors--yours or anyone else's. Maybe I'm the one that's been doing you the favors all this time and you never even knew it. 'Cause you do and say all the right things, you know, but Baby, that's ice water you got runnin' through your veins."*

## 6. LISTENING TO WHAT OTHERS SAY ABOUT THE CHARACTER

*"What shall I say on this recommendation?" Ms. Williams asked. "I've checked out his grade point average and the other records. Everything's in order."*

*"Fine, fine," replied the dean, tapping his fingers absently on the edge of the desk. "Well," he said. Then again, "Well. I guess we have to say something, don't we, Ms. Williams? Mr. Burnett is a--well, how can I say it?--a rather difficult young man to pin down. He has all the necessary qualifications--more than he needs, really--and yet, one gets the feeling that--What is it? I don't want to let my personal impressions weigh too heavily. But--what is it, Ms. Williams? I can't quite put my finger on it, can you?"*

## 7. SHOWING THE REACTIONS OF OTHERS TO THE CHARACTER

*Jack could hardly believe that Rod was actually apologizing. Imagine Mr. Wonderful himself admitting that he was wrong! He glanced quickly at Kevin to get his reaction; he wore the same I-never-thought-I'd-live-to-see-the-day look on his roommate's face that his own face must have shown. Well, maybe tigers DID sometimes lose their stripes!*

## 8. SHOWING THE CHARACTER'S REACTIONS TO OTHERS

*What a jerk, he thought. What an impossible, incredible jerk--with that stupid out-of-style jacket and those baggy pants that hit his shoes at least an inch above where they belonged. "Highwaters," somebody had called them. That was good: high waters; a flood of ignorance and poor taste. Wouldn't you think that someone in his position would at least know how to dress and not look like a funny-paper character?*

## PORTRAYING MINOR CHARACTERS

What we have been saying in the foregoing pages about developing a three-dimensional or well-rounded character, a character whom we know and can therefore portray in considerable depth, applies only to the main character, the protagonist, who has a problem and tries to solve it within the confines of a short story. Minor characters cannot and should not be dealt with in the same way. In the first place, there is not space enough in a short story to develop other characters in depth, and even if we took the time to do it, we would then have as many other plots as we had characters — the making of a novel. A short story deals with only one plot — a single character with a single goal which is blocked by some obstacle.

Minor characters are kept fairly simple, as a rule, and one-dimensional. It is not advisable to develop them in depth except to the extent that they affect the actions and reactions of the protagonist. For example, if the main character's obstacle is another person — that is, if the conflict involves a clash of two personalities — then we need to have enough background information on the conflicting character, and he must be dealt with in sufficient depth, so that the problem facing the protagonist is clear enough for understanding and credibility.

### Individualizing a Minor Character

A mere walk-on character does not have to be described in any depth at all. Other minor characters, who may not be crucial to the action but are nevertheless a necessary part of it, may be treated superficially; yet, they must be individualized in some way if they are to come alive and be believable and realistic. One proven method of individualizing a minor character is borrowed from the cartoonist. Consider the artist's method when he creates a caricature. He depends largely on exaggeration of one or two features, so that the person being caricaturized is recognizable, but his features are out of proportion. The writer may borrow this method, as great writers have done for hundreds of years, to make a minor character seem real and completely unlike any other character in the world, not merely a *type*. Think, for a moment, of caricatures you have seen of recent American presidents. Notice which facial features have been drawn out of proportion.

Your purpose in caricaturing a minor character in a story will not be for humor or satire, however, but to make him unique, to make him stand out from other characters as an individual. You may introduce a character, for example, by describing him as "a squat little man whose eyes seemed too close together and whose fingers reminded one somehow of claws." Or you may describe a woman with "a nervous voice that ran up and down the scale like a comic song." Whenever you refer to this character in the story, making reference to the original description will be an effective way of insuring the individuality of that character.

Another way of achieving this goal is by making him imperfect. (This method is useful for the main character, as well.) To say that a young woman "would have been beautiful beyond belief except for the mark above her right eye which gave her a continually quizzical look," or that "he had an annoying habit of repeating the last few words of everything you said," is to insure that your minor character will come through as a distinctive individual, even though he is not dealt with in depth.

### Handling a Crowd

Occasionally, it is necessary to include a fairly large number of characters. The protagonist, for instance, might be the leader of a teenage gang, consisting of fifteen or twenty young men. Should all of them be named, identified, or described? Absolutely not! Your story would become so unwieldy that you would give up quickly in despair. Even if you were writing a novel, it would be a mistake to try to include so many personalities. In a short story, you are even more limited. Yet, it is helpful to know the approximate number of persons that make up the group.

One way to deal with this problem is to select two or three persons in the group, give them names and individualize them, and let the others remain anonymously in the background. It will be sufficient, then, for the reader to know that twelve or fifteen other people were also involved.

It is important, however, to avoid "concert actions" and "the everybody syndrome". People do not operate like Siamese twins, thinking, acting, and reacting in perfect unison. Even in violent mobs, where actions seem to be simultaneous and unified, each individual is acting for himself. It is more realistic to show one or two characters cheering, booing, laughing, or running, and then indicate that others joined in this action, than to take the easier way out and simply say, "Everybody laughed." Even in a mob scene, concentrate on the reactions of several individual characters whose comments and actions are indicative of the mood of the whole crowd rather than on the crowd itself as one nameless mass. Such characters do not have to be named; they can simply be "a man in overalls holding a small child on his shoulders" or "a determined-looking girl holding on to the arm of a young man."

### Controlling Numbers

Many inexperienced writers have the tendency to admit too many characters into their stories. In most cases, three or four identified characters should be the limit in a short story. (Some stories require even fewer.) All of them should be absolutely necessary to the story in some way. Sometimes it is possible to eliminate extra characters by combining two or three into one. If you have a series of actions performed by three people which could just as easily be performed by one, ask yourself, "Are these other characters really necessary to this story?" Each character should have a definite — and necessary — reason for being there. If the story would not be changed in any important way if he were taken out, then by all means, eliminate him. Each character must be able to justify his presence. Think of him as a paid actor in a live stage performance; assume you are paying him by the hour. Is he earning his money, or is he just an "extra"? Is he worth what he is being paid to keep him on hand? Keep the number of characters to the fewest that you can get by with.

Sometimes a character who is important to the story is nevertheless "offstage" most of the time. His influence may be great, but his physical presence may not be necessary. If this is the case with one of your characters, consider the possibility of having all the information about him which is necessary to the action introduced indirectly, perhaps through the dialogue of other characters. In this way, his presence will be felt, but he will never have to be brought "on stage" as an actual character.

### Avoiding Confusion

The naming of characters can be important, as was mentioned earlier. Concerning minor characters, avoid the possible confusion that can result from the wrong names. It is difficult enough to individualize them without robbing them of their identity by a confusion of names.

One way to avoid this confusion is to be consistent in what a character is called throughout the story. While the protagonist may be called William by his mother and Bill by his peers, it is not advisable to offer alternate names with minor characters. If you begin with the nickname Chuck, let this minor character remain Chuck throughout, not Charles sometimes, Charlie, or Mr. Williams.

Another way to avoid confusion is to make sure that your characters do not have similar names. Names beginning with the same consonant, such as Donna, Della, and Dottie; names with similar endings, such as Toni, Sherri, and Luci; names that rhyme, such as Nick and Dick; or names of the same length, such as Burt and Tod, may require the reader to search back to earlier parts of the story to learn which character is indicated. There is no justification for setting up this kind of unnecessary difficulty for the reader.

## DESCRIPTION WITH A PURPOSE

Description for its own sake should be avoided. Unless it serves a specific purpose, it should be considered superfluous. One very useful purpose of description of a character is to reveal personality. It is meaningless to describe the color of a person's hair or eyes unless something unusual about them helps us to understand how he perceives himself or how others perceive him. Unless these features reveal something of the character's conceit or sense of shame, for example, it is needless to mention them. It may be helpful to describe the way the person wears his hair to indicate perhaps that he is stylish, extreme in his habits, conservative, bold, or mousey. The way he uses his eyes, or their habitual or occasional expression, tells us more about his disposition than their color reveals. The color of his eyes is meaningless, unless they are described as "cold blue", "earth brown", "steel gray", or something similar. Descriptions of height, weight, and body build are often useless, but if such descriptions tell something about the personality, then they may be used to good advantage.

Clothing, too, can be used effectively to reveal personality. When it is described, it should usually be for this purpose, not for its own sake. Clothes, we repeat, do not *make* the person but do reveal a great deal about the one who wears them. Avoid extremes (you do not want to create a stereotype), but do describe the meaningful and relevant details of clothing that will help the reader know the wearer better.

Description, in addition to revealing character, may suggest mood. A writer may describe a character indirectly or set a mood for his behavior by letting the reader see his surroundings. A person of cheerful disposition may be shown in a cheerful setting, with vivid yellow and orange and plentiful sunlight surrounding him. The room he occupies may be in complete disorder (which, in itself, should tell us something), but the disorder itself may be cheerful and bright. The time of day or night and a description of weather conditions may suggest that the character is in a sunny, pleasant, reflective, capricious, or troubled mood, or that the events to come are hopeful or unfortunate.

The writer who learns to include description for a useful purpose, a good reason other than that he writes it well or likes the way it sounds, has a powerful tool in his possession, but he must be aware that this power is dulled if it is overused or used for the wrong reasons. When description becomes superfluous, the reader's interest begins to wander, and it is difficult to recapture it.

Descriptions are often more effective when they are introduced indirectly at various natural points throughout the story as the need arises than in one big chunk at or near the beginning.

## AVOIDING VALUE JUDGMENTS

It has been said that "beauty is in the eye of the beholder." What is, therefore, *beautiful* or *just* or *interesting* or *true* to the writer may not be considered so by the reader. Such descriptions are inexact in that they are highly subjective and have to do with one person's system of values. Don't expect the reader to take your word for it when you describe a character as "weird" or "phony", or a situation as "dull" or "unfair". This advice goes back to our earlier observation about showing and telling. It is best to describe a person or situation in such a way that the reader can see him or it for himself and come to his own conclusion. If you do your job well as a writer, he will reach the conclusion you intend him to reach, but the knowledge will be his own, not a second-hand opinion, and he will believe in it.

If you want to indicate that a character is eccentric, conservative, narrow-minded, or what have you, place him in several situations in which his eccentricism, conservatism, or narrow-mindedness becomes apparent from his actions, reactions, thoughts, or words.

## DEALING WITH AGE

It is a general misconception that writing about children is easy; it is, in fact, one of the most difficult kinds of writing to do. Recreating the child's mind and vision and accurately reproducing his vocabulary requires a rare insight, indeed, and few adult writers are capable of capturing on paper the essence of childhood. Yet adults do write children's stories, many of which are highly successful, so this comment is not meant as discouragement, only as a warning that the task is not as easy as it often seems.

Equally difficult is the depiction of any age more advanced than the writer has personally experienced, either by having attained that age himself, or by living in close proximity and being capable of empathizing with an older person. It is a rare child, indeed, who can walk in his own mother's or father's shoes; he is too close to the problem to view it with objectivity. Indeed, he often *is* the problem and will not gain any real insight until he is himself a parent.

Dealing with old age is a different matter. What constitutes middle age or old age to twenty-year-olds is interesting in itself, and often inaccurate. The danger of insufficient knowledge is likely to lead to stereotypes. Relying on television depictions of an eighty-year-old man or a fifty-five-year-old woman signals trouble. There is little in television drama that provides a true picture of real-life people, and to base your view of what it is like to be fifty, sixty, seventy, or eighty years old on these presentations is a mistake. If you write about what you know from your own experience, you will be better off than if you depend on second-hand experience. If you have had first-hand experience with older people, you are qualified to write about them, and what you have to say may make a very meaningful contribution to new insight and understanding of this neglected and misunderstood age group.

It is important, early in your story, to provide some clues to the age of your character. This is not to suggest that a paragraph or two be set aside for the purpose of discussing age, but rather that a hint be dropped to indicate the age group fairly early. (It is seldom necessary to include exact age information, except where the age itself is an issue. Then the information can be included indirectly in dialogue or in some other unobtrusive way.) Unless the reader is able to infer a general age group accurately, he may be jolted unnecessarily later on to learn that the man he assumed was college age is actually a grandfather. Remember that information indirectly introduced is often more effective than that which is pointedly stated.

## INTRODUCING A NEW CHARACTER

When a new character comes on the scene, the reader should meet him as he would in real life — not in great depth, but in terms of a few momentary impressions. Some brief physical description may be in order here, especially the features that are most striking to one seeing him for the first time. The first impression is all that one needs to see, not an in-depth examination. Further description should be subtle and should include only those impressions that matter to the story. (Those impressions, if reported from the point of view of another character, need not be accurate. The character reporting the impressions may later refer to his first impressions and reinterpret them in light of new knowledge.)

## A FINAL WORD

A believable character is *consistent* in his behavior. His actions are always "in character". He does not come up with surprises, actions that are not in keeping with what the reader knows of him.

A believable character is also *motivated* to do whatever he does. If there is a change in his behavior or attitude, as there often is in the protagonist, sufficient reason is shown for that change.

Furthermore, a believable character is *plausible*. Real, live people are neither saints nor monsters. They are a combination of positive and negative forces, with one or the other side winning out, but they are not all bad or all good.

Characters can be described as either "flat" or "round", depending upon the degree of depth to which they are developed. A "round" character is complex and many-sided, as the protagonist should be. A "flat" character is characterized by one or two traits and can be summed up in a single sentence, as most of the minor characters are.

Both types are necessary to fiction, each character being handled in enough depth to justify his role in the story. Even the flattest character, however, can be individualized, as has been mentioned before, so that his personality is unique.

Characters can also be described as "static" and "developing". A static character does not change in any significant way from beginning to end. Usually, the protagonist is a developing character, in that he does make a change — not necessarily a very obvious one, but a change, nevertheless. That change may be only a new awareness of what the problem is, or a decision to change the course of his behavior. Whatever the change may be, it should be within the possibility of that character; it must be sufficiently motivated by the circumstances in which the protagonist finds himself; and there must be sufficient time for that change to take place.

## SUMMARY

The creation of the main character should be the writer's first consideration. The plot will then grow logically from the character created. Before any writing is done (other than note-taking), the protagonist should be thoroughly thought through.

The writer should explore his own family and acquaintances for models, remembering that the character which will eventually evolve will bear only a partial resemblance to the original model.

The main character should be revealed through indirect means, through more showing than telling.

Minor characters may be individualized through minor flaws and by the avoidance of confusion through sound-alike names.

Characters should be kept to the minimum number possible.

Individual actions should be reported when a crowd is involved.

Only those aspects of physical appearance and dress which help to reveal character should be included.

Value-judgments should be avoided.

Only first-hand experience with various age groups should be considered as a solid basis for reporting on them.

New characters should be introduced in the same way that they appear in real-life situations.

The changes in the protagonist should be consistent, motivated, and plausible.

Chapter 2

## Following the Road Map

To many writers, the necessity of having to think of a plot is the most frightening aspect of creating a short story. The first inclination is to look for something different and new — something far removed from the humdrum of everyday and the typical fare of the soap opera. But the truth is that there are only a few plots to be found in fiction; one can change the time and place and add variations here and there, but the basic plot has been used over and over again from the earliest days of storytelling to the present. There is, indeed, nothing new under the sun, as far as plots are concerned. It is the finer points of storytelling, not the plot, that make the difference and create from an old idea freshness and originality. If an entire class were given a plot outline and told to write a story based on it, there would be such wide variations that many readers would not recognize the basic similarities. If a plot seems stale and overused, it is the treatment of the plot, rather than the plot itself, which is at fault. Well-developed characters whose motivations and psychological makeup are handled with understanding and skill can be introduced into the most ordinary situations and create an unforgettable story unlike any other. It is important to realize that a plot outline can be a great help, not a ready-made hindrance to be avoided like a plague.

Some kind of action is a necessity in fiction. The plot may be intricately woven or it may be so slim as to seem nonexistent, but some movement must be involved. The action may be mental or physical, but something must happen; some series of events must take place. Otherwise, the result would be an essay, not fiction. A short piece of writing which contains only thoughts, observations, and reflections can hardly be called a short story of the traditional type.

To be sure, not all modern stories follow a rigid formula; some move forward from one point to another almost imperceptibly. Others represent a "slice of life" — perhaps a typical day (but usually a significant one) in the life of the protagonist. Perhaps the reader understands that the most important action will take place after the story ends, very likely as an outcome of what has happened — or not happened — within the story itself.

Not every student will wish to write his story according to a formula, and none should be forced to do so. But many students are grateful for the security of a road map to guide them successfully from one development to the next and on toward a solution of the original problem. It is for such students that this chapter is included. At the same time, it must be pointed out that the plot outline is basic to most stories, even many which may not seem to have one.

A plot outline represents a writer's road map. You would not think of setting out on a long journey into unknown territory without knowing which direction to go, what highway to take and where to turn off. Without a road map, you would wander aimlessly, make many wrong turns, end up on dead-end streets, and only by the sheerest luck arrive at your intended destination. A plot outline gets you started in the right direction, keeps you from making wrong turns, and guides you successfully to the end of your story.

But where does a writer look for a plot? The best answer to that is: Within his own experience. Just as the proverbial grass in the neighbor's yard looks greener than your own, the lives that other people lead (especially fictional lives) often look more interesting, too. That must mean, then, that to someone else, *your* experiences are interesting. As a writer, try looking at your own life from the outside; discover the uniqueness of it, the universality of it. The earth is populated by millions of people, but you are the only individual anywhere who possesses the experiences that you have known! Nobody on earth is more interesting that you are!

Write what you know best. You have heard that advice before because it is very good advice. Find your plot in your own life situation, past or present, or in the experiences of a close friend or family member. It's easy and it's fun.

The same advice applies to the selection of time and place. Unless you are an experienced writer who is willing to put years of research into the discovery of historical backgrounds and cultures, you cannot expect to recreate successfully and convincingly the speech patterns, manner of dress, daily habits, and numerous details of living of other times that will make your story seem true. The writer of historical fiction usually knows a great deal more about his background than he includes on the printed page, but what details are given are authentic and credible, based on years of painstaking research. The most remarkable aspect of Alex Haley's phenomenal novel, *Roots*, is perhaps his recreation of daily life among his tribal ancestors in the African village of Juffure. Skipping over details of time and place is not a reasonable alternative to dealing with them. Unless you know what you are writing about, it would be wise to avoid the terrain of Alaska during the Gold Rush or the surface of the moon or Mars. While it may be possible to fake it with many readers, there is always someone who *knows.*

When I was in my late teens living in St. Louis, I wrote the first draft of a novel. Hoping to conceal its autobiographical nature, I chose for my locale the city of Pittsburgh. I had driven through Pittsburgh once and stopped there briefly, and one similarity of the two cities remained vividly with me — their dirt. In those days, we burned soft coal in our furnaces, and the resulting soot drifted through the winter air like snowflakes and encrusted everything we used with carbon. I did not realize then that Pittsburgh's soot came from a different source and reacted altogether differently, nor did I consider the unmistakable differences in landscape, industry, speech patterns, and daily routine. Several years after completing this ill-conceived novel, I came to understand that it was futile to try to fit one city into the boundaries of another as if one were a copy of the other. No matter what similarities two locations may seem to have, one cannot be substituted for another. If I had stuck with the streets I knew so well, the local landmarks, and the kind of life I lived during those St. Louis years, I might have been able to create a work that others might have enjoyed sharing, but because I had tried to build on a false foundation, all else was doomed to crumble.

In thinking about your plot, keep in mind that a short story is not a novel. Keep it simple — and do not feel apologetic about its simplicity. Remember that you do not have the space to develop more than one plot; therefore, you will want to confine all aspects of your characters' personalities, all their actions, all their thoughts, all your description, and every sentence of dialogue to the movement of one unified plot from beginning to end.

Remember, too, that you, the writer, must maintain complete control of your material. Even though the plot may center around a real-life experience, you cease being a participant and become instead the creator-controller as soon as you begin your transfer from fact to fiction. Since you are not writing an autobiography, the facts you begin with will soon begin transforming themselves into something else entirely, so that what you finish with will not be at all the experience with which you started. While the actual truth has meaning to you, the artistic truth, which is developed in the story, will be something different. Unless you are willing to distort and change the actual truth for the sake of the artistic truth, perhaps you had better write autobiography instead of fiction.

Being in control of your material as writer, you must train yourself to be an amateur psychoanalyst, not only observing people's outward actions and spoken words, but also exploring their hidden and secret selves and interpreting the nuances of their speech, their unrecognized motives, the meaning lurking behind their smiles or frowns. If you are writing about yourself or someone close to you, this will be difficult to do because one cannot always be objective in such cases. Here is where imagination takes over as you begin to make up fictitious reasons and hidden meanings to explain certain actions.

Chapter One discussed the importance of getting to know the main character before any consideration of plot. If that has been accomplished, then the development of plot becomes simpler, for it is clear that a particular character is likely to face certain kinds of problems while another character will face very different ones. It is in these problems that the conflict lies.

## GOAL

In literature classes, most students have heard conflict in fiction discussed in terms of opposing forces: man against man, man against nature, man in turmoil with his own emotions. A simpler way of identifying the basic conflict in a story is simply to ask the question, "What does this character want that he is prevented from getting? What is standing in his way?"

The first question will identify the protagonist's goal. However, it is important to recognize that there are often two closely related goals rather than one. There is an immediate goal and an ultimate or long-term goal, a revealed goal and a hidden goal, an apparent or superficial goal and an underlying goal. Describe them however you will, the two goals are frequently there. The second one has to do with factors (often unrecognized by the character himself) explaining the first. A college freshman may want a certain expensive car so desperately (even though he has no real need for it) that he is willing to go to any length to get it, even stealing it, if necessary. The car is obviously his revealed, immediate, recognizable goal. But *why* does he want it so desperately when he has little need for *any* car, let alone this particular one? Is it because he believes this car alone will bring him the attention and favor of girls (or a particular girl) who have ignored him in the past? Or does he feel inferior to his roommates because their parents are professional and his are laborers and he feels that this car will bestow status upon him? Is his *real* goal, then, social status or attention? The protagonist may not understand why he behaves the way he does, but the writer must learn to delve deeply into the subconscious existence of his character to learn what makes him tick. The reader may share this super-knowledge, this insight into motives, with the writer, but the protagonist may never identify the source of this emotional need, or he may later gain this insight through some incident related in the story. Such new self-knowledge may well be the solution to his initial conflict.

The immediate (recognizable) goal should be indicated fairly early in the story. The very first paragraph, even, is not too early to provide some hint as to what the protagonist wants. Indirectly, through dialogue or some significant action, however small, the character may indicate his desires. The student whose goal is a new car can be shown in the opening scene, for example, browsing through a magazine and lingering over a picture of a car, perhaps tracing its outline longingly with his finger. Pictures on his bedroom wall can serve the same purpose, or he can be heard in conversation with someone on the telephone making comments about the car he would like to own. However the subject is introduced, the reader should not have to wait until the story is a fourth of the way to the finish before he knows what it is really about. Indicate fairly early what you intend the immediate goal to be. *(This advice does not apply to the long-term or hidden goal which must be revealed through subsequent action and dialogue.)*

The immediate goal must be of great importance to the protagonist. He must want what he wants almost desperately. If his interest is so mild that he merely shrugs his shoulders and gives it up if it proves too difficult to attain, then it is not strong enough to bear the weight of a story. If the goal is something quite trivial and transient, perhaps you had better think about it again and ask yourself if it is important enough to provide the basis of a short story on which you will be spending many hours of thought and hard work. The answer to that will depend on the character you are writing about. If you have developed him as a person to whom trivial concerns take on great meaning, then, by all means, you should proceed with such a goal, but before you do, be certain that you are dealing with triviality intentionally.

The immediate goal, in most cases, must appear to the protagonist to be attainable, though difficult. It may not be at all within his reach, but he does not know or will not accept this fact. Or the immediate goal may be attainable, but the ultimate goal may not be, and since the protagonist is not aware of his subconscious yearnings and cannot identify the source of his discontent, he does not recognize the futility of his quest. The ten-year-old girl who wants to visit her divorced mother in another state will act and work toward that recognized goal, believing the obstacle to be her father's unreasonable objections. She may fail to achieve her goal in the end, finding the visit itself beyond her means, or she may manage to visit her mother only to find her real problem to be that her mother does not want her. The underlying goal may then become a part of her conscious knowledge. Perhaps some compensating factor may eventually soften the cruelty of this situation, but then again, it may not. Not all life experiences have happy endings, and there is no reason that a piece of fiction must.

One final bit of advice regarding the goal: Don't lose track of what it is. As you write, that goal must be kept in mind constantly. Just as a driver must continue to answer the question, "Where am I going?", the writer, too, must keep his destination in mind or he may become hopelessly lost.

## OBSTACLE

What the protagonist wants and what prevents his getting it make up the conflict of the story. He is hell-bent on getting to a certain destination, but something or someone is blocking his way. What will he do to get around that roadblock, believing that the obstacle is surmountable?

First, *the obstacle must appear to the protagonist to be real and formidable.* It may, indeed, be a figment of his imagination, but he is not aware of that. To him, the problem is actual and difficult to solve. For example, a young woman wants more than anything else to become a doctor, but her family is in no position to help her financially, even through undergraduate school. She can see no way to obtain the necessary education to realize her life's dream; yet she feels that somehow she *must* or her life will have no meaning. This is, indeed, a real and formidable obstacle. On the other hand, a student may want desperately to excel in a certain subject so that he may qualify for certain opportunities later, but he sees as an obstacle the fact that he has never been able to make higher than average grades in this subject and believes himself incapable of doing better. This obstacle may not be as real as he perceives it to be. The reason for the mediocre grades in the past, which may have gone unrecognized, may be poor study habits or some other such problem over which the student has some control. As long as he does not realize this, however, the obstacle will appear to be very real and very strong.

Second, *the obstacle — or what the protagonist perceives to be the obstacle — should be apparent to the reader early in the story.* If there is an underlying problem of which the protagonist is unaware, the reader must be let in gradually on this secret knowledge. For example, Ted needs to make a certain grade in his English class in order to continue his financial aid or scholarship, but his instructor refuses to let him make up an exam he missed. His future action will no doubt be directed toward winning this instructor's sympathy and persuading him to change his mind. The real obstacle, it turns out, is Ted's inability to accept responsibility for his own actions, which he may discover later in the story. Let's say that he is successful in getting another chance, takes the exam, and fails it miserably. Only then does he recall that the reason he intentionally missed the exam when it was originally scheduled was that he had not studied for it. But the reader knew where the problem lay all along as he watched the student frantically gathering other students' notes and exam papers and witnessed his oversleeping on mornings when he should have been in class.

Third, *the obstacle must have a direct relationship to the goal.* This point seems so obvious that it hardly needs saying. Yet, in our experience, we have found that students occasionally lose sight of their destination and erect roadblocks that have little or no bearing on that particular road. Keep in mind that the obstacle must stand in the way of the protagonist's reaching *that* goal, not some other one.

## ACTION

It stands to reason that, if the character wants something desperately, something which he feels he can get in spite of the obstacle standing in his way, he will do something, take some action, to get around the thing standing between him and his goal. The obstacle will not go away by itself; he must do something to help himself.

*The action which the protagonist takes to get around the obstacle must have a direct relationship with what it is that he wants.* It cannot be unrelated. If you go astray on this point, the story is irretrievably lost. Here again, this relationship should be perfectly obvious, but inexperienced writers often drift from the highway and are never able to get back.

Furthermore, *the action should be performed by the protagonist,* not some outside force. Although there are a few exceptions to this rule, you will probably be on safer ground if you abide by it. It is because the character is highly motivated that he is willing to devise some way of trying to accomplish his goal. It is better if he is not simply the passive recipient of someone else's actions. It is better, also, if the action is not a coincidence that just happens at the right time.

In addition, *the action must not present such an easy solution to the problem that the story ends there.* If the obstacle is too readily removed, then it really was not so formidable, after all, and without a real problem, there is insufficient material for a story. We must assume that the easy solutions have already been tried and have failed.

Another point to keep in mind is that *the action must go beyond mere wishing or hoping or continuing what has already been tried.* It usually must be also more than just a decision to do something; it must be the action itself. Such a statement as, "She decided to keep on trying to convince him that her way was best" is not the kind of decisive action that will move a story along.

## COMPLICATION

If the action taken solves the problem right away, one is led to wonder if the problem was real in the first place. The solution comes too easily, and the reader is likely to feel cheated. The action, then, should not solve the problem but should create, instead, a new problem or complication. For example, a college senior, finding that she is pregnant, wishes to marry and raise her child in a family setting, but her boyfriend sees marriage as a drawback to his career plans and refuses to do anything but help her with an abortion, which she does not want. Having strong views on the subject, she is determined to have her way. She acts by appealing to his parents, whose religious beliefs oppose abortion. Will this solve her problem? Not likely. The chances are that this action will create new problems. The young man may be so angered that he withdraws from her completely, accusing her of such ulterior motives that she is filled with a terrible sense of guilt and self-doubt. Now, she has not only the question of her pregnancy to deal with, but her mental turmoil, as well. And so, "the plot thickens."

The complication that results from the protagonist's action must be a natural and logical consequence of that action. Be wary of introducing chance or coincidence as a complicating factor. We are dealing with a chain of cause-and-effect relationships. One part of the story hinges on the part just preceding it, which, in turn, hinges on the part just before that. If we keep that in mind as we write, we can avoid some of the unrelated occurrences that sometimes come in the writing of beginners.

## CRISIS-CLIMAX-TURNING POINT

The showdown that the foregoing action leads to is the most crucial point in the story. If you have followed the road map carefully, you will have a character who has tried to get around the obstacle that blocks him from his desired goal by doing something which, instead of solving the problem, has gotten him in deeper than he was before. Now where does he go from there?

Obviously, something must happen to turn the situation in one direction or another so that the problem can be resolved. But how do we get the protagonist out of a seemingly hopeless situation? Well, more action, of course. If it was action that complicated the problem in the first place, then further action will finally either resolve it or prove the case to be so hopeless that nothing can be done about it.

Somewhere along the way, the character may face a moment of truth. He may come to realize that what has happened to him is an indirect (or direct) result of his own folly or blindness, or perhaps someone else's. It may be at this point that the turning point is reached. On the basis of this new self-knowledge (or new understanding of another character), he will probably try to extricate himself from the predicament in which he finds himself. There is no magic formula for introducing this important moment of truth or awakening; that will depend entirely upon the kind of character that has been created and the surrounding circumstances. But however this turning point is brought in, it must be credible and real.

Here, especially, we cannot emphasize too much the danger of relying upon chance or coincidence to resolve the problem. While coincidence or chance may very well get the story into motion in the beginning, it is rarely acceptable in the later stages of the story. Killing the main character off in an accident is usually a cop-out to avoid dealing with the problem in a more logical way; if this is not true, the reader is likely to suspect that it is anyhow. Equally unacceptable is the sudden introduction of a new character who just happens to hold the solution in his hands.

The Latin term, *deus ex machina* (god from machine), refers to solution by coincidence. I recall many extreme examples of this which I witnessed as a child during Saturday movies where adventure serials were shown. One chapter would invariably end with the hero hurtling from a mountaintop, with not a savior in sight and nothing below but treacherous rocks lapped by angry ocean waves. The invitation to "come back next week" never failed to lure us back to the darkened room. The following week, the moment of doom would be flashed on the screen again. Then, just in the nick of time, as the super-hero was about to crash upon the jagged rocks below, a huge bird, or some other miraculous force, would emerge from nowhere and dive beneath him, breaking his fall and bearing him safely to the shore. This is an extreme example of *deus ex machina*, of course, but even in its modified forms, it should be avoided.

Let us say another word of caution about coincidence. The well-known observation that "truth is stranger than fiction" cannot be overstressed. Coincidences do occur in real life with amazing frequency. We could all tell stories of happenings that occurred in such a way that they were hardly believable; yet, we know for certain that they *did happen* just that way. We cannot argue with fact; but fiction is *not fact*. What we are forced to believe when we see it with our own eyes just may not be acceptable in a story that we know from the very start is fiction. Sometimes there is a great temptation to include the surprising, the bizarre, or even just the accidental happening to liven up the story; if we can testify that that happening did occur in real life, we feel justified in including it. But it just won't work. Many a potentially good story has been ruined because of the factor of incredibility; readers just will not swallow some of the things inexperienced writers sometimes try to force upon them.

Let me tell you a remarkable story which I know to be true. A teacher of my acquaintance, who was at that time probably about fifty or fifty-five years old, was accustomed to frequenting, on her lunch hour, the drugstore or five-and-ten near the high school where we both taught. She was not a particularly popular teacher, but was dedicated to her work and was known to be demanding, but fair, in her classroom. She was also considered friendly, in a gruff sort of way, and she had earned the respect of her students. It was surprising, then, to some of the young people who knew her, that she sometimes failed to return their greeting when they saw her in the neighborhood outside school. She gradually gained a reputation as a person who was friendly enough when she had to be, but really didn't want to be bothered with students on her own time.

One day, when a student spoke to her at the nearby drugstore, the woman neither returned the greeting nor looked blank (a reaction which had been reported by others), but surprised the young person by asking, "Who *is* this Mrs. X?" After a few minutes of shock, the student realized that he had mistaken someone else for his teacher. He finally told the stranger that the look-alike Mrs. X taught at the school across the street.

When the stranger entered the office at that school and asked to see Mrs. X, the secretarial staff doubled up in laughter and demanded to know what kind of stunt Mrs. X was trying to perform. Then, after some reluctant convincing, one of the staff directed the woman to Mrs. X's room.

I wish I had been there to see these women's faces when they confronted each other in a living mirror! This was no accident; they knew they had to be closely related, but how? A long and painstaking search of records eventually turned up this information: The women were identical twins who had been separated at birth and adopted by different families. One had spent the major portion of her adult life in that city; the other had lived many years in South America and only recently had moved to the very neighborhood of the very city of the very state where her sister worked!

Unbelievable! Too much of a coincidence to have really happened! But the truth is that it *did* happen in real life. But just try to get away with that in a short story and you will be laughed right off the editor's desk into the nearest wastebasket. No need to tell the doubter that "that's the way it really was." The literal truth and the artistic truth are sometimes very different, and the aspiring writer will do well to realize that he must be a *creator*, and not simply a *reporter*.

## RESOLUTION

Whether or not the protagonist eventually reaches his goal is a decision that you, the writer, will have to make. Many stories end happily and leave the reader with a glowing feeling of satisfaction. However, many a happy-ending story, in which the protagonist gets what he wants in spite of the obstacle(s) in his way, is far from satisfying to the reader and leaves him with the impression that the story could not have ended this way and was only contrived.

The outcome of the story should depend on the kind of character the protagonist is, as well as the events that have occurred up to this point. Is it logical to assume that a character who has bumbled his way through the story, making all the wrong decisions, will come out well in the end? Anything is possible, of course, but is it likely? Do the foregoing details justify the ending?

The term *poetic justice* might better be called *dramatic justice*, since today it has nothing to do with poetry. This is something quite different from justice in the legal sense.

In an excellent story entitled "Footfalls," by Wilbur Steele, the protagonist is an old blind man who eventually commits murder after many years of waiting for his intended victim to return to the town where a great deception took place years before. Not one of the townspeople brings charges against the old man, nor does the reader condemn him, because he has been made to feel so sympathetic toward the man and his cause that the murder seems, in a dramatic sense, entirely just. Whatever kind of outcome is chosen for your story, the reader should be able to feel that it is just and inevitable.

The ending usually answers the question, "Does the protagonist finally get what he wants?" But this cannot always be answered with a simple yes or no. With a word of warning against the kind of ending successfully used in "The Tiger or the Lady," we would like to point out that an indeterminate ending is right for some stories. Perhaps the problem is such — and the character's personality is such — that any definite resolution of the problem would be unthinkable. We do not mean to encourage the use of the indeterminate ending simply as an escape from dealing with the problem honestly and fairly. It should not be used simply because the writer cannot think of any more satisfactory ending. But if the story calls for one, do not hesitate to use it. The fact that the protagonist is powerless to resolve his problem may be the whole point of the story.

Let us suppose, for example, that Cherie wants to be a model, but is told that she is overweight. She goes on a crash diet and, as a result, suffers a recurrence of a former illness. While she recuperates, only partially cooperating with medical instructions, hoping to get well and keep her weight down, too, we see her at the end of the story still daydreaming over fashion magazines, totally unwilling to accept the fact that she cannot have it both ways.

At the end of most stories, and as a result of the actions in it, the protagonist is in some way, however subtle, different from when the story began. But remember the old adage that a tiger does not lose his stripes (or a leopard his spots). People do change, of course, but the change must be entirely believable if the story is to have any impact on the reader. A new awareness or understanding is often change enough, a new insight which was lacking before. In view of this new awareness, the character may vow to change. The reader may know, in his heart of hearts, that the protagonist will never be completely successful in his efforts to reform his behavior, or if he is, the change will be very gradual, but he is at least left with some hope for the future, and that is all that is necessary. To give a character a radical change of personality or habit within the narrow limits of the time and place of a short story is likely to be a mistake.

If the protagonist is unsuccessful in attaining his goal, is there perhaps some redeeming factor that will make his situation more bearable in the future? In real-life situations, the answer to this question is often affirmative. One does not attain the wealth — or power or beauty or recognition — he desires, but he does perhaps gain courage, fortitude, or humility. Or he learns that his original goal was not worth the effort he used to seek it. He may learn to value, instead, some possession that he has hertofore taken for granted — his sight, perhaps, his health, his family, or whatever. On the other hand, he may fail in this effort, but the reader may be left with the hope that, under different circumstances and at another time in the future, he may, indeed, get his heart's desire.

## THEME

Many stories have a recognizable theme; that is, they are told to illustrate a particular point. That point is not necessarily a moral teaching or a lesson to be learned; it may simply be a statement of the way things are, according to the real or assumed beliefs of the controlling mind. The theme may be some bit of wisdom or truth about the nature of the world or humankind. It may reflect the author's or the protagonist's philosophy of life and, therefore, be open to debate or argument.

Two writers may begin stories with the same conflict in mind; then the stories may go in quite different directions, depending on the theme. For example, let us put two boats at sea in a raging storm and show each sailor struggling for survival. One writer, whose theme is that "nature is kind," will direct his action in a way that will prove this point, and no doubt everything will work for the protagonist's survival. The other writer, whose theme is that "nature is hostile to humankind," will provide actions to prove that point. The protagonist will probably not survive, and his destruction may be so devastating that it will seem to be the result of intentional malevolence. For the sake of illustration, let's add a third sailor in a storm and say that this writer wishes to illustrate the theme that "nature is indifferent to humankind." The protagonist may survive or not survive, but all incidents leading to the resolution of the conflict will prove that there was really no rhyme or reason — no divine design — in what happened. Nature was neither friend nor foe; and that is what the third writer is trying to say.

Sometimes the theme of a story is stated by a character through dialogue; other times, it is not stated at all, but left up to the imagination of the reader, who is expected to draw his own conclusions. Seldom in modern stories does the author make his point directly.

The writer would do well to consider whether or not his story is being told to make a point. If his story has a theme, he should be well aware of what it is and select his events accordingly. It is the theme, more than any other single part of the story (other than the selection of a protagonist), which will determine the direction of the action.

A well-chosen title often helps to reveal the theme. A few words quoted from a familiar piece of literature may be effective as the title of an original story. Perhaps those particular words seem to have no bearing on the story; it may be the words that are omitted are the ones which add meaning. A writer should not overlook quotations from other writers' work as a source for a title. (The Bible and the works of Shakespeare have provided numerous titles, including "Cast the First Stone", which is included in this book.)

## SUMMARY

A few more words about plotting, in summary.

The protagonist's goal is often two-fold, consisting of an obvious or recognized goal and a hidden goal. (The writer, but not the protagonist, needs to keep both goals in mind.) The recognized goal should be revealed early in the story. It must be of great importance to the protagonist, and it must appear to be attainable, though difficult.

The action which the protagonist takes should show a direct relationship between his goal and the obstacle that stands in the way of his getting it. It should be a true action, not simply hoping or trying or continuing a plan that has already been proved ineffective. The action should be performed by the protagonist himself, not some outside person or force. This action must not present a ready solution to the problem; it should, instead, create a new problem or complication.

What we have been discussing is a road map for what might be considered a formula story. While many writers prefer a great deal more freedom than this formula allows, it is helpful to realize that such a plan or outline — which may be altered at any time if it becomes unworkable — can help the writer avoid simply rambling on and on with no particular destination in mind.

Many stories which may not seem to follow a sequential plan actually do; just because a story does not read like a soap opera does not mean that it is plotless. The difference is usually in the degree of subtlety involved and the skill with which all elements are worked together into a unified whole.

Some stories, especially psychological ones, successfully omit the complication, but without the goal and obstacle, which send out an urgent call for action, it is doubtful that a story can result. If you prefer to omit some of the development after the first three items — goal, obstacle, and action — it may be difficult to sustain interest to the end, but many professional writers have done it, and perhaps you can, too.

## THE STORY OF THE PRODIGAL SON        (Adapted from the Revised Standard Version of the New Testament)

*There was a man who had two sons; and the younger of them said to his father, "Father, give me my share of property." And the father divided his savings between the two sons. A few days later, the younger son gathered all his belongings and took a journey to a distant country, and there he squandered his money in loose living. And when he had spent everything he had, a great famine arose in that country, and he began to be in want. So he went and joined one of the citizens of that country who sent him into his fields to feed the swine. And he would gladly have eaten the garbage that the swine ate; and no one gave him anything. But when he came to himself he said, "How many of my father's hired servants have bread enough to spare, but I am dying here of hunger. I will arise and go to my father, and I will say to him, 'Father, I have sinned against heaven and before you; I am no longer worthy to be called your son; treat me as you would one of your hired servants.' " And he*

*got up and went to his father. But while he was still a distance away, his father saw him and felt sorry for him, and ran and hugged and kissed him. And the son said to him, "Father, I have sinned against heaven and before you; I am no longer worthy to be called your son." But the father said to his servants, "Bring the best robe quickly and put it on him, and put a ring on his finger and shoes on his feet, and bring the fatted calf and kill it, and let us eat and make merry; for this my son was dead and he is alive again; he was lost and is found." And they began to make merry.*
(Luke 15:11-24)

If you are a student of the Bible, you know that this is not the end of the story, but if we were to introduce the reactions of the brother, we would be getting into another story, another conflict, so let us stop here.

Reading between the lines and fleshing out the bare outline that the New Testament provides, let's examine this story in terms of its plot. The main character is a rebellious young man, perhaps jealous of his brother and eager to gain his independence. What is his goal? It is freedom to lead his own life. What is the obstacle in his way? It may be his father's insistence that he live according to his rules and dictates. What is the action that the young man takes? He takes his share of the family wealth and leaves home.

Now what complication results from this action? He cannot find a job as easily as he thought he could. (We may assume that he has never had to work before and is not really equipped for a job. Furthermore, he has no experience to commend him.) He spends his money foolishly, and when it is gone, he is broke and unable to provide for his necessities. He finally comes to realize that he was better off at home under his father's care and protection than he is now, and he decides to go back home.

Does he succeed in achieving his goal? Yes, he does get his freedom, but he was not ready for it. He probably realizes, as a result of his actions, that his father is not such a bad person after all.

Is there a theme to this story? Yes, there are at least one or two, possibly more. We learn from this narrative that what we want is not always the best thing for us. We may also learn that we sometimes misjudge the motives of others and miss their capacity for understanding.

## A STORY YET TO BE WRITTEN

Let us take another example to make sure we understand how a story may be plotted. It cannot be emphasized too strongly that the identification of the main character is extremely important and deserves more attention than is given here. (Refer to Chapter One for guidelines on the analysis of character.)

1. **Who is the Main Character?**

   A seventeen-year-old girl, cute, but not pretty. Rather petite. Stylish dresser, but not extreme in her clothing. High school senior. Good writer; likes to write, but mother has always been super-critical of her efforts. Best subjects are English, Spanish, and anything requiring verbal skills. Occasionally submits articles to the neighborhood political organization for young people to which she belongs, but not often. Plans to go to college and become a lawyer or psychologist.

   Parents are divorced; has little contact with father, who is a successful businessman in another state. Mother is prominent club woman and writer; she has a paid job with an organization and is fairly well known (though not famous) as a contributor to slick magazines.

   Girl has a strong sense of independence; is sometimes hostile to authority, including her mother's, but is not in any sense an open rebel. Is somewhat argumentative; is usually a clear thinker. Is a good organizer; has an instinct for leadership. Studies well only what seems worthwhile or interesting to her. Grades are slightly above average. Has friends and gets along well with her peers.

   Has a habit of shading her eyes with her right hand when trying to make a point in conversation; she does this most often when she is thoughtful and very serious.

2. **What is Her Goal?**

   To be her own person, not her mother's daughter; to get out of her mother's shadow and make her own decisions.

3. **What is the Obstacle?**

Her mother's reputation as a writer and organizer, and her mother's expectations of her, as well as other people's expectations that she will be like her mother.

4. **What Action Does She Take to Overcome This Obstacle?**

She subconsciously stops competing with her mother by concentrating heavily on school subjects and activities unrelated to her writing. She neglects the subjects in which she could most easily excel.

5. **What Complication Results from This Action?**

Her grades drop and her mother punishes her by refusing her the use of the car for some of her activities unrelated to school. She also threatens that the girl will have to work and help herself through college unless her grades improve.

6. **How Does She Handle This New Development?**

She so resents her mother's stand that she gets a job *then* and quits school. The job? Writing for a neighborhood newspaper.

7. **Is She Finally Successful in Getting What She Wants, or Not?**

No. Her writing talent is "discovered" and she is offered an important editing job after she graduates from college (or completes two years). Her mother's wishes for her future become her own and she realizes, now, that this is the kind of work she really likes. However, in order to pursue a writing career, she will continue to walk in her mother's shadow and work under her authority and criticism — at least for awhile.

8. **Is There Any Compensating Factor Which Helps to Soften Her Defeat?**

Yes. She comes to terms with her own abilities and discovers it is unnecessary to resent her mother's success. She knows what *she* can do, and that is all that matters. She is now willing to return to school, go to college, and major in English or journalism. She realizes that her mother is interested in her development, even though she is often overbearing.

9. **What Theme Does This Story Illustrate?**

People are happiest doing what they were intended to do (or what they are best equipped for), or we do well when we stand on our own merits and are not influenced by the faults or failures of others.


**EXERCISES**

1. (Oral) In groups of four or five class members, select one of the following plot situations for discussion. You will be given the first three steps of the plot outline. Then (a) flesh out the character so that you know a great deal about him; (b) decide on what logical action might grow out of the conflict, as stated; (c) decide what possible complications might arise to make the plot "thicken"; (d) discuss what climax the series of events might lead to; (e) conclude the story by deciding whether the character was successful or at least compensated for defeat; and (f) discuss possible themes that the story could illustrate.

Try not to repeat the details of stories you have read or seen televised, but do not be concerned if the story sounds familiar. Keep in mind that the apparent goal and the hidden goal are often not the same. Be careful to look beneath the surface for motivation; this is important.

   A. A high school star athlete wants a career in sports, but his parents oppose his attending college on an athletic scholarship, wishing him instead to devote the major portion of his time to studies that will lead to a more dependable and predictable lifetime career.
   B. A shy young woman who has always played second fiddle to her sister wants to make her parents proud of her, but her sister is always her superior in appearance, the social graces and achievement.
   C. A ten-year-old boy wants to visit his father in another state, but the father is not

interested in having him come.

D. The class clown, who is always noisy, full of practical jokes, and the life of the party, wants to date a certain girl, but she seems to be unaware of his existence.

E. A teenage girl is overly-conscious of her size. She is taller than most of the boys she knows and is often the victim of sexual remarks about her well-developed body. She would like to be a less conspicuous size, but she sees her physical development as irreversible.

F. A young woman who was adopted as a child wants to locate her biological parents, but she can find no clues to her identity.

G. A young adult who has always been obese would like to lose weight permanently, but various diets have proved only partially or temporarily successful.

H. A man in his late twenties or early thirties is economically secure, upwardly mobile, and reasonably satisfied with his marriage and family life, but he still finds himself attracted to other women. He would like to be a faithful husband, but he cannot seem to control his habit of straying into other sexual arrangements.

I. A young lesbian wants to come out of the closet, but realizes that the shock would probably kill her ailing mother and cause her father to disown her.

J. An only child living in a somewhat childless neighborhood wants a dog or cat, but is allergic to animal hairs.

K. An elderly widow wants to maintain her own home and independence away from her children, but she will soon be physically unable to remain alone.

2. (Written) Starting from the beginning, create your own character (perhaps the one you worked with in Chapter 1), and carry him through ALL of the steps of plot development. *Do not omit any of the steps.* Be sure that each step is closely related to all the steps that precede it. (As you write a complete short story, you may wish to omit some of these steps, but it is useful to know how to work with all of them so that you can make omissions skillfully with a firm knowledge of what you are doing.)

3. Evaluation. (Oral) The instructor may choose to select a few plot outlines from those which have been turned in, or he may shuffle them and distribute them to groups of four or five students for review. (The students' names may be removed or omitted.) As a group, then, read and discuss the plot outline you have been given and evaluate it in terms of how logically it evolves and to what extent the various parts relate to each other and contribute to a unified series of events.

## Chapter 3

## Beginning the Journey: The Initial Situation

### THE INITIAL SITUATION

Many writers have difficulty getting started. How and where should the story begin, they wonder. Through the trial and error method, they may be lucky enough to hit upon just the right approach. But many a story with great potential fails from the very start. If the beginning is bad, there is little that can be done to redeem the poor start later on. What is more, it will hardly matter what follows the poor beginning, in many cases, because the reader will have laid the work aside after the first few paragraphs. YOU MUST ENGAGE THE READER'S INTEREST AT OR VERY NEAR THE BEGINNING OF THE STORY OR YOU MAY NOT ENGAGE IT AT ALL.

Furthermore, YOU MUST KNOW WHERE YOU THINK THE STORY WILL END BEFORE YOU CAN DETERMINE WHERE AND HOW IT SHOULD BEGIN. If you have followed the advice on plotting, you have already planned your road map and are only now ready to begin the journey, the writing itself. If you have not followed that advice, you are likely to be in trouble already. This is not to say, of course, that the plot outline cannot be changed. Often characters begin to take over the story and lead their own lives, to the surprise of the writer who thought he could dictate and control their actions completely. When this happens, it is a good omen and probably indicates that you have done a good job of creating lifelike and believable characters. By all means, let such a character move in his own direction and avoid trying to force him back into the pattern of behavior that your plot outline calls for. But when you see that the action is changing, it is important then to stop and rewrite or rethink your plot outline in that new direction. Letting yourself just drift with the events without any idea of your destination may work out well but the chances of success are slim.

There are, of course, various places where a story may begin, and probably all of them have worked well for some writers at some time. The chronological beginning, however, is seldom the best. It would take too long to get to the conflict and would introduce events that probably would not catch the interest of the reader. Many readers find it annoying to have to plow through paragraph after paragraph of background and introductory material to get to the problem with which the story deals. It is always possible, and usually necessary, to bring in some background information at some point, but the beginning of the story is not the recommended place.

Description, either of character or scene, often occurs at the beginning of a story, but if you choose this kind of beginning, do it with extreme caution. Ask yourself *why* you are beginning with this description and what purpose is served by doing so. If it is to establish a mood, you may have chosen well. If you feel that the character's appearance is of major importance, or the insight which might be gained by seeing him in his surroundings, then by all means start with description that serves that purpose. But description for its own sake, while it is to be avoided in other places as well, is *most* detrimental in the beginning paragraphs. It is a sure way of losing a large number of readers.

There are other ways of beginning which you may find work well for you, but keeping in mind that the opening paragraphs are some of the most important ones in the entire story, let us explore one sure-fire method that you can depend on.

BEGIN RIGHT IN THE MIDDLE OF THINGS. Start the story by showing the protagonist in a moment of significant action or conversation. Sustain this scene until the situation is firmly established in the reader's mind. (During this opening scene, it is often possible to provide some clue concerning the conflict.) Then bring in later whatever background information is necessary to indicate what prior events led up to the present situation. (Additional background information can be introduced from time to time as the story progresses.) Then return to the present scene and play it through to a normal conclusion.

Notice that we said *significant* action or dialogue — significant, that is, in terms of the conflict around which the story will revolve; significant in terms of the kind of person the protagonist is and his relationship to the conflict.

Keeping this advice in mind, read the following beginnings of stories by college students and judge for yourself why they are effective:

*(1)      Edith burst into the room, letting the screen door bang shut behind her. Tossing her crumpled sweater in the general direction of the sofa, she flopped down into the nearest chair which complained noisily with the sound of creaking springs. A groan came from the next room.*

*"Edith, why can't you come into the house like a lady?" her mother scolded as she appeared in the archway. "You know that little Victorian chair can't stand that kind of punishment."*

*Edith turned away with a resigned here-we-go-again expression, at the same time knocking the ash from her cigarette onto the already scarred table top. She crossed one stockinged leg over the other, indifferently touching the run that extended the length of her left leg.*

*A gray kitten tapped playfully at the knotted shoestring dangling from the girl's scuffed oxford. Edith kicked carelessly in the direction of the kitten's paw.*

*(2)      The Reverend Mr. Cyrus Steele sat rigidly on the unyielding cushion of his straight-backed chair and stared ahead into the gloom. Subconsciously, the fingertips of both hands met in a characteristic gesture of self-approval. Daylight had waned and finally faded completely away, but he was unaware of the darkness of the sky beyond his single bare study window, or of the shadows that had gathered in the narrow room.*

*(3)      "Thank God, it's over," Bill thought as he boarded the Delta jet for Detroit. He smiled absently at the stewardess who welcomed him aboard and made his way gradually down the aisle to the coach section. He was glad there weren't too many people aboard. He always liked to sit in a window seat and hated it when none was available. Even after four years in the Air Force, from which he had just been discharged, he still enjoyed looking down on the landscape through a haze of fleecy clouds.*

*He seated himself and automatically fastened his seat belt, smiling at his reflection in the window. Freedom. Oh, how good it was at last! He was vaguely aware that someone had taken the aisle seat — a woman, he thought, but he did not bother to look. He just wanted to relax and enjoy the ride.*

*(4)      I sat crouched in a fetal position with utter darkness surrounding me on all sides like invisible walls. In fear and unable to move, I pondered the blackness of night. It must truly be man's primordial terror. I theorized how much like hell that isolation was. It didn't really matter whether I opened my eyes or kept them closed. My head swam and my senses were useless in that void. Shivering, I felt my consciousness wavering and I longed for the welcome light of dawn.*

*(5)      The slam of the wood frame door, its torn screen clinging for dear life, broke the early morning silence. Lola Johnson, her ever-present Miller and Rhodes shopping bag in hand, stepped quickly across the rickety porch and down the few steps onto the sidewalk below.*

*Keeping a steady gait, the short, squat lady headed south on Fifth Street toward Broad, buttoning her sweater as she went. You could never tell about spring mornings in Virginia, and if there was one thing Lola Johnson couldn't abide, it was being cold. Besides, the best way for a young lady of sixty-two to reach sixty-three was to take precautions.*

*She crossed the street and adjusted her pillbox hat as she saw a friend approaching.*

## QUESTIONS

1. In each of these initial situations, what kind of person do you suppose the character to be? What personality traits would best describe him/her?
2. What possible conflict could each of these characters face? Where do you think the story might go from this kind of beginning?
3. In which story-situations are you given some clues to age? How old do you assume each of these characters to be?
4. In which of these initial situations is description used most effectively? What purpose does this description serve? Is it, in this case, an effective way of beginning a story?

5. In each of these situations, how well can you judge the mood of the character? Where are clues provided?
6. Are you sufficiently interested in each of these beginnings to want to read on? To what do you attribute this interest or lack of interest?
7. In which examples are seemingly minor details helpful? Why?

## THE TRIGGERING ACTION

You will recall that, in our plot outline, we indicated that our main character wanted something which he was prevented from getting and took some action which he believed would get him around the existing obstacle. In Chapter 2 we listed some hypothetical conflict situations. One concerns a high school star athlete who desires a career in sports but whose parents object to his attending college on an athletic scholarship. It is likely that this young man has held this ambition for years, perhaps since early childhood. Why, then, is this goal *just now* becoming of such urgency that he is going to be forced into action to overcome the obstacle? The answer lies in a change of status; he is about to graduate, and the familiar ambition must now be acted upon or relinquished. His forthcoming graduation is the "triggering action" that will force him to do something *now*. Another word for this triggering action is *motivation*.

Another hypothetical situation in Chapter 2 concerns a young woman, adopted as a child, who wishes to locate her biological parents. If we assume that she has wanted to do so for many years, we must ask, "Why has she not taken some action before? Why is this goal suddenly so urgent *at this particular time* that she is now ready to do something about it when she has never done anything about it in the past except to wish?" In other words, what triggering action now motivates her? Perhaps she has just discovered that she is pregnant and wants to be able to pass on to her child some sense of its roots. This would be the kind of change in her status that would call a short story into being.

If, however, this young woman has *not* had this goal until recently, we must then ask what has just occurred in her life to make this goal suddenly important to her. Perhaps she has just discovered accidentally that she is an adopted child and the shock of this information requires some immediate action.

The point is that situations which have existed for a long time require some kind of recent change to make the problem so urgent that wishing is no longer enough; decisive action must be taken, and it must be taken *now*. The obese person who wants to lose weight has probably always wanted to lose weight but is now motivated by some recent change that makes the loss of weight urgent.

In writing the initial situation of your story, keep in mind the necessity of a triggering action. An excellent place to begin the story is shortly after the protagonist has become aware of whatever change or new discovery is going to force him or her into action.

## REVIEW OF METHOD

1. Show the protagonist in a moment of *significant* action or dialogue.
2. Sustain that scene until the situation is firmly established.
3. Introduce enough background information to indicate briefly what brought the character to the present moment.
4. Return to the opening scene, play it out, and bring it to a close.
5. Be sure to create a triggering (motivating) action to account for the urgency of the present conflict.

## WRITING EXERCISE

With a particular character in mind, write your own initial situation. (You should have in mind a tentative plot outline although you may choose not to write the entire story.)

## Chapter 4

## On Stage, Everyone!

### WRITING IN SCENES

You have thought your character through so thoroughly that you know him more intimately than you do your best friend. You have plotted your story so that you know the direction it will take. You have written your initial situation and thus gotten the story off to a start. What next?

You will avoid much of the frustration that writers often feel if you will think of your story in terms of scenes. How many different locations and moments of time do you think will be necessary to move your story through all the steps of action and bring it to a conclusion? Unless you consider this problem early, you may find yourself floundering helplessly and doing a lot of unnecessary writing in the process.

Without developing a full plot, let us imagine the situation of a young man who goes to college during the day and works a night shift to support his wife and young child. He is trying to do too much, and his heavy schedule is catching up with him. His grade point average has been dropping, and he has been on probation for several semesters. Now he faces the possibility of having to drop out of school. We might consider him in the following locations at the times indicated:

*Scene 1: In his bedroom alone just after receiving a notice in the mail.*
*Scene 2: At the lunch (or breakfast) table with his wife a half hour later.*
*Scene 3: The following morning in his history class.*
*Scene 4: That evening at work.*
*Scene 5: A week later alone at his desk.*
*Scene 6: The next day in his advisor's office.*
*Scene 7: That afternoon with his wife in their apartment.*

There could be additional scenes, although probably not more than one or two. In *your* story, there might be fewer scenes than we have indicated here. There is no set number of scenes that will work best in all stories. The thing to remember is that all the action that occurs should take place in some particular place at some specific time.

### SETTING THE STAGE

Becoming conscious of scenes will make you more stage-conscious as you think through your story and write it. Imagine that you are writing a play instead of a short story; every scene must be "blocked". If this were a play, what scenery and props would you provide? What furniture would be needed in the room where the action takes place for each scene? Where are windows and doors located? If other characters enter or leave, from what direction do they come in, or where do they exit? Where is the character who dominates that scene sitting or standing? What is the condition of the room? Mentally block out each character's position in relation to other characters and the setting you have provided. Then remember that, while a playwright takes care of these details by including specific directions in parentheses, the short story writer must provide them within the context of the story itself.

### INCLUDING DETAILS

Let's assume that the husband in Scene 2 (Let's call him Jim) enters the kitchen as the curtain rises. Is his wife (Let's call her Karen) already there? Exactly where is she, and what is she doing? Is she feeding the baby perhaps? Is she also attempting to prepare Jim's breakfast or lunch at the same time? If you want your scene to be realistic and visible to the reader, small details pertaining to the room, its condition, and its occupants will be helpful.

### GETTING ON AND OFF STAGE

In becoming stage-conscious, remember to get your characters offstage once you have gotten them on. This is often a good way to bring a scene to a logical close — by letting one of the characters leave the room. By mentioning a person's departure from the stage, you will avoid confusion in the reader's mind since, after all, the only stage he can visualize is the one you create with words.

The same advice that applies to getting a *major* character offstage applies to minor characters as well. It is easy for a writer to forget a minor character after he has served his usefulness, but he must not be left just standing there simply because the writer forgot to remove him. Get him offstage in the same way that you would remove a more important character. Often this can be done in only a few words, such as: "After Jack had stormed out of the room . . . ."

## REPORTING DETAILS

Let's examine two versions of the same scene and try to determine which is more effective.

*(1)      Jim decided not to tell his wife about the notice just yet. Maybe he would be able to think of something in a little while.*

*"Hi again," he said.*

*"Ready for your lunch now, Hon?"*

*"Yeah, I guess so. Hey there, Skipper. You eating again?"*

*"What was in the mail?" Karen asked.*

*Jim did not know what to say. At first he pretended not to hear as he kept playing with the baby. Karen asked the question again.*

*"Oh, nothing much," he said. And then to change the subject, he added, "This soup sure is good. What'd you do to it?"*

*(2)      Jim decided not to tell his wife about the notice just yet. Maybe he would be able to think of something in a little while. He tucked the letter securely inside his wallet, took his jacket from the hook, and headed for the kitchen.*

*Karen was there balancing a spatula in one hand and trying to cajole Skipper into one more spoonful of applesauce with the other. The child's highchair, placed beside her chair, was already covered with food he had spilled and was playing in gleefully.*

*Jim marvelled at his wife's patience. "Hi again," he greeted her as he pulled out a chair for himself.*

*Karen smiled back at him. "Ready for your lunch now, Hon?"*

*"Yeah, I guess so," he replied. He looked appreciatively at the steaming bowl she placed on the table. Waiting for her to join him, he turned to observe his son. "Hey there, Skipper. You eating again?" The child made a happy gurgle in reply.*

*Karen gave Skipper a spoon to play with and joined her husband at the table. Helping both bowls, she asked, "What was in the mail?"*

*Jim did not know what to say. At first he pretended not to hear as he smiled at the baby's spoon-banging routine. Karen asked the question again.*

*"Oh, nothing much," he said, making it a point to fill his mouth with crackers. In a moment he exclaimed, "This soup sure is good! What did you do to it?" Before she could answer, he crammed another cracker into his mouth.*

Now let's assume that this conversation comes to a close and Jim has successfully avoided answering Karen's question about the letter. How can we get him offstage and bring this scene to a close?

*He drained the last drop of coffee from his cup, at the same time pushing back his chair. "Sure was delicious," he said as he tousled Skipper's hair. "I'll see you about 4:30. Gotta stop by the library for a few minutes." He leaned over and kissed Karen. "Gotta rush now."*

*"Bye, Hon," she said. "Have a good day." She rose and started cleaning off the table as Jim gathered his notebook and dashed toward the outer door.*

The second version, with the addition of the final section of the scene, is much more visible and realistic than the first, isn't it? We are able to see the little family in a specific setting. The small details help to make our characters come alive and convince others that this lunch-time conversation really did take place. Of course, revealing these details requires more words, but the additional care pays off in the end. Taking shortcuts is certainly easier for the writer, but the scene is less convincing. The main character has been taken onstage (for this scene, the kitchen on a weekday) and then taken offstage. All that is necessary now is a transition to the next scene.

## MAKING A SMOOTH TRANSITION

A transition from one scene to the next may be short or long. Since a story is usually a combination of narration and dramatization (that is, *telling* and *showing*), two dramatic scenes may be linked by a fairly long section of narration. On the other hand, the transition may be composed of just a phrase, or sentence or two (*"That afternoon after his classes were over . . . ."*), that will cover chunks of time unimportant to the movement of the story. These sentences or phrases can provide a smooth transition that will satisfy the reader by letting him know how much time has passed between scenes and *how* that time was passed without going into a play-by-play description of everything that happened. (*"On his way to the campus, Jim wondered what he could do, but once he got to class, there was no time to think of personal problems. The day went by rapidly and before he knew it, it was time to go home for a quick dinner and nap and get ready for work. That night as he punched in, he felt unusually tired and wondered how he would be able to make it through the late shift. But somehow, by the time he got to his ten o'clock class the next day, he felt strangely refreshed."*)

In four sentences, we have gone from one morning to the next. Not only have we provided a transition from one time and place to another, but we have done it without confusing the reader. When we see Jim performing now in his history class, we are ready to witness this new scene with clarity and understanding.

## WRITING EXERCISE

1. Using the same characters and situation that we have been discussing, write a transition of no more than four sentences, linking any two of the later scenes.
2. Choose any of the scenes except Scene 2 and write it in the same kind of detail which has been illustrated in the second version of the kitchen scene. Be sure to block the scene first in your own mind and make the imaginary stage visible enough to create an illusion of reality. Get your character(s) onstage and off at appropriate points.

## Chapter 5

## The Way You See It
### (Point of View)

One of the most important decisions a fiction writer must make is his choice of the point of view from which his story will be told. Every set of events is interpreted by the person through whose eyes these events are seen. Recall the widely varied versions of an accident as told by those who see it; no two people see exactly the same details or place the same values on what they think they have observed. Sydney Harris, the popular columnist, often reports on the various ways in which the same person or situation is viewed, showing how opinions shift according to who is doing the reporting. One's own child, for example, may be considered "spirited" by his family but "undisciplined" or even "wild" by outsiders. A great deal depends on who is doing the seeing and the telling.

A novelist may tell his intricately woven story from a multiple point of view. Sometimes he follows the protagonist's point of view for several chapters, then switches for several more chapters to the point of view of another important character, proceeding then to even a third character's point of view, returning again to the point of view of the first character. This change from one point of view to another is more likely to appear in a novel than in a short story and is not recommended for the beginning writer of short fiction. This is because of the limitations of space and the difficulty of giving the characters credibility in so short a space. It is better for the writer to decide on one point of view only and stick to that throughout the story.

But which point of view is best? What points of view does the writer have to choose from? There are several possibilities:

1. First person
   a. Primary
   b. Secondary
2. Third person
   a. Objective
   b. Omniscient
   c. Limited

### FIRST PERSON

In the first person story, one of the characters refers to himself or herself as *I* and *me*. The storyteller appears to be telling a story in which he himself was in some way involved. It has the ring of truth about it — a kind of built-in authenticity — because the "I" in the story was there. This point of view is often so convincing that a casual reader is likely to mistake the story for autobiographical truth instead of fiction.

#### First Person Primary

In the first person primary point of view, the "I" in the story is the main character, the protagonist. It is his own story, presumably, that he is telling. It is the "I" who faces an obstacle and must somehow work "my" way around it to try to accomplish "my" goal.

Many writers are tempted to choose this point of view because they feel the reader will be less likely to question the credibility of events, but there are some serious limitations which should be considered. The first person narrator can report only what he has seen or knows, or what has been reported to him by some other character; he can never know what someone else is thinking unless that someone else puts his thoughts into words that he can hear. Furthermore, the first person narrator cannot be anywhere else than where he, as one individual, is. He cannot leave his own consciousness and peek into other rooms, other houses, other cities without being there physically. So while the first person story sounds very convincing, it is extremely limited, and the writer who chooses it unwisely will find himself devising ways of getting necessary information to the narrator by obviously contrived means which readers are not likely to accept.

#### First Person Secondary

In the first person secondary point of view, the "I" is not the main character but a less important one. Sometimes his only purpose for being in the story is to testify to events he observed as an eye-witness. He may be a close friend of the protagonist, a relative, an acquaintance, or even a stranger, but he must be in close enough proximity to the main character to be able to get the information necessary to tell the main character's story. There are not many stories which are told most effectively from this point of view, but for some stories it seems the *only* way. Individuals do not see themselves as others see them, and usually do not understand themselves or their motives for behavior as well as they would like to believe. A minor character is sometimes in a better position to be objective about the main character and interpret his behavior than the main character himself can do.

## THIRD PERSON

No character in a third person narrative appears as "I"; each one is either "he" or "she" throughout. While the third person points of view do not have the built-in sense of authenticity that the first person story does, it can often provide that sense in more subtle ways and lead to a convincing story with fewer problems.

### Third Person Objective

In the third person objective point of view, the writer is a reporter. He records what he sees others do and what he hears said in conversation between characters. He does not attempt to get inside any of the characters' minds; he does not report what is thought or felt, because thoughts, feelings, and perceptions cannot be known by an objective observer. A story told entirely from this point of view is quite difficult to write; words and actions must be reported in such a way (in such depth and with such selectivity) that the reader has enough information to draw his own conclusions about the inner workings of the characters' minds. Skillfully handled, this point of view can be extremely effective, but inexperienced writers should be cautious in using it by itself since the demands it makes upon the writer are great.

The objective point of view is most useful in combination with other third person points of view. It permits the writer considerable latitude in reporting events and dialogue beyond the presence of particular characters, providing the opportunity for deeper insight and understanding.

### Third Person Omniscient

The third person omniscient point of view is the most permissive of all. *Omniscient* means "all-knowing" or "knowing everything"; the narrator can wander into and out of any and all the characters' minds at will. He can report not only what he sees and hears, as in the objective point of view, but also what various characters see, hear, feel, and react to at any time he chooses.

This omniscient point of view has been used successfully by professional writers, and some books and articles on creative writing suggest its use by less experienced writers. From our experience, however, it is doubtful that this point of view should be attempted in the kind of short story that is likely to be written for the average college class. The brevity of the story just does not allow for the kind of mental gymnastics a reader would have to go through when quick shifts from one point of view to another are made. It is difficult enough to portray one character in depth; to try to create depth in other characters by delving into their mental processes would be, we feel, a mistake. Such shifts might also tend to lead the writer astray, taking him down byroads that lead away from the concerns of the main highway. Once we begin to concern ourselves with a minor character's thoughts, feelings, and motivations (beyond what he tells us in his own words or shows us through actions), we are likely to forget who our protagonist is and find ourselves with the ingredients for two plots — the main character's and the minor character's — instead of the one we started with.

### Third Person Limited

The third person limited point of view, properly handled, comes closest to the first person narrative in terms of creating an illusion of reality and authenticity. The protagonist remains "he" or "she" throughout the story, but the writer gets into his or her mind frequently, reporting not only what he says and does, but also — and more importantly — how he feels and what he is thinking. This is similar to the omniscient point of view except that the omniscience is *limited* to only one character. All other characters are dealt with objectively. We hear them speak and we watch their actions, but we are never told what they are thinking and feeling; only the protagonist provides us with this secret knowledge.

This point of view has all the advantages of the first person primary narrator without its limitations. It provides an opportunity to portray the protagonist in great depth. Because it can be combined with the objective point of view, we are able to go beyond the main character's presence whenever necessary and see and hear what others are doing and saying. Making a transition back to the presence and consciousness of the protagonist is not difficult, and we are thus permitted to tell *all* the story without resorting to mechanical — and unconvincing — means.

The third person limited point of view, in our opinion, is by far the most useful and convincing choice, offering the most advantages and the fewest pitfalls. For the most effective short story, with few exceptions, this is the point of view which we would recommend.

## EXAMPLES OF VARIOUS POINTS OF VIEW

Let us look at five versions of a little story adapted from AEsop's Fables. They will help to illustrate the differences we have discussed.

### (1) FIRST PERSON PRIMARY

*One day while I was resting in the woods, I was awakened from sleep by the tickle of something moving quickly across my chest. When I opened my eyes to investigate, what should I see but a tiny Mouse. I quickly grabbed him between my paws and prepared to gobble him down.*

*But before I could get him to my mouth, he started apologizing profusely. "Oh, pardon me, King Lion," he cried. "Forgive me this time, and I will never forget it. One day I may be able to do you a favor in return."*

*Can you imagine that? What could he ever do for me? "Do ME a favor?" I asked. "That is really a good joke." I really shouldn't have laughed so, but I just couldn't help myself. I had been feeling rather grumpy before I went to sleep, and the Mouse's audacity was so refreshing that I felt suddenly very generous and decided to let him go.*

*The little rascal was so grateful that he stumbled over his own feet trying to get away.*

### (2) FIRST PERSON SECONDARY

*I was perched comfortably in a tree one day watching a Lion below me lying on his back taking a nap. Suddenly I noticed him twitching for no reason that I could see. Taking a closer look, I detected a small object not quite as large as myself scooting back and forth across the Lion's chest. It was not until the Lion awoke and caught him between his great paws that I saw it was a Mouse. It seemed to me that the Lion was about to pop the little fellow into his mouth but suddenly stopped. It appeared then that the Mouse must have said something, but I could not hear what it might have been. All I know is that the Lion went into uncontrollable fits of laughter. Then the Mouse got away, whether with or without the Lion's consent, I could not tell.*

### (3) THIRD PERSON OBJECTIVE

*One day when a Lion was asleep, a little Mouse began running back and forth across his chest. The Lion awoke, grabbed the Mouse with his huge paw, and opened his mouth as if to swallow him.*

*"Oh, pardon me, King Lion," the Mouse cried. "Forgive me this time, and I will never forget it. One day I may be able to do you a favor in return."*

*"Do ME a favor?" the Lion said. "That is really a good joke." The Lion laughed and laughed. "I was feeling rather grumpy before I went to sleep, and your amusing little remark has made me feel so much better that I am going to let you go."*

*"Oh, thank you, thank you!" the Mouse exclaimed, as he scurried beyond the Lion's reach.*

*(4) THIRD PERSON OMNISCIENT*

*One day when a Lion was asleep on his back, he became aware of a tingling sensation on his chest. He tried to put it out of mind, but it was so persistent that, before he knew it, he was fully awake.*

*What did he see but a tiny Mouse! What audacity! the Lion thought. How dare this creature, not even big enough to make a decent meal, approach the important person of the King of the Forest himself! He would get rid of him in a hurry. Grabbing him between his paws, the Lion prepared to do away with this annoyance.*

*The Mouse, knowing that the jig was up, decided to humble himself. "Oh, pardon me, King Lion," he apologized. "Forgive me this time and I will never forget it." He hoped he was making his voice sound properly subservient. He knew these brutes all too well. They liked to take advantage of someone they knew they could defeat. Only flattery and pretended subservience would win him a reprieve. "One day I may be able to do you a favor in return," he continued, careful to notice the Lion's response. He knew the Lion might think him too presumptious, but he thought his offer was worth a try. He was relieved to hear the Lion laugh.*

*"Do ME a favor? That is really a joke," the Lion laughed. He could not imagine how such a tiny, unimportant creature could ever do him a favor. He should have felt insulted, but the remark was so ridiculous that he could not bring himself to resent it. Furthermore, he recalled how grumpy he had felt before his nap and was secretly glad to have this little upstart lift his spirits. He could afford to be generous since this tiny thing would not even make a decent mouthful.*

*"Go on, go on," the Lion said, continuing to laugh.*

*"Oh, thank you, thank you!" the Mouse exclaimed, as he scurried beyond the Lion's reach. He could afford to be subservient a few minutes longer if it meant his safety. After all, he knew his strengths and was fully aware that, as small as he was, he possessed talents that even the self-styled King of the Forest could not boast.*

*(5) THIRD PERSON LIMITED*

*One day while a Lion was asleep on his back, he became aware of a tingling sensation on his chest. He tried to put it out of mind, but it was so persistent that, before he knew it, he was fully awake.*

*What did he see but a tiny Mouse shivering in fear. What audacity! How dare this creature, not even big enough to make a decent meal, approach the important person of the King of the Forest himself! He would get rid of him in a hurry. Grabbing him between his paws, the Lion prepared to do away with this annoyance.*

*"Oh, pardon me, King Lion," the Mouse said. "Forgive me this time and I will never forget it." Why was it that beings were so quick to apologize for sins they committed so willingly only a few minutes before? Apologies made under the threat of punishment were really rather meaningless. But the next sentence was so unexpected that it was funny.*

*"One day I may be able to do you a favor in return," the Mouse boasted. Do HIM a favor? A mere mouse do a LION a favor? How ludicrous! How laughable! He could not contain his amusement. He really should have resented such audacity, but remembering the grumpy mood he had been in before his nap, he decided to be generous and let the little creature go.*

*"Oh, thank you, thank you!" the Mouse exclaimed, being true to his inferior breed and running for dear life.*

In case you are wondering about the outcome of this fable, the Mouse did indeed come to the Lion's rescue later by gnawing through the ropes that bound him. In the original, this story is followed by a stated moral, which should be quite obvious to the reader.

**EXERCISES**
1. (Oral) Go back over each of the five versions of "The Lion and the Mouse" and indicate which features qualify it for that particular point of view. Pick out words and phrases, wherever possible, that provide clues.
2. (Written) Select a very brief story with which you are familiar (fable, nursery rhyme, or fairy tale, for example) and retell a portion of it in your own words, using all five points of view. (Be sure that the story you select involves two characters in some kind of conflict.)

## CONSISTENCY OF POINT OF VIEW

Occasionally a writer shifts from one point of view to another for special effect. J. D. Salinger's story, "For Esmé — With Love and Squalor," for example, begins with the first person primary point of view, then shifts to third person. This change is made deliberately to coincide with the abrupt changes in time and the protagonist's traumatic experience and mental condition. Even though this shift is highly effective, the beginning writer should be wary of following Salinger's example.

Opinions of experts vary on the advisability of shifting from one point of view to another. As we stated before, the larger scope of a novel permits a great deal of freedom in this regard; a piece of short fiction may not permit such freedom. The average length of a short story is only between 2,500 and 3,500 words, and many of the stories written for a college class may be even shorter. Keeping in mind the audience for whom this book is intended and the likelihood that many of the short stories will not run to the maximum length, we must point out that shifts in point of view are likely to be hazardous for the student writer. They tend to make the story awkward and uneven and often lead to unnecessary confusion. IT IS OUR ADVICE, THEN, THAT THE POINT OF VIEW SHOULD REMAIN CONSISTENT THROUGHOUT THE STORY. Even such a seasoned author as Mark Twain occasionally violated the third person limited point of view, making for some unconvincing and improbable passages. For less experienced writers, we can expect the difficulties to multiply if the point of view is violated.

Select your point of view carefully, weighing its advantages and disadvantages for the particular story which you have in mind. If your story, for example, is psychological, it is doubtful that a completely objective point of view is your best choice. Probably the third person limited point of view, combined with the objective, will serve your purpose best. If, on the other hand, your story involves only one named character and there is no need for any objective reporting, the first person primary narrator will probably be most effective. The content of each story should determine which point of view will be best. But once you have made the choice, stick to it and avoid the temptation to vacillate. (The exception to this advice is that the objective point of view may be used in conjunction with either of the other third person points of view without being considered a violation.) If you choose wisely, you will solve one of the major problems facing fiction writers.

## Chapter 6

# The Way You Say It
## (Dialogue)

In order to follow the development of a play, a reader must rely almost entirely on what the characters say and do. Except for stage directions (which are printed in parentheses and are there only for the benefit of the actors and directors and are not intended for the audience), all the information which is given is in the form of dialogue — characters speaking, usually to each other, but occasionally aloud to themselves when no one else is present. No narration, no explanation, no interpretation is provided. The spoken word is everything.

In a short story, the reader has the additional benefit of passages of narration, as well as narration intermingled with dialogue, to move the action along and to provide insight into the characters' minds. Dialogue loses none of its power, however, simply because it does not make up the entire story. Several points should be kept in mind for the writer working with dialogue in short fiction.

Of the many advantages of dialogue, two in particular should be noted. First, dialogue can provide information indirectly, letting the reader know things that otherwise would have to be told through narration. In addition, it can help to portray a character through what he says to and about others and the way he says it, as well as what others say to and about him. (See Indirect Methods of Characterization in Chapter 1.)

Several points might be helpful in the handling of dialogue.

## USE BALANCE

In many stories, it is advisable to work toward a fairly even balance between dramatization (which depends heavily upon dialogue) and narration. A story which relies too heavily on narration is likely to be dull and unconvincing in that it may lack the sense of immediacy that dramatized action possesses. On the other hand, in a story which has too little, or no, narration, the scenes may seem quite disconnected. It is difficult to read a story in which almost every sentence is dialogue; its excessive use becomes monotonous and annoying, and the story tends to become too lengthy.

## AVOID WASTE

In general, dialogue should be saved for dramatic passages that can be presented best only through this medium. Greetings and passages of small talk often can and should be eliminated from dialogue and merely indicated quickly through narration. *(Example: After they had greeted each other warmly, the two quickly decided on a booth in the corner and headed toward it.)*

## DEVELOP A KEEN EAR

Convincing dialogue is not easy to write. Your ability to transfer to the printed page convincing conversations can be sharpened, though, if you train yourself to listen well. Practice paying close attention to the way your friends and family members talk, and get into the habit of translating the spoken into the written word, keeping in mind that the two are not the same. This will mean putting aside temporarily what you have been taught in English classes about avoiding sentence fragments and rambling, run-on sentences. In reporting conversation accurately, it is not your purpose to write "good English" so much as to make your characters come alive. In real life, few people speak in grammatically correct, well-constructed sentences all the time. They ramble; they abbreviate; they get side-tracked from the main point. They slur their speech, often dropping final consonants, running words together, and relying heavily on contractions and colloquialisms. They pause; they break; they repeat; they keep going without a break and speak in incomplete sentences. Learning how to report these speech habits in writing takes practice, time, and skill, but your mastery of these techniques will pay off in rich dividends and prove well worth the trouble.

The use of a tape recorder can be helpful in your study of the spoken word. It is a good idea, too, to read aloud passages of dialogue which you have written and listen to the way they sound. (Be careful, though, to read what you have actually written, not simply what you hear in your mind.)

## INDIVIDUALIZE SPEECH PATTERNS

Not all individuals talk alike. One's age, education, profession, region, and ethnic and socio-economic background, as well as one's parents' backgrounds, may have some bearing upon a person's speech, and the writer needs to be aware of possible differences between characters due to any of these factors. At the same time, one should be aware that there are differences within the same family, same region, same ethnic group from one individual to another. The creation of stereotypes is to be avoided in speech, as well as elsewhere. Speech differences are far more subtle than careless or hasty writers would have us believe. In real life, it is likely that vocabulary, emphasis, and phrasing, more than pronunciation of words alone, denote the differences to be brought out. Unless a writer is highly competent in recognizing and reproducing dialects, it is better not to use them at all and to depend rather on other factors within the story to bring out differences.

It smacks of snobbery to assume that a truck driver in casual conversation sounds less literate than a college student, an office worker, or even a teacher. It must not be assumed that all inner-city black people, Italian immigrants, or Oriental-Americans sound a certain way. Unless it is important to the characterization of a *particular* person to point out his lack of education, his age, or his ethnic background, it is probably better not to try to indicate a marked difference in his speech. Relying on speech *alone* for such information shows a weakness in the writer's artistry; if such information is important, then speech is only one of *several* ways in which such information can be revealed.

Fake spellings, a characteristic of some comic strips, especially are to be avoided. Practically everybody in the United States pronounces *was* as "wuz" and *enough* as "enuf". Many words can be represented by similar phonetic spellings, but these are meaningless when used as an attempt to indicate social status or educational background, and there is no justification for their use.

It is wise to keep the speaker's age in mind so that his vocabulary and speech patterns will not be inconsistent with that age.

## VARY SENTENCE PATTERNS

One way to avoid monotony in dialogue, as well as elsewhere in your writing, is by varying your sentence patterns. Instead of beginning most sentences with the subject, followed by the verb and complement, begin sometimes with a participial phrase, a prepositional phrase, a dependent clause, or something similar. The rhythmic flow of words will be smoother and more interesting than if you follow the same kind of sentence structure in all your writing.

Vary the position of the identifying label, too. Place it sometimes at the beginning of the sentence, sometimes in the middle (especially if you wish to indicate a dramatic pause), and sometimes at the end of the quotation.

> *Examples:* "*That's enough now! Just cut it out!*" *she yelled.*
> "*That's enough now!*" *she yelled.* "*Just cut it out!*"
> "*That,*" *she said,* "*is enough now. Just cut it out.*"
> *She yelled,* "*That's enough now! Just cut it out!*"

Any good handbook can make further suggestions regarding kinds of sentence patterns and the elements of style. If monotonous writing is one of your problems, it might be a good idea to consult one of these.

## IDENTIFY THE SPEAKER

A reader deserves to know who is speaking without having to retrace his steps through several sentences by reading backward. There are few things more annoying than having to read sentence after sentence of dialogue with the speakers frequently changing and no indication of who is speaking when. While it is neither necessary nor advisable to identify the speaker every time it changes, a conversation should not be allowed to go on for too long before the reader is reminded of who the speaker is. Every few exchanges should be identified by name or some other recognizable designation. (Jean might be identified as "the girl"; the physician, whose name is Dr. Kimberly Reid, might be referred to in one place as Kim, in another as simply "the doctor".)

There is nothing wrong with repeating "he said" with some frequency. Readers are so accustomed to the use of this phrase that they are not nearly so likely to find it monotonous as a writer might think. Furthermore, when it becomes obvious that the writer is going out of his way to find substitutes for the familiar "he said", sometimes coming up with quite outlandish ones, he only calls undue attention to a weakness in writing that would otherwise go unnoticed. Avoid the temptation to go overboard on variety simply for variety's sake.

Sometimes, however, other words are better than "she said" because they indicate *how* something is said. To *ask* or *exclaim* or *murmur* or *shout* something adds meaning to the words themselves; such verbs, judiciously chosen, tell *how* something is said and eliminate the need for unnecessary adverbs. Do look for other words to tell *how* the words are spoken, but not just to avoid saying "she said" if that phrase will suffice.

In looking for substitute words, remember that one can *say* words, *ask* in words, and *reply* in words, but one cannot *smile* words or *shrug* words. Such actions as smiling and shrugging must be reported separately and not tied into the identifying label.

> *WRONG:* "I don't care what you do," he shrugged.
> *RIGHT:* "I don't care what you do." He shrugged.
> He shrugged. "I don't care what you do," he said.

Another caution: Be careful of your use of the pronoun *he* or *she* to indicate a speaker, especially if it is not clear which male or female character you are referring to. If two or more members of the same sex are involved in the same conversation, such pronouns will not lessen the reader's confusion but only add to it.

### ADD VISIBILITY

Long passages of dialogue, even with the speaker clearly identified, can become monotonous. They tend to make a story seem more like the radio drama of a bygone day than a live performance on a modern stage, unless some precautions are taken. One way to avoid such monotony is to break up long passages of speech by one character by interjecting some mention now and then of small bodily movement and/or facial expression. LET THE CHARACTER BE SEEN AS WELL AS HEARD. Give him visibility. Remind the reader of his gestures, his movement on the "stage", his thoughtful pauses. Such information, along with the spoken word, will help him to come alive for the reader and, at the same time, eliminate the possibility of monotony.

> *Example:* "Well, what I was really trying to say," he continued, *nervously fingering his tie,* "is this." He turned away from the window and faced the girl. "Look here, Leah," he said. "Don't make it any harder for me."

Even when the quoted passages are not particularly long, it is important to let the "audience" *see* the character, as well as hear his words. Keep the reader aware of where the character is when he speaks and of what he is doing and how he is looking at the time. Such small details will help the character to become real and credible in the eyes of the reader.

### WATCH THE MECHANICS

#### Capitalization, Punctuation, and the Paragraph
Take time to memorize a few simple rules for handling dialogue.

1. Only a character's exact words (direct quotation) go within quotation marks, not the gist of what is said (indirect quotation).

   Direct quotation: *He said, "I have always had a preference for cities."*
   Indirect quotation: *He said that he had always had a preference for cities.*

2. Quotation marks operate in pairs. Once you begin a direct quotation, you must remember to bring it to an end. However, if a quotation carries over into more than one paragraph, use quotation marks at the *beginning* of *each* paragraph, but at the *end* of only the *last* one.

3. When it is necessary to include a quotation within a quotation, use single quotation marks for it.

*Example:* *Jack said, "I remember his exact words. He said, 'If I'm not back in half an hour, go on without me,' so I left."*

4. Each time the speaker changes, a new paragraph must begin. This rule applies without regard to the length of the sentence, even though it may be only one word.

*Example:* *"I will probably go to the movies after I finish my homework," Joan said.*
*"Do you think you can go?"*
*"Probably," he answered.*
*"Good," she said.*

5. Information closely related to the speaker belongs in the same paragraph as the words he speaks.

*Example:* *"Do you think you can go?" she asked. She hardly dared to hope that he might.*
*"Probably," he answered.*
*She did not wish to sound too eager or too pleased. She purposely paused. Then she said, "I'm glad," trying to sound as if she didn't care.*

6. The identifying label, or "tag", is set off from the quoted words by a comma or commas, except in those instances in which the quotation ends with a question mark or an exclamation point.

*Example:* *He repeated, "You don't know what you're saying, do you?"*
*"You don't know what you're saying, do you?" he said.*
*"You don't know what you're saying," he said, "do you?"*

7. The rules of capitalization which apply in general writing apply also to dialogue. Capitalize the beginning of the entire sentence; capitalize also the beginning of the *quoted* sentence. Do not capitalize parts of the sentence which do not begin the sentence (unless there is some other reason, such as a proper noun, for using a capital letter).

*Example:* *He repeated, "You don't know what you're saying, do you?"*
(*He* is the beginning of the overall sentence. *You* is the first word of the quoted sentence.)
*"You don't know what you're saying," he said, "do you?"*
(*You* is the first word in the overall sentence, as well as the first word in the quoted sentence. None of the other words *begins* a sentence.)

8. Periods and commas are always placed *inside* the quotation marks. (It does not matter whether a period ends the quoted sentence, the overall sentence, or both; it still is placed *inside* the quotation marks.)

*WRONG:* *"It would be foolish", she said, "to wait any longer".*
*RIGHT:* *"It would be foolish," she said, "to wait any longer."*

9. Colons and semicolons are always placed *outside* the quotation marks.

*WRONG:* *All he says is, "I can't recall;" perhaps that's all he knows.*
*RIGHT:* *All he says is, "I can't recall"; perhaps that's all he knows.*

10. Question marks, exclamation marks, and dashes are placed according to their use — sometimes inside and sometimes outside the quotation marks. If they apply to the quoted words only, place them inside. If they apply to the overall sentence, place them outside.

> *Example:* *Tom threw the glove down and yelled, "I've had it!"* (Only what Tom said is exclaimed, not the entire sentence.)
> *I'm sick of hearing you say, "I don't care"!*
> *Are you ready to watch "The Price Is Right"?* (The quoted words are not the question; it is the overall sentence that is the question.)

### More About Punctuation Marks

Exclamation marks should be used sparingly. They are meant to indicate strong feeling. Strong beliefs, surprise, anger, or fright might be reasons for using this mark of punctuation, but unless you mean for the words to be shouted, screamed, or exclaimed, you probably should not use an exclamation mark but a period instead. The writer who peppers his sentences too liberally with exclamation marks is saying in effect that the words themselves have failed to do the job for which they were intended and he is therefore trying to compensate by using eye-catching punctuation. It just doesn't work, and the weakness of the writing becomes even more evident than if the writer had not advertised his failure.

The dash is used to indicate a sudden change of thought or to set off a parenthetical statement. In dialogue it is also useful to indicate that a character's speech is suddenly interrupted. For example, if one character is speaking and before he finishes what he intended to say, another character cuts him off, the dash is the proper mark of punctuation. On the typewriter, it is made by two hyphens coming together, with no space between the two hyphens or between the hyphens and the words.

> *Examples:* *I knew--at least, I always thought I knew until today--all the symbols on the chart.*
> *"If I had only known, I would have--"*
> *"You would have done nothing," he interrupted.*
> *Bess and I--Bess was my roommate in college--always got along well.*
> (Parentheses could be used here just as well as dashes.)

Avoid the temptation of using an ellipsis (three spaced periods indicating that a part of a quotation has been omitted) when a dash is called for. The ellipsis is useful when a writer is quoting from a book or other passage of literature and wishes to leave out a portion of the author's quoted words, but it is not a substitute for a dash.

### WRITTEN EXERCISES

Copy the following passages of dialogue, inserting capital letters and proper punctuation where they belong. Also indicate where new paragraphs should begin by indenting at those points. (Be careful to place punctuation marks clearly before or after quotation marks as required, not directly above them.) Each sentence is set apart from the next. You will have to decide who the speaker is.

1. *wait he shouted, running after Lisa and waving his arms frantically*
   *where do you think you're going*
   *Lisa turned slowly and glared at him with contempt*
   *wouldn't you like to know she asked her voice calm*
   *just don't follow me, that's all*
   *I will follow you wherever*
   *you will not she interrupted*
   *you will go back and wait*
   *you will go back and wonder but you will not follow me*
   *Bill knew that she had won again*
   *he said I really don't care anyhow*
   *then he turned and walked back to the house, trying to look unconcerned*

2. *stop he cried you may go no further*
   *but what if*
   *do as I say he interrupted it is not for you to decide*
   *I said at least let me ask you this*
   *have you seen a truck go by with al's repair shop printed on it*
   *yes I think so he answered grudgingly*

*I smiled then*
*I knew I was on the right track*
*and was the driver a little old man with wild hair*
*stranger he said you ask too many questions*
*now go*
*I went but not before saying thanks anyhow*

3. *it was Charles I think who spoke next*
   *at least that's the way I remember it now*
   *do you know he asked where your children are at this moment*
   *everyone looked surprised everyone that is except his wife*
   *but Mrs. Dow looked more surprised than anyone else*
   *yes of course, she said with one eyebrow raised*
   *my daughter is with your son as if you didn't know*
   *Charles smirked triumphantly before continuing*
   *that is exactly the point he purred*
   *you don't know any more than I do*
   *what if I should tell you*
   *but he never finished the sentence for just at that moment the young people burst into*
        *the room looking as if they had been scared out of their wits*
   *shut up all of you the boy shouted*
   *just shut the hell up for once and listen*

Chapter 7

## The Backward Glance

Have you ever caught yourself remembering some person or event you have not thought of in years and wondered why the thought occurred just then? Perhaps you have played a game in which you were given a word and asked to say the first thing you thought of after hearing it. The answers might have seemed so unrelated that you wondered why you gave them.

The sudden, unexplained recollection of the past and the word evoked, without any apparent connection, are not as strange a combination as they might seem. Part of the psychiatrist's technique is to ask his patient to "free associate". He or she may ask him to say whatever comes to mind. In the course of a fifty-minute session, while the mind rambles from one thought to another, seemingly without direction, the patient may discover, to his surprise, that his unrelated thoughts and comments are not really unrelated at all. ONE THOUGHT LEADS TO ANOTHER; NOTHING IS OUT OF CONTEXT. Thoughts of the forgotten past are called to the surface of recognition because some present thought has brought them to mind. Just as there is some kind of motivation for one's words and actions, there is also motivation for thoughts and memories, although one does not always recognize what it is. Two of the most useful techniques in story-telling take advantage of this ability of the mind to link past and present experience.

In Chapter Three, it was pointed out that the chronological beginning of a story is seldom the best place to begin. Within the confines of one short story, it is inadvisable to begin with the protagonist's early childhood and bring him through his entire life in order to reach his present predicament. Yet, there is a great deal of background information which needs to be included, since present attitudes and behavior are so crucially influenced by past experience. There are several methods by which isolated episodes from the past can be selected at will and introduced as necessary without bogging the story down. One of these is the flashback.

## FLASHBACK

In addition to enlightening the reader on past events which have some bearing upon the present situation, the flashback may also serve as an effective link between one point of action and another. In addition, it may help to illustrate a point and, at the same time, lure a memory out of the misty past and fire it with present urgency. Furthermore, it can provide insight into a character or situation that would otherwise require narration.

Everybody is familiar with the flashback. In a movie, it is often achieved by a brief musical interlude, a fade-out, or a fuzzy distortion of the picture so that it is immediately clear to the viewer that the present action has been interrupted and the character is now reliving a scene from the past. At the end of the memory sequence, the picture is again distorted, and it is clear that the present action has been resumed. The writer, unfortunately, does not have trick photography to fall back on, but must achieve a similar effect with words alone. The writer who learns the technique will find it extremely useful.

A number of writers and teachers agree on some useful guidelines, the first being that the transition into and out of the past must be unmistakably clear; the reader must never have to guess what period of time is being depicted. There are several ways to insure this clarity.

1. The character should be involved in a specific activity, but it must be a quiet one — an activity conducive to daydreaming and letting his mind wander. Driving along a street with no conversation to demand his attention, waiting for a traffic light to change, or listening to music would be that kind of passive activity. (Perhaps listening to a boring lecture in an uninteresting class would be another.) Any activity which does not demand the character's full attention will qualify.

2. Provide a take-off point, a memory link, that will logically lead the character back to the past. This is where free association comes in. We remember some incident of the past because something in the present reminds us of it and makes the connection. Be sure to indicate what that present link, that take-off point, is.

3. Some writers use such devices as a series of periods at the beginning and end of the flashback, or underlining (equivalent of italics) of the portion of writing which represents the flashback. Either or both methods are simple and useful (if not the most effective) ways of keeping the time clear.

4. Introduce the flashback by using a word or phrase that involves remembering. ("Once again she recalled...," "his mind drifted back to that day ten years before when...," or "she relived that hour when....") Sentences that begin this way are signalling devices which alert the reader that a flashback is coming.

5. Shift from the past tense to the past perfect tense. Since stories are told in the simple past tense, the writer must indicate that the flashback represents an even earlier period in the past. This is achieved by using the helping verb *had* with the past participle. For the first few sentences of the flashback, until it is clearly established that a different period of time is being represented, the writer uses the past perfect tense, reverting to the simple past tense as soon as this can be done smoothly. ("Helen *found* herself drifting back to the birthday party of her eighth year. She *had been* surprised to learn that her cousin Ted was not coming. Mother *had come* into her room the first thing that morning with the bad news. "Honey," she *said*, "I know how much you were counting on seeing your cousin Ted today, but I'm afraid you're in for a disappointment." "Oh, no," Helen *groaned*. "Don't tell me....") Notice that as soon as it is clear that this conversation took place in the past, the verb tense returns to the normal simple past.

6. Use the word *now* to return to the present, along with some mention of the original memory link which led into the flashback, whenever such a return seems natural. Or provide a sudden noise, the changing of a traffic light from red to green, or any reasonable method to bring the character out of his daydream and back to the reality of the present moment.

7. Once the transition has been made from present to past, remain completely in the past until it is time to make the transition back to the present. Do not vacillate between the two time periods.

The second point to keep in mind is that the flashback should be represented as a vivid memory, and as such, it needs to be shown (dramatized), not simply told about (narrated).

## ILLUSTRATION

Read carefully the following passage, repeated from Chapter Three, which contains a flashback, and examine it according to the guidelines which have just been discussed.

### First Version

*"Thank God, it's over," Bill thought as he boarded the Delta jet for Detroit. He smiled absently at the stewardess who welcomed him aboard and made his way gradually down the aisle to the coach section. He was glad there weren't too many people aboard. He always liked to sit in a window seat and hated it when none was available. Even after four years in the Air Force, from which he had just been discharged, he still enjoyed looking down on the landscape through a haze of fleecy clouds.*

*He seated himself and automatically fastened his safety belt, smiling at his reflection in the window. Freedom. Oh, how good it was at last! He was vaguely aware that someone had taken the aisle seat--a woman, he thought, but he did not bother to look. He just wanted to relax and enjoy the ride.*

*In a few minutes, he heard the motor purr and the jet maneuvered itself down the runway for take-off. Once it began to cruise, Bill's tension subsided and he let his thoughts drift to Brenda, who was waiting for him in Detroit. Well, no, she wasn't waiting for him. Or rather, she wasn't expecting him today. He had not told her exactly when he was coming; he needed some time to himself before he saw her.*

*Bill was distracted by some movement in the seat at the end and turned to watch the woman fish for something in her purse. Eventually she pulled out a slim cigarette case, and he noticed her hands. Her fingers were slender and long like Brenda's and tipped with the same shade of pinkish nail polish that Brenda wore. He remembered those hands, clasped together in resignation that day four years ago when he had told her he was leaving........*

*"It's your decision, Bill," she had said. "You know I don't want you to go, but if you really want to, then you should."*

*"I don't want to," he answered. "I just think it'd be better that way. Let's face it. My father wouldn't give me a dollar to buy lunch, so you know he's not going to send me to school. At least I'll be able to get an education in the Air Force."*

*Brenda smiled a sad, one-sided smile. "Well," she said, "I waited that time when you were in the hospital, and I waited when you were working in Chicago that summer, so I guess I can do it again."*

*Bill felt a little sorry for her. She was trying to be so brave, but all the time he knew she was going to miss him like everything. He got up from the porch step where he had been sitting and stood behind her chair, touching her soft hair as gently as he could.*

*"It'll be different this time," he promised. "Honest it will. As soon as I get out, we'll get married, okay? Then I'll never have to ask you to wait for me again."*

*Her hands lay helpless in her lap, the long, pink-tipped fingers tense against the struggle he knew she felt........*

*Now another pair of hands, touching the flame of an expensive looking cigarette lighter to a cigarette, brought his attention back to his present predicament. "That was a long time ago," he thought. "Things are different now." Feeling suddenly very weary, he eased his seat into a reclining position and closed his eyes.*

Notice that:
1. The flashback is dramatized, not narrated. It is "acted out", not told about, just as the rest of the story is acted out.
2. Bill is doing something in a specific place, but it is a passive activity. He has just settled down for a plane trip.
3. A memory link has been provided, the hands of the woman in the aisle seat which reminded Bill of Brenda's hands. At the end of the flashback, the word *now* signals the return to the present.
4. A word meaning *remember* signals the coming flashback. "He recalled those hands touching her face that day four years ago when he had told her he was leaving."
5. The flashback is set off from the rest of the story by a series of periods at the beginning and end.
6. The past tense shifts to past perfect. "Her fingers *were* slender," "polish that Brenda *wore*," and "He *remembered*" now shifts to "she *had said*" and "he *had answered*," shifting back to the simple past tense, once the new time frame has been established.
7. We know that the flashback has ended when the word *now* appears and we return to the memory link. "Now another pair of hands. . . ."

## EXERCISES
1. (Oral) Read the following version of the same story and discuss it in terms of its handling of the flashback. Which of the two versions is better? Why? Are there other elements of this version which make it more or less effective than the first one? Discuss them, if there are.

### Second Version
*"Thank God, it's over," Bill thought as he boarded a Delta jet en route to Detroit. William C. Merrick had been officially discharged from the United States Air Force.*

*Bill smiled at his reflection in the window. "Freedom, oh how good it is," he thought as he fastened his seat-belt.*

*Once the jet began to cruise, Bill's tensions began to subside. He thought about the young lady who was waiting for him in Detroit. She wasn't actually waiting for him today because Bill did not tell her when he was coming. He wanted some time to himself before he saw her.*

*Bill tilted his head slightly to the left and gazed at the woman beside him. Her hands were slender and her fingers were long. She wore a pinkish color of nail polish: the same color Brenda wore.*

*He remembered how Brenda had held the side of her face as if she had had a toothache.*

*"Bill, it's your decision. I don't want you to go, but if you want to go, you should go,"
Brenda said.*

*"I don't want to go. I just think it would be better if I did go. Let's face it; my father
wouldn't give me a dollar to buy lunch, so you know he's not going to send me to school.
At least I'll be able to get an education in the Air Force," Bill said.*

*"I have waited for you while you were gone before. I guess I can wait for you again,"
Brenda moaned.*

*"But it'll be different this time. As soon as I'm discharged, we'll be able to get married,
and I'll never ask you to wait for me again," Bill promised.*

*He watched her hands as she lit her cigarette. He looked out the plane window at the
fluffy-looking clouds. "That was a long time ago; things are different now," he thought. He
put his chair in a reclining position and went to sleep.*

2. (Written) Using a portion of the story you are now writing (or creating a scene from a
story you may have in mind), write a paragraph involving present action, make a
transition into a flashback, and after the flashback, return to the present for a sentence
or two, bringing the scene to a close.

## STREAM OF CONSCIOUSNESS

A less frequently used device for introducing information about the past economically is
the stream-of-consciousness technique which has been used so effectively (although
sometimes confusingly to the reader) by such authors as William Faulkner, James Joyce, and
Virginia Woolf. A more sophisticated technique than the flashback, it is not necessarily
recommended for the novice, but the more adventurous or advanced student is invited to
experiment with it.

Some readers are annoyed, and many are initially confused, by this kind of writing
because it lacks the clarity of the flashback. There may be no clear points of transition
between past and present, no guidelines to follow for easy understanding, and no more logic
than governs the wanderings of the subconscious mind. The passage may cut across both
time and place indiscriminately and unexpectedly, mingling past and present without
warning (or with only such warning as is provided by ellipses). The sentences may be
incomplete and rambling because the drifting mind does not think in orderly fashion or in
complete sentences. Only short snatches of words may appear, sometimes seeming to be out
of any context whatever. It is often necessary for the reader to do a double-take. Several
readings may be required before any sense can be made of what is going on. But the
persistent reader may find that, if he is willing to take the trouble to try to unravel the
mystery, he is much more deeply involved emotionally than he ever dreamed he could be
with a piece of fiction. (Such was our experience with the difficult fourth section of William
Faulkner's "The Bear" the first time we read it.) Such an involvement, when it occurs, is
well worth the trouble to which a reader must go.

The important thing to keep in mind, if you wish to use a passage or two (or more) of
stream of consciousness in your story is this: It is like the flashback and the psychiatrist's
technique in that memories are induced by some specific detail of the present. One thing
leads to another. Something in the mainstream of the story reminds the character of
something else which may have been heretofore forgotten — and perhaps painful.

Some writers who use this technique, however, modify it to such an extent that it
closely resembles the flashback and is no more difficult to follow. Let's examine two such
examples of the stream-of-consciousness technique written by students.

In the first, the protagonist is a widow of about forty-five who, forced to look for work
after many years as a homemaker, finds her age and lack of experience in the work world a
handicap. Looking from the window of her furnished apartment, she remembers another
spring in her childhood and then returns to an incident that has been symbolic in her life.

*The room was hot and dark and stagnant, but beyond the open window, the fragrance
of cherry blossoms hung, and even though it was only May, the air pulsed with the lazy
drone of summer sounds. The branches moved almost imperceptibly, hypnotically, and
Lila's eyes drooped heavily under their spell. Where else? What other time and place?*

*In the schoolyard that spring the pink and then the cherries tight and green but the children wouldn't leave them alone, and then dark red and round and full against the flat green leaves. Ripe on the green leaves . . . . Dark straw, it was, kind of sailor with a wide brim off the face and a ribbon streamer down the back--green grosgrain--and the cherries on the band. Before I started school, or maybe kindergarten--no one else on the porch or anywhere around--no one to play with. And cold, about October maybe, late and cold and I just stood there freezing and nothing to do and alone and she wouldn't let me in. Shut out . . . . I could hear their voices in there but couldn't make out the words. But I knew when he came out he'd say no. Always the same. A lot of new reasons, different words and hands making different gestures, but always the same. No, no, no, no, no. Not here. Not now. Not ever . . . . That poor man in Riverdale with all those medical bills and nothing but his pension now after all those years, and she probably won't even live. Genevieve, I think. No, Geneva, Mama's name . . . . Why was the fresh air so important? Couldn't she see? Didn't she care? Did she ever? . . . . Little kid just wandered off. Mother inside washing. Just walked off the porch and kept going. They ought to cover up those dangerous holes. What's the law for anyhow? The kids don't read the signs. Do they care? Long as they're making money they take shortcuts and nothing's safe and some poor kid locked out to get fresh air . . . .*

*I would've bought it but I didn't like the color. Can't stand green. Don't you have it in yellow or pale blue, I said, some nice bright spring color? Well, I'll look again tomorrow. Something without flowers. Why do they always put flowers on hats? So silly all decked out in buds at my age . . . .*

*She raised her right hand to her face and felt around her eyes. I wonder if that new cream is really any good for wrinkles, she thought.*

Notice in the above passage how one thing leads to another. Lila is sitting in a stuffy room (specific locale), aware of several things in her surroundings, but it is the *cherry blossoms* that serve as a memory link. The questions, "Where else? What other time and place?" serve as a transition into the memory. The double space also acts as a separator of now and then, as well as the reference to "*that* spring."

The cherry blossoms on the tree (present time) remind Lila of cherries in the schoolyard of her childhood. Once she has followed the trail to her childhood, she is quickly led to another childhood memory of a hat with artificial cherries which she was wearing during a painful experience of being lonely, cold, and shut out of the house. The memory of being shut out reminds her, in turn, of being shut out in another situation (perhaps being shut out of job opportunities as a middle-aged widow). If this interpretation is accurate, and Lila is, indeed, a middle-aged or older widow who is economically insecure, it is her own situation that now causes her to recall a newspaper article she has recently read about an elderly man whose wife's illness is draining his meager income. The wife's name sticks in her mind because it is similar to her mother's name. And now we are back to the original memory of herself as a child being shut outside the warm house *by her mother.* Her mind leaps at what might have happened to her if she had wandered off the porch — what *did* happen to another little girl of present times (another newspaper story, undoubtedly). Suddenly, today's newspaper tragedy melts into her own emotional tragedy. This newspaper child, whom she likens to herself, reminds her again of the hat she associates with her childhood loneliness and rejection. Now we see Lila in a hat shop rejecting a hat because it subconsciously reminds her of the symbolic hat of her early years. She does not realize why she does not like the hat offered by an unsuspecting salesperson; she thinks it is because of her age — which causes her to come back to the present through her awareness of her wrinkles.

Quite a roundabout trip, isn't it? And yet, we get some valuable insight into the workings of Lila's mind and the experiences which have influenced her that we could hardly expect to get so economically in any other way.

In the second example, taken from "Cast the First Stone", included in its entirety in the appendix, a troubled man, suddenly realizing that he has been indirectly responsible for a controversy that is tearing his church apart, returns to his neglected hobby, which is wood-carving.

*Now he sat down on a low stool, picked up a ball of steel wool, and absently began to rub one edge of the wood with a steady, circular motion . . . . Sitting in the pew with Mama--just a little fellow. The knothole in the wooden seat back--such a funny roundness. Rough and smooth at the same time. Liked to trace it around and around with my fingers. She didn't care much. Kept me quiet. Not like the time I yelled out when Papa was lying out there in front. Why was he sleeping there in front of all those people with his clothes on? A funny bed, I thought. Take care of Mama. Yes, Papa. Yes, sir. The sheets damp. His forehead flushed, wet. Hot hands. Stay in the church, son, do the Lord's work. Yes, Papa, Yes, yes . . . . Yes, I can!*

*Still a month away, the deadline. The women--would have to be the women--they'd do it. Mrs. Clark and Mrs. Johnson next door and the Winstons across the street--expecting me to call them anyhow today. Just run by there instead and they'd offer me a cup of tea and I could say--well, don't quite know what I WOULD say, but it'll come. I've got to make them see.*

The man under stress works on a wood carving; the circular sanding motion reminds him of the way that, as a child, he used to trace the knothole of the pew in church with his fingers. The memory of the church pew, in turn, reminds him of his father's funeral. Now he is a child again, in his memory, and reacts as he did then to the mystery of death. Recalling his father's death carries him backward slightly to his father's final days and the deathbed admonition to the boy to "stay in the church" and "do the Lord's work." Finally, it is the memory of the father's last words that suggests a solution to the present problem. Just as he has been the cause of the problem in the church, this character now realizes that he holds the key to its solution.

### SIMPLE NARRATION

It is not necessary to utilize either the flashback or stream of consciousness in your story. If these techniques are not handled well, they may be better omitted. There is another way to introduce information about the past, and that is by simple narration. Such passages may be introduced during a lull in the action, or they may be brought on by something that has just occurred. The protagonist may be involved in some passive occupation in a particular place, as in the flashback, or a scene may have just come to an end. As with the flashback, the writer shifts from past to past perfect tense, narrating now instead of dramatizing whatever information is necessary to give the present situation meaning. Unlike the flashback, the past perfect tense is sustained. A simple transition will indicate to the reader that the character has returned to the present situation.

*Wendy rushed into her room and shut the door. The handwriting on the envelope looked vaguely familiar, and somehow it excited her, but she could not quite place it. Anxiously she tore it open and read the single sentence scrawled unevenly across the lined paper.*

*"Meet me Sunday same time same place. Evan."*

*Evan! Of all people! Why him? Why now? And where did he get the audacity to assume that, after all this time, he could just walk back into her life this way and find her waiting? She sank down on the bed wearily, wondering what she would do. She really did not want to see him ever again, she told herself, but in the back of her mind was a faint glimmer of hope that he might have changed.*

*She and Evan had been a twosome all through high school. They had been the couple that everyone knew would make it. They were the envy of everyone in their crowd. Everything had gone smoothly for awhile--too smoothly, probably. Even her mother, who seldom liked any of her friends, had found him charming and well-mannered, and her father had enjoyed talking to him, often making complimentary remarks about what he referred to as Evan's get-up-and-go. Not that he had been all goody-goody. Far from it. What Mom had never guessed was that in the back seat of a car Evan became an octopus. And Daddy would never have surmised good old Evan could outdrink and out-cuss almost any bum on skid row when he set his mind to it and lie as smoothly as the most hardened criminal, all the while retaining a smile of innocence and purity.*

*In fact, it had been just this dual quality about Evan that had first disturbed her. Then the gap had widened when she found out how frequently he had deceived her. As ideal as he always seemed to others, she had eventually cracked his exterior and found revealed beneath it a core of such rottenness that she could no longer respect or trust him. By the time the summer after graduation had ended, they had made a clean break and he had moved away to Landsport, presumably to take a job.*

*Now, five years later, here he was back again, acting as if nothing had happened and no time had passed. Wendy picked up the sheet of paper and looked at it again, half hoping that the familiar scrawl would suddenly disappear like invisible ink, half feeling a rush of anticipation at the possibility of once again being crushed in his arms.*

## A FINAL REMINDER

Three methods of introducing background information, or significant segments of the past, into the present action of a story: the flashback, the stream-of-consciousness technique, and simple narration. Any combination of these may be used effectively.

The major portion of the story, however, should take place in the present. While many successful stories are told largely through flashbacks (or one long flashback, as in the story within a story), it is often preferable to use this technique selectively and sparingly, the basic episodes being presented in vivid dramatic scenes linked together with smooth transitional narration. Background information may be introduced as required, but the main action moves along in the present.

A final word of warning: Neither the journey into the past nor the background information should be introduced too close to the beginning of the story. If the flashback appears in too prominent a position or is presented more vividly than the present action, perhaps it would be better to consider beginning the story at a different point.

# Evaluation Guidelines

As short stories are completed as a classroom assignment, the instructor may wish to have other students involved in the evaluation process. For this purpose, students may select pen-names to conceal their identity. Only the instructor need know the authors' real names. The students may also be instructed to type their stories on spirit masters, if there are available facilities for duplicating them and distributing them to all the members of the class. Each item may be checked off on a scale of one to five.

As a guideline for discussion, copies of the following form may be distributed.

1. PLOT
   Triggering action (Is it clear why it is necessary to take some action, at this particular time, to solve a problem that is perhaps of long duration?)
   Identification of goal, obstacle, and related action (Are these items clearly identifiable?)
   Resolution of conflict (Is the problem solved in a justifiable and emotionally satisfying way?)
   Credibility (Is the sequence of action believable and true to life?)

2. CHARACTERIZATION
   Depth (Is each character analyzed in sufficient depth for his role in the story? Is the protagonist understood in depth, and is he three-dimensional?)
   Credibility (Is each character believable?)
   Motivation (Is there clear motivation for each action performed by a character? Is the main character, in particular, moved by some identifiable force or event to do what he does?)
   Consistency (Does each character act "in character"? Are his thoughts, words, and actions in keeping with the kind of person we are led to believe he is?)

3. POINT OF VIEW
   Appropriateness (Is the point of view from which the story is told the most effective one that could have been used?)
   Consistency (Is the point of view consistently observed throughout the story? Is it free from unintentional or inappropriate violations?)
   Clarity (Is it clear which point of view, or what combination of points of view, the writer has selected?)

4. DIALOGUE
   Identification of speaker (Is it always possible for the reader to identify who is speaking without confusion and without having to backtrack several sentences?)
   Punctuation and paragraphing (Has the writer mastered the skill of reporting dialogue properly?)
   Fidelity to living speech (Is each character's speech believable and natural-sounding? Is his manner of speaking appropriate for his position in life? Has the writer avoided stereotyping his characters through their speech and refrained from artificial and meaningless spellings?)
   Frequency according to need (Is there as much dialogue as the story seems to demand? Is the reader permitted to witness conversations for himself instead of simply being told about them? Is the dialogue reserved for meaningful exchanges and not wasted on the mere niceties of social intercourse?)

5. DRAMATIZATION AND NARRATION: BALANCE
   (Is there a sufficient balance between what the narrator tells and what the reader can witness first-hand? Is dramatization used for the most crucial points of the story, narration being reserved for binding the scenes together and moving the plot along at a reasonably fast pace?)

6. VISIBILITY
   (Is the reader able to "see" what is going on, as if the characters were moving across a visible stage? Can he see the characters in motion as they speak and think and

interact with one another? Are the settings visibly presented so that the reader can visualize every location where action takes place?)

7. **TRANSITIONS**
   (Are the transitions from one place to another and one time to another handled smoothly? Are the transitions from present to past and back to present clearly indicated?)

8. **FLASHBACKS AND OTHER MEMORY DEVICES**
   (Has the writer been selective in the material presented from the past? Have the transitions been smooth and free of confusion? Do they achieve what they set out to do?)

9. **DESCRIPTION**
   Purpose (Does all the description serve a useful purpose in the story?)
   Helpfulness (Does this description help the reader in any concrete way?)
   Authenticity of setting (Does the setting, as described, appear to be authentic?)

10. **SYMBOL, IMAGE, AND IRONY**
    (If the writer has chosen to use symbolic elements, repeated imagery, or irony, is it effective? Are enough clues provided so that a careful reader will be able to understand what is meant?)

11. **THEME AND TITLE**
    (Is the title appropriate to the story? Does it suggest to the reader, or help to emphasize, what the writer is trying to say? Are all the events of the story in keeping with what the theme is assumed to be? If you were to see this title in a table of contents, would you turn to it right away?)

12. **OVERALL UNITY**
    (Do all parts of the story work toward a unified whole? Is the story free from extraneous material?)

13. **INTEREST**
    (How well did the story hold your interest? Did the opening paragraphs urge you to want to read on? Even if you have not experienced a similar problem, were you able to lose yourself in the story?)

14. **COMMUNICATION**
    (Were you able to understand what the writer was saying? How well did he communicate his ideas to the reader? Was the story free from problems that stand in the way of clarity and coherence?)

15. **MECHANICAL SKILLS**
    (Was the story relatively free from common technical problems, such as misspelled words, unintentional sentence fragments or run-on sentences, faulty construction, misplaced modifiers, etc.?)

16. **ADDITIONAL COMMENTS**
    (What other observations can you make about the effectiveness of this story? What did the writer do especially well? What suggestions can you make for improvement?)

## Wasted

**By Parth Galen**

I sat crouched in a fetal position with utter darkness surrounding me on all sides like invisible walls. In fear and unable to move, I pondered the blackness of night. It must truly be man's primordial terror. I theorized how much like hell that isolation was. It didn't really matter whether I opened my eyes or kept them closed. My head swam and my senses were useless in that void. Shivering, I felt my consciousness wavering and I longed for the welcome light of dawn. . . . . .

I was aroused only very slowly. A bright diffuse light showed pink through my eyelids. I opened them to see where it came from. As my eyes began to focus I could make out a high green roof of leaves broken here and there by the pale blue of dawn. I sat up wearily, coming out of my troubled sleep, and looked around me. I was completely surrounded by massive trees. Bewildered, I tried to figure out where I was. I couldn't remember the preceding day at all. I rose slowly to my feet to get a better look at things. I wondered why my limbs ached as from a great labor when I staggered against the nearest tree.

Looking down at myself, as at a stranger, I was puzzled by my clothes--a soiled flannel shirt and faded Levi's. They weren't mine. Or were they? I looked to the trees again. It was a forest but I did not know that place or how I got there. I checked my pockets for possible clues but they were all empty. Now my mind raced to the most startling realization of all. I couldn't even remember who I was! The full force of my position swept me into a gnawing fear of the unknown. The vastness of the forest and the void that was my memory combined to assault my very reason.

I walked slowly, looking about at the myriad tall trees all around me. The place was completely beyond my reckoning. A genuine terror gripped me. I kept asking myself the same questions over and over--Who am I? Where am I? Why?--with no answers forthcoming. It was all gone and I was here, alone and afraid. I tried to think of possible reasons for my plight--car accident? plane crash? foul play?--but there was nothing except an incredible mental block. After a few more moments of wondering I realized the futility of racking my brain for a memory that wasn't there. I decided to worry about my amnesia later and turned my mind to the more pressing task of getting out of that damned forest.

As I pondered which way to go, the forest seemed to press in on me. It was stifling in there, and darkness loomed in every direction. I called a loud clear "Hello" but the sound fell muffled as soon as it left my lips. I hesitated uncertainly, imagining half-formed things lurking in the shadows and intertwining leaves above, phantoms of my forgotten childhood.

I couldn't discover any visible path after checking the immediate area so I resolved to follow the sun. It was then rising high as the morning drew on. Determined, I plunged into the undergrowth and tried to keep a straight course. The tangle of briars and thorns tore my shirt and viciously scratched my arms and face. The salt of my perspiration stung the already smarting wounds. I struggled on in the muggy heat for what seemed miles. My own body heat attracted swarms of mosquitoes which exasperated me to no end and the forest showed no signs of thinning.

I had begun my trek with an uneasy confidence, relying on the sun as my direction-finder as well as time-keeper. Now my path was darkened even as mid-day approached. The trees thickened and became taller, shutting out the guiding light.

My fear grew with the darkness. Was that the same exposed rock I had passed an hour ago? How could I make any progress traveling in circles? I felt I had to keep moving or the mosquitoes would eat me alive. Not only that, I realized I had only a few hours of daylight left to find my way out--if there was a way. The forest seemed to have a will of its own. Did that tree move? I felt the peculiar sensation that someone or something was following me, but when I whirled around to surprise it, there was nothing. As I forced myself to keep moving, my senses seemed now dulled, now painfully acute. Aieee! A mosquito crawling in my ear! I slapped the side of my head wildly and it stopped buzzing. Still I ran on. My fluttering heartbeat and the blood rushing at my temples was unbearable. I stumbled and fell heavily against a tree. I stopped my ears and closed my eyes. My clothes clung wetly to me like a second skin, and my hair was damp on my forehead.

When I could stand it no longer, I cried out and started running wildly, heedlessly through the gathering darkness. I ran, driving myself as the adrenalin coursed through me, for minutes, hours, an eternity. Suddenly I noticed that no undergrowth barred my terrified flight now. I could not remember when the terrain had changed. Yet it seemed as if the lower branches and snakelike roots were trying to grab me or trip me up. Stumbling, I cursed the forest and blundered on.

Looming up ahead, rays of sunlight stabbed down through the thinning trees. I could feel the land begin to slope downward. Steeper and steeper it became so that I could not stop my downward plunge. It was all I could do to keep from crashing into trees and ducking from vines. A wall of undergrowth suddenly appeared and I threw my arms across my face. I crashed forward through the bushes, tearing my clothes as I did so. Then there was nothing--no trees, no undergrowth, no darkness. I opened my eyes and the violence of the sunlight blinded me. I slipped and slid downward on a bed of thick grass. The slope still increased as I shaded my eyes trying to see what was happening. I rolled over an embankment and fell headlong into ice-cold water. The shock of the cold water revived me and I came up gasping. I was standing knee-deep in a narrow, clear brook. I waded upstream a few feet to where I could see beyond the embankment. The forest had ended abruptly and I was clear at last.

Climbing out of the water I lay down on the grassy bank, still heaving from the desperate effort in the forest. The sky was clear and blue overhead and I was amazed to find that the sun had not yet reached noon; it was still beyond the trees. I had lost all conception of time and direction in the forest. Here it was but mid-morning. Birds sang cheerfully overhead and frogs croaked nearby. I returned to the water and cupped my hands to drink slowly from the cool water. I discovered that most of my cuts and scratches were only superficial as I bathed them. Gradually the terror of the wood subsided. Soon I felt almost content until I suddenly realized that I was still lost and without memory. I climbed back up the embankment to survey the open land across the brook.

I could see vast acres of fenced fields and pasture. Just on the edge of the horizon I could dimly discern a red spot in a sea of green which I took to be a barn. I was elated. With new courage and a clear sense of direction and purpose, I would make for that farm. There would be people there who could help me. I scrambled down the bank and began wading slowly across the brook, testing its depth with each step. I was arrested halfway across by a new and ominous sound that silenced the birds and frogs.

I couldn't be sure, but it sounded like the far-off baying of hounds, away back in the forest. I paused, listening for a couple of more minutes. They were getting closer. Hunters? A posse? My mind raced again. What could they be after? I listened. The yelping hounds seemed eager; they must have had a scent.

My heart leaped into my mouth. My God, no! I tried once again to recall the night before. My blank memory, compounded by a creeping fear, afforded me no answers. Even if they were not tracking me, I didn't want to be caught trespassing. I couldn't come up with a reason; I just felt that I shouldn't be there. The baying of the hounds was getting perilously close--just on the other side of the underbrush, they seemed.

I had to snap out of my indecision and hesitation. I splashed frantically the rest of the way across the brook. At the top of the opposite bank there was a fence and a sign that gave me all the reason I needed for running for my life: NO TRESPASSING--VIOLATORS SHOT ON SIGHT. Any way I looked at it, I was their prey; I was a fugitive. I vaulted the fence with some effort, for my legs were heavy with the wet Levi's. Soon I was running so hard I felt as if my lungs would burst. Unable to move farther, I paused. I turned, panting violently, to scan the distant line of trees along the brook.

To my horror, I saw a group of red-jacketed men and the glint of metal. Gunbarrels! The agitated hounds were running back and forth along the top of the embankment. My heart sank as I guessed the truth. A split second after this realization came, the hunters spotted me and slid down the bank with a shout. The furious baying of the hounds was redoubled.

Now for it, I thought. Once again I launched myself into a flight of terror. My fear possessed me and drove me on. My legs, driving like pistons beneath me, exploded with sheer animal power. Yet the relentless howling never seemed to recede. Still I kept up my dizzying pace. I tried to leap another fence and choked back a cry of agony. The barbed wire lacerated my thigh and the burning pain raced through me. I dared another momentary pause to staunch the bleeding and found myself in a deep-rutted lane heading for the farm. I took it to be no more than a quarter mile away. My leg throbbing, I gritted my teeth for the last dash. Behind me the hounds were gaining.

Within minutes the barn loomed up immediately ahead. My legs felt leaden as I plodded into the barnyard. Except for a few chickens, the place looked deserted. Perhaps the owner was one of my pursuers. At any rate, the aid I hoped would be here was non-existent. My only refuge was the barn. I ducked into it and cowered like a beaten cur. My limbs shook and my eyes refused to focus. As my head cleared, I saw the first hounds bounding toward me. The hunters had evidently loosed them for the kill. I just barely managed to slam the sliding door shut, catching the foot of the lead hound. The rest crashed snarling and howling into the door and each other, cut off from their victim.

Peering through a crack in the door, I watched the hunters form a cordon bristling with ready shotguns. They were taking no chances. A cornered beast is the most savage of all. I couldn't rationalize my plight nor did I seem to care any longer. If I tried to get out of the barn by another exit the hounds would nail me in seconds. If I stayed where I was *they* would enter by those same exits. All escape was thus cut off. My destiny awaited me in that yard. The air was electric with tension as I steeled myself for a spring. I would go down fighting.

With a shout I threw open the door and leaped into the midst of the hounds, kicking and flailing my fists. I stumbled forward trying to throw them off and screamed as one brown hound sank its fangs into my calf. I heard a shrill whistle and the hounds fell back. Only then did I fully realize my position. I was on my knees in the center of the yard with a dozen shotguns leveled at me.

A few feet in front of me and in the center of the cordon, a tall man, with his face hidden in shadow under the brim of his hat, gave the order.

"Waste him."

I was stunned by a blinding flash and a deafening blast. I was hurled backward by its force, but there was no pain. I rolled, groping in the dust, trying to rise. I could see where my flesh had been shredded by the buckshot, yet I couldn't feel any pain. With the will but not the strength, I gave up trying to stand. I only wanted to face them and get it over with. I extended my arm outward toward them, palm up and fingers trembling, working my hand in a gesture pleading for mercy. I wanted to say, "Finish it!" but the heavy saline taste of blood choked my throat. It finally came--one more thundering, murderous report--as if all the shotguns fired as one. I sank down into the dust, my blood mingling with the earth, red in my eyes, down, down, down. Out of consciousness, passing from one world to another. . . . . .

I was floating in a dimension between life and death, between wakefulness and sleep. Then I awoke, panting and sweating, still gripping the dust of the barnyard. But when I looked at my hands there was nothing, and I knew I had passed out of a dream. It was always that way, the same goddamn dream haunted me whenever I was thrown into solitary confinement.

How many times have I escaped this hell only to be brought back, beaten, chained, or thrown into the black isolation of the "hole"? I remember the words in the dream, so calmly uttered: "Waste him." And I die, gratefully.

But there is no death here, unless it is an endless one. I know the darkness and these four close walls are my tomb. My tortured mind burns with the knowledge that I will escape again and once more see the light.

## Cast the First Stone

### By Hilton Neale

The Reverend Mr. Cyrus Steele sat rigidly on the unyielding cushion of his straight-backed chair and stared ahead into the gloom. Subconsciously the fingertips of both hands met in a characteristic gesture of self-approval. Daylight had waned and finally faded completely away, but he was unaware of the darkness of the sky beyond his single bare study window, or of the shadows that had gathered in the narrow room.

He had done what he had to do. He could find no leniency in his heart to condone the irresponsible behavior of a straying sheep. It had come to his attention a week before that

John Randall, chairman of the board of trustees at Bethany Church, was involved in a scandal. Of course, all of Medville knew that John's marriage was not a happy one, that Mrs. Randall had tormented her husband unceasingly for twenty-eight years, wearing away his manliness with constant harrassment and petty criticism, until she had finally reduced him long since to a silent, faceless shadow. Everyone knew, too, that she had kept him in perpetual debt with her extravagance. Still, one married for better or worse, and if he lacked the strength to control the tongue-lashings of the once-lovely shrew he had so proudly taken to wed in her softer and more subtle youth, that was his cross to bear. It didn't give him license to alter his vows in order to pursue Nell Halport, a quietly plain little thing half his age.

When the truth came out, Cyrus had had no choice but to make an example of him. The church could not permit its officers to flaunt their sins and continue to serve. John's resignation had been requested at the official meeting the night before, and if he had not been such a fool as to try to make explanations and excuses, there would have been no need to bring into the open all the sordid details which Cyrus had felt it his duty to inquire about and verify. The whole incident had left him with a feeling of utter disgust, for it was beyond Cyrus' comprehension that a man might waste his emotions on a mere woman and not be a fool.

As for himself, there were only two things that Cyrus ached for with an uncompromising passion. One was the new church building for which a drive for funds was currently in progress. For the ten years of his present pastorate, he had raised his voice above the chugging of nearby trains that always chose the climax of his sermon for passing, and had struggled against the growing, insidious blight of the neighborhood. Finally, with the congregation moving gradually to more pleasant outlying areas, he had been able to persuade his reluctant parishioners that the time had come to build on a new site. So far, he had been gratified by the financial response, but there was still a long way to go, and there was not much time left if they were to get the desirable location which they had selected.

The other goal of Cyrus Steele--and perhaps the more deeply rooted--was to keep his church free from sin. He himself had walked down the straight and narrow way of unquestioned virtue all his days, never looking to left or right except to beat relentlessly from his path any threat to his uprightness. He had married Martha more for her impeccable reputation and her steadfast ways than because of any romantic illusions; he was not a man for frivolity. He had also been well aware of her warm simplicity and outgoing friendliness, which he knew would be an asset in his calling.

Whenever parishioners had been known to stray, Cyrus had seen to it that they were dealt with severely. Nobody could say Cyrus Steele didn't preach what he practiced and practice what he preached. No one could say that *he* wasn't a watchdog for the Lord.

Martha and he had not always seen eye to eye on this matter, but he had never failed to have his way. John Randall was no exception. If he chose to live outside the dictates of the church and decent society, then he must bear the consequences. What Martha thought about it really did not matter. He had never been able to alter that foolish strain of sentimentality in her. Yet, while she had often disagreed with him, she had never openly defied him.

Cyrus was aroused from his recollection of the past few days' events, secure in the justification of his disciplinary actions, by the distant ringing of the telephone. He rose and switched on the lamp. The clutter of his desk annoyed him. He busied himself tidying and sorting the mail that needed response, the clippings, and the notes for next Sunday's sermon to be based on the text: "And be not conformed to this world; but be ye transformed by the renewing of your mind, that ye may prove what is the good, and acceptable, and perfect, will of God."

Presently he heard a gentle tapping on his closed door and knew it was Martha bringing his usual glass of milk and the evening paper.

"Come in, Martha," he said.

The door opened quietly. Cyrus did not turn. After a moment's silence, he wondered why she did not enter.

"What are the headlines?" he asked, feeling a shade of annoyance.

"I don't know."

"Hasn't the paper come yet?"

"Cyrus," she said, "the headlines aren't important tonight. Emily Proctor just called.

Mr. Randall's been let go from his job."

He noted the hint of reprimand in her voice but decided not to acknowledge it. She would feel that it was *his* fault. But how could he be held responsible for the consequences of the man's own transgressions?

"That is regrettable," he replied shortly. "One should weigh the cost before he decides to indulge in illicit pleasures."

"But don't you think," she said, "the cost would've been high enough anyhow even if he'd just been left alone? We're all human, Cyrus. You know very well that with the kind of nagging he's had to put up with all these years, only a saint could've escaped such a pitfall."

Cyrus did not look up. He went on stacking the last pile of papers neatly in one corner of his desk, making sure all the edges were lined up evenly with the end of the blotter, slowly passed his hand over his thinning gray hair, rearranged his rimless spectacles over the coldly penetrating gray eyes, and sat down deliberately at his desk. His fingertips found each other.

"Martha." He enunciated carefully and slowly. "Am I to understand that you condone this man's disgusting conduct? Would you have me close my eyes to something all Medville is gossiping about--and he a pillar of the church, or seeming to be? Is this the kind of example you would set before our young people? More power to the Enright Company for insisting their employees live respectable lives! He's done his dirt; now let him pay for it."

"I know he's done wrong, but he's not a young man any more. You could intercede--"

"All the more reason," he said, "for not acting like a fool."

"Oh, Cyrus, I don't understand you sometimes." She sighed. Her tone told more of defeat than exasperation. "I knew about this long before you did. It isn't right, it isn't moral, but that girl gave him the only joy he's ever had in his life. Do you remember how he--"

"You knew about it?" he shouted. "You let this thing go on right under your very nose--"

"I knew and I understood a little what he suffered. And he did suffer in more ways than one. He wasn't an immoral man, you know, and to do what he did and try to live with his conscience . . . I hoped he'd work it out. I hoped it wouldn't have to come to this. But yes, I knew. He even talked to me about it once--in confidence, you know."

"He talked to you? The--the--*cur*! To you and not to me?"

"What good would it've done? What's happened would have just happened that much sooner, that's all. I tried to help him. That's something you would never have done."

"Martha, I refuse to have you talk to me this way. I'm disappointed. I'm gravely disappointed in you."

"Yes," she said and turned away. "I suppose you are."

Medville had an unpredictable reaction to John Randall's "resignation" from the trustee board and his dismissal from the Enright Home Improvement Company for which he had been a highly dependable and skilled cabinet maker and carpenter. In the week that followed these events, Mrs. Randall had left her husband in a final act of disapproval and indignation. John was not at church that Sunday to hear the minister's remonstrances, which everyone knew were intended for him. He had followed the ways of the world and therefore stood in public disgrace. But there was some doubt as to who constituted "the public" other than the Reverend Mr. Cyrus Steele. For it was later rumored that several members of the congregation said their customary greetings on the church steps after service and then, individually and secretly, went from the Bible-flapping sermon on the sins of conformity to the home of Mr. Randall, whom they found in the midst of befuddlement in a cluttered and lonely living room. They had been surprised and embarrassed to meet there, but after the first few awkward minutes, they busied themselves, as if by common consent, with tidying the house, preparing a meal, and coaxing him to get some rest.

Martha was not among the after-service visitors. Her absence from home at such an hour on a busy Sunday would have been difficult to explain, as would her presence in the Randall home at all, after her husband's verbal attack. But the women of Medville knew who was responsible in the following weeks and months for making certain that John did not neglect his meals. And certain odd jobs that had been indefinitely postponed in many neighboring homes suddenly became a matter of the direst urgency. During the daytime, when husbands were conspicuously absent, many households were the scene of surreptitious activity. In general, the men, preoccupied by more urgent matters, did not even notice that the back stairs no longer creaked or that their wives had ceased to nag them about new shelves in the basement.

What at least one husband did notice, however, was the sharp decrease in church attendance, especially when his first sermon was followed shortly thereafter by another, no more subtly veiled than the first, on the Seventh Commandment. Along with this decline came a noticeable drop in the payment of voluntary pledges for the new church property. Cyrus was plainly agitated and more than a little mystified that such a promising beginning should now, at the crucial last minute of opportunity, face possible defeat. He was vaguely aware of Martha's aloofness and lack of conversation at the dinner table, where once the trivialities of every day had been pleasantly--even if one-sidedly--discussed. Of course, that didn't matter too much. She had disagreed with his outspoken stand on the Randall business, but she had disagreed before and it always blew over. He was not a man to be unduly concerned with the reactions of others. As long as he knew he was right, no one else's opinion mattered.

"Didn't see the Wilson children at Sunday school," he commented.

"No," she said.

"Not sick, are they?"

"Not as I've heard." Martha was appraising the pattern on the tablecloth.

"Still a little early for the Newtons. Don't suppose they're back yet."

"Mm .... Guess not." She absently dabbed at the mashed potatoes on her plate. Finally, she laid down her fork and looked at her watch. Before Cyrus had finished his meal, she rose from the table and went into the kitchen where the muffled clatter of pans indicated the next job to be done. Cyrus reached for his third biscuit, broke it open and buttered it, replaced the top, and bit into it vigorously.

As dearly as Medville loved a funeral and enjoyed detailing the earliest symptoms of illness and the final throes of agony, the putting away of Nell Halport was a quiet and lonely affair. Her life had been inconspicuous until her involvement with John Randall had received such wide publicity. She had lived with her widowered father on the outskirts of town all her young life, too busy with chores in a household bursting with lively younger brothers and sisters to finish high school herself or take part in the activities of others her age. She was a plain girl who went to town only on market days, quickly returning to the small farm to resume her endless duties and cares. No young, handsome admirer had ever felt his life incomplete without her. No romance had brightened her youth except the thrill of every rising sun when she looked above the head of the one cow the family possessed, murmured her inarticulate yearning, and gazed beyond at the greening hillside and the promise of the day.

One day two years before, when her father had suffered a near-fatal heart attack, she had conversed briefly with John Randall who had come to offer help and comfort and had taken away with him more quietness and peace than he had known existed. From that day on, he had been a beggar in his need of her, and she had been, at first reluctant, and then generous in the sharing of her quiet strength.

Their child, a tight-fisted, red-faced little monkey of a boy, had lived for two hours after his thin, peevish wail first protested against a world in which the wages of sin was death. The mother had lived only long enough to see that his unfocused eyes were brown, and that a curl of reddish hair the color of John's protruded from the base of an otherwise bald skull. There had been no time to summon the father; the labor pains, perhaps hastened by too rigorous activities on the farm, had preceded the doctor's calculation by six weeks. Nell had suffered and died alone except for the inexpert help of a neighboring farm wife who had cut the cord, slapped the transient breath from the newborn infant, and bathed him for his brief sojourn from the unknowable to the eternal.

The next day, a joint funeral was held unannounced at the Potter Funeral Chapel with Nell's father, a few farmers and their wives, and an itinerant country preacher present for the final rites. And John. By the time Medville got the news, only a freshly-dug plot of earth bore evidence that one woman in all the world had made the fruitless years of John Randall full and warm for so brief a spell.

For Cyrus Steele, the death of Nell Halport was the climactic verification of his lifelong views. But he could not fully enjoy the victory of his rectitude. The little tragedy of two insignificant sinners was overshadowed by the teetering of one of his dearest dreams. The campaign for church funds was running far short of its goal. Of course, even if the lovely, wooded site in Melmore Gardens was lost, there were other desirable locations. But he knew that the underlying reason for this failure would be likely to doom any subsequent effort. To be so close to the realization of this dream and then to fail! To desire so passionately the new structure far from the trains' staccato jerking and the screams of dirty, lost children. . . .

He could not escape knowing that the Randall business was somehow at the bottom of his present frustration, but he did not consider himself at all responsible, and the connection was not a thought to be dwelled upon nor explored. No matter how passionately he desired the new structure, whatever disappointment he might experience, he was not a man to compromise on a matter of integrity. He knew that he was right to insist upon certain moral standards in his church; the church was for the pure in heart, not the flagrantly unworthy, and if the bricks of the present building all crumbled around the heads of the members and himself, then crumble they must, but he would not be moved. If part of the membership secretly sympathized with John Randall enough to neglect their pledges, then they were sinful, too, and he would ferret them out. Let them all rot in their false loyalty. He would do his duty to God and then leave them in their predicament. There were other churches to be had.

John Randall entered the Procter home by the side door, wiped his feet carefully on the mat, and walked across the tiled kitchen to the table. Mrs. Procter had called him earlier to say that she and a neighbor had been detained on their shopping trip to town and might not get back before his arrival. He was to let himself in--the people of Medville rarely locked their doors--and help himself to the lunch she had left covered in the refrigerator. By that time, she said, she should be back to show him what she wanted done.

John ate his meal slowly, savoring every mouthful. Then, running hot water, he added his dishes to the ones in the sink, washed and dried them carefully, and stacked them neatly on the sideboard. Mrs. Procter had not yet returned, and he looked around to see what he could do. Now that the dishes were clean, the spotless kitchen needed no further attention. Pushing open the swinging door which led into a large, sunny hallway, he made his way to the living room. A smudge filmed a small portion of the large mirror above the table, and he took a clean cloth from his pocket and dabbed at it. The faint sound of a door closing came to him from the front of the hall. Mrs. Procter must be back from town. But the first voice he heard was not hers. Her neighbor must have come back with her. He was about to reenter the kitchen when the sound of his own name made him stop. He should have moved on or made his presence known as soon as he realized they were discussing him, but his feet felt weighted with lead.

"--been and gone."

"--such a pity, Emily--persecuted without mercy."

"never understand--he'll pay for it." The words came clearer now. "He's paying already. He'll never get that church he had his mind so set on. The people just won't stand for it, that's all. Him so high and mighty and holier than thou all the time. Well, let him be, but even the Master didn't look down his nose none when some poor human stumbled. Is he better than Him, does he think? As if the poor soul ain't been punished enough. His wife and--"

"Course, Emily, you know that was a blessing in disguise. That woman--"

"Yes--yes, guess it was, but a body gets used to a way of living and misses it something awful even when it's bad. But imagine that poor little thing dying like that, so frightened and in disgrace, that never hurt no one, and that innocent little baby, too--no chance at all, none. Now I'm not saying all that was the Reverend's fault or nothing, but that poor Mr. Randall's paid a dozen times over for what he done. It just ain't right, Bess, a man's got to pay and pay ten times over for the same crime. Did you see how few people was there last Sunday?"

"Humph. Yes. And from the talk afterwards, I'd say there won't be half that many next week. And the collections!"

"Well, I really can't say as I care much what happens now. Don't feel right somehow listening to him preach his high-sounding sermons. And I know it's not Christian to think it, but I just don't feel like paying my hard-earned money to a church where a poor body's only welcome if he hasn't got no sins at all. The good Lord knows there ain't a perfect one among us. It just ain't right."

"Yes, the good Lord knows it," Bess agreed, "but Reverend Steele hasn't been told yet.

Emily, you're the first one's come out and said it, about the money and all, but I know it's what every living soul in town's been hinting at. I've been fighting it in myself, but I can't help--"

"Was that the back door closing?" Emily went to the kitchen but no one was there. "I don't know," she said. "Just the wind, I guess. But Mr. Randall's been here, all right. Why, bless my soul, look how he cleaned up in here. Guess he got tired of waiting. It's such a shame, really, such a shame--and him such a mild, sweet soul."

"Yes, and not a mean bone in his body," Bess said. "Why, most men in his place would've been mad at the world and 'specially put out with Reverend Steele. But he's never said a word against anyone at all. All I heard him say once was, 'He only did his job the way he saw it. And I reckon he's right. I had no call to do it.' "

"No, he wouldn't be one for hard feelings. It ain't his way."

"No," Bess agreed, "it's not his way at all."

John left Emily Procter's home with clouded eyes and a worried frown. He had not waited to do the job he came to do, but he knew that wasn't important now. He had a bigger job to do. He had to think, and he always thought best when he worked with his hands. Had he been aware of the excitement in his hurried pace, he would have been surprised, for the house he rushed to was so overpowering with its memories and shadows that he always approached it now with apprehension. But today he opened the door without his usual dread, not even hearing the click that always now brought such a hollow loneliness.

For the first time in several months, and not knowing what he did, he went down the basement stairs to his workroom, hesitated in front of his bench, and then tenderly, with an almost maternal concern, with both hands stroked the massive piece of wood that stretched almost the length and width of the room. Before his misfortune, he had wanted to make something for the new church and had worked with great zeal for many arduous hours toward that end. When, as a member of the board, he had first seen the architect's drawings, he had been struck instantly with a vision of a large, stark, simple cross above and behind the altar; the design of the sanctuary seemed to demand it, and he had almost felt the stone-hard African mahogany under his skilled hands and shaped and smoothed it in his imagination before he was even aware of his desire. But later, after it was started, he had not felt worthy, until this moment, of even looking at his project or bearing to defile it with his touch.

Now he sat down on a low stool, picked up a ball of steel wool, and absently began to rub one edge of the wood with a steady circular motion . . . . *Sitting in the pew with Mama . . . just a little fellow . . . The knothole in the wooden seat back--such a funny roundness. Rough and smooth at the same time . . . Liked to trace it around and around with my fingers. She didn't care much. Kept me quiet . . . Not like the time I yelled out when Papa was lying out there in front. Why was he sleeping there in front of all those people with his clothes on? A funny bed, I thought . . . Take care of Mama. Yes, Papa. Yes, sir. The sheets damp. His forehead flushed, wet. Hot hands . . . Stay in the church, son, do the Lord's work. Yes, Papa . . . Yes . . .* Yes, I can!

Still a month away, the deadline. The women--would have to be the women--they'd do it. Mrs. Clark and Mrs. Johnson next door and the Winstons across the street--expecting me to call them anyhow today. Just run by there instead and they'd offer me a cup of tea and I could say--well, don't quite know what I *would* say, but it'll come. I've got to make them see. Make them understand. I could say--well, we'll see, we'll see. Make a list first--the key ones, ones that'll run to the others, talk a lot. Let's see. Mrs. Hargrove, Mrs. Mills, Mrs.--Mrs.--oh, if it works! If it only, only works!

About four weeks later, the Reverend Mr. Cyrus Steele beamed broadly across the chasm between his pulpit and the pews and unconsciously brought the tips of his fingers together. He cleared his light, rather high-pitched voice to speak again.

"And now, good friends," he said, "before we dismiss, we wish to make public the announcement we all have been waiting and praying and working for--waiting quite breathlessly, some of us." Near the rear door a child coughed several times. "We had some rather troubling times and hope seemed pretty dim, and there were days when we didn't think we'd be able to stand here this morning and tell you the good news.

"But we came through, friends." He flapped his Bible shut vigorously. "We've topped our goal, and our representatives will meet tomorrow morning at the First National Bank at ten o'clock to make the transaction official. The land is ours, by some miracle of the Lord's.

"And it only goes to show, good people, that sometimes we act like foolish, straying sheep and have to be led by rather stringent leadership back to the righteousness of the fold. For God doesn't want his church built on a foundation of sinful laxity and conformity to the ways of the world. He made us in His own image, and He insists that we church people assume the role He wants for us as the leaders of righteousness in the midst of the world's wickedness." His fingers found each other again across the closed leather-bound Bible. A train whistle tooted once in the distance and then again a little louder than before.

"I tell you, friends, it's good to look out into the audience and see before us attentive faces rather than empty pews, and it makes us proud and happy to know that we are all of one accord."

Emily Procter's glance strayed to the empty pew of Mr. and Mrs. John Randall. She turned to whisper something to the occupant of the seat beside her, but Bess's head was tilted slightly forward and her mouth was open. Only the chugging of the passing freight cars made her first snores inaudible.

## Early Winter

### By Renée Walton Schwall

Leigh set the tea kettle, half full of water, on the burner and flipped the burner knob to high. Sighing deeply, she pulled her bathrobe tighter around her slender frame, took her cup and saucer, with a solitary teabag in it, over to the kitchen table and sat down across from her brooding husband. Absently, she gazed out of the kitchen window at the dreary sunless morning. Again she sighed, thinking of how dull the weather had been this month. Ever since the baby had been born in early January, not a day had gone by without the seemingly eternal darkness of mid-winter and the seemingly endless screams of a newborn infant.

"Sure you don't want any tea?" Leigh asked softly.

"No thanks," her fair-haired husband replied, his head still buried in a cluttered pile of papers and books.

"Joe, you know you shouldn't go to school on a completely empty stomach. You know that today is one of your long days."

"I know. Don't have time this morning. Old geezer in my physics course is laying a heavy exam on us this morning and I didn't have time last night to study when I got home from work. Just pack me a sandwich. I can eat that before I go to work this afternoon."

Leigh rose from her chair and turned toward the refrigerator to begin preparing a simple but nourishing lunch for her husband. As she reached for the loaf of bread a sudden scream rang out through the tiny apartment.

"Oh, Jesus! Just what I need! I've got this huge test coming up and I can't even have any peace and quiet to study for it! Don't just stand there! Go shut the kid up!"

Leigh stood by the refrigerator planted to the floor. She looked at Joe, who had now taken the time to look up from his books. His face had anger in it and it was something she was unaccustomed to seeing. His eyes were narrowed and their blueness had gone ice cold.

"I said, don't just stand there! I've got to study! I don't have time this morning to play nursemaid!"

Leigh felt her own eyes well with tears as she felt Joe's angry gaze turn into one of accusation, as if it were her fault that the baby had chosen this particular moment to wake up. She felt her feet moving under her as she turned away from Joe and hurried to try and calm the baby.

Little Joey lay screaming fitfully in his crib. Leigh picked him up and rocked him in her arms as she carried him over to the changing table and unfastened his diaper. Even though little Joey was being changed, his crying still would not let up, and as Leigh pinned the fresh diaper on him she knew she had to hurry back to the kitchen to start his formula for his breakfast. She set the baby, still wailing fitfully, in his crib and returned to the kitchen.

"Where are you going?" she asked, as she saw Joe standing in the kitchen with his jacket on, busily cramming his books into his knapsack.

"Can't get any work done here with the baby screaming like that. It really gets on my nerves. I'm going over to the library where it's quiet."

"But your lunch--"

"I don't have time to wait. I'll pick something up before I go to work tonight." He slung his knapsack over his shoulder and put his gloves on. "Damn! And I'm the one who is trying to save money."

"Joe, I'm sorry--"

"Well so am I." They stood facing each other as Leigh tried to think of something to say that would break the terrible tension that she felt was between them.

"I'll see you at midnight then?" Leigh said as she saw Joe's angered face relax.

"Yeah," he muttered softly. "See ya." He moved close to her and she felt the warmth of his lips brush against her cheek as he turned towards the living room. The sound of the tea kettle was soaring to the same pitch level as the baby's screams as she heard the front door squeak open, then close with a defiant thud.

A feeling of emptiness was starting to creep through her as she turned and took the tea kettle off the stove. She poured the boiling water into her tea cup and listlessly dunked the tea bag in and out of the water, watching the clear water grow gradually darker with each dunk.

Deciding to let her tea cool a bit, she went back into the bedroom to comfort the baby. She picked up her crying son and returned to the kitchen with him. With Joey on her left hip and her right hand free, she began preparing his formula. When the formula reached room temperature, Leigh put it into a bottle and sat at the table and fed Joey.

When the nipple of the bottle reached his mouth, Joey stopped crying and hungrily sucked at his breakfast. Leigh watched her son take his nourishment and amazed herself thinking about what a beautiful baby he had become. When he had first been born she had thought that he looked somewhat like a picture of Winston Churchill that she had seen in her high school history book. He had been bald and round-faced and ugly. But now when she looked at him she could see a strong resemblance to Joe, and, sometimes, when the baby yawned, she thought that she could see a likeness to her youngest brother when he had been a baby.

As Joey finished the remaining drops of formula, Leigh tossed a towel over her shoulder, set the bottle on the table and picked the baby up and started to pat him firmly on the back. As she did this her thoughts again turned to amazement at how dependent this little life was on her. She thought back to her own mother and wondered if she had experienced this same feeling. "Of course she did," Leigh thought. "Only she never thought I'd outgrow that dependency." She eased back in her chair, still patting Joey and recalled a time about a year before when she had come home from school, to find her mother sitting at the kitchen table waiting for a confrontation.

Leigh had come home and had burst into the house and had rushed to the telephone to call Joe when she had discovered her mother sitting at the table. She had guessed by the look on her mother's face that another lecture was about to begin.

"Leigh, put down that phone right now!" Mrs. Ryan commanded.

"I told Joe I'd call him as soon as I got home from school."

"I think that Joe can wait a little while longer. You and I have something very important to discuss."

Leigh replaced the receiver to its cradle, and came to sit opposite her mother at the table where she anticipated the topic of discussion.

"Now, Leigh," her mother began cautiously, "I know that things have been pretty rough on you with your father and I being divorced and all, but this thing with Joe--honey, you've got to realize what you're doing."

"I know what I'm doing," Leigh responded, feeling annoyed by her mother's interrogation.

"Now we're never going to get anywhere if you're going to take *that* attitude."

"What attitude?" Leigh said trying to make her voice sound as defiant as possible.

"That--oh, it's not important. What is important is that your step-father and I think that you and Joe are getting a little too serious with each other. Really, Leigh, what am I supposed to think when I come home from the grocery store and find all the doors locked and you and Joe sitting on the couch draped all over each other with your clothes all in a mess? My God, every time I walk in the door, you two look like a couple of kids that just got caught with hands in the cookie jar. And suppose it hadn't been me that came home? Suppose it had been one of your little brothers? Jesus! Do you have any idea what kind of impression that could make on them?"

Leigh did not answer but sat wondering, angrily, why her mother was making such a production out of this issue. After all, she *was* sixteen years old and perfectly capable of making her own decisions.

"Now your step-father and I have been discussing this and Bob and I feel--"

"Did you know that's the second reference you've made to Bob? This is none of Bob's business!" Leigh screamed, partially in anger at her mother's conspiracy with her step-father and partially in fear of incurring her single-minded step-father's wrath. "Bob is not my father! He has no right to tell me what I can do and what I can't do! He has no right at all!"

Mrs. Ryan listened to this verbal assault on her husband. Standing up and pulling herself up to her full five-foot-two-inch height, she delivered a stinging slap to Leigh's cheek.

"Dammit, Leigh, I'm not going to sit here and listen to you attack Bob like this! That man works fifty hours a week to put a roof over our heads and food on our table! The least you could do is show a little respect!"

"Respect!" Leigh spat out the word. "Respect for what! The man treats me like a child! You both do! I feel like a caged animal!"

"Well," Mrs. Ryan said sitting down again and fumbling for a cigarette from the pack on the table, "I'm afraid that if this carrying on with Joe continues, we're going to have to forbid you to see him. I won't have this in my home." She lit her cigarette and inhaled.

"*Your* home! *Your* feelings! What about me? Don't I have a right to decide what I want to do with my life?"

"Yes, but for the moment I think you're doing the wrong thing."

"But, Mother, you're treating me like--"

"A child?" her mother finished. "Isn't that the way you're behaving right now? Just like a spoiled little child that can't have her own way? Don't think you can run our lives, Miss High and Mighty! Bob and I can ground you for so long your hair will be grey before you can go out again." She ground out her cigarette with an air of authority.

Frustration peaking, Leigh tearfully fled from the kitchen to the sanctuary of her own room, her mother's final words ringing in her ears. She ran to her bed, slamming the door behind her. She sat sobbing and wondered why her mother and step-father disapproved of her relationship with Joe so strongly. Surely they could see that he was her whole world. He was her constant companion, lover and best friend. Although he was four years older than she was, he never ceased in making her feel every bit the adult she felt she was. Joe would listen to her when no one else either cared to or had time. She could trust him with her darkest secrets and she needed his quiet strength. She felt peace in herself only when she was wrapped in his arms. Leigh only wished that her mother and step-father could see things from her side. If only they could see how much she and Joe were in love, their attitude would surely change. Their attitude would have to change soon, though, she thought. She picked herself up off the bed, went to her dresser and looked in the mirror. She gazed intently at her tear stained face and vowed that nothing her mother and step-father could ever do would stop her from seeing Joe. Her and Joe's plans were much too important to her to let them stand in the way.

Finding a kleenex, she dabbed at her eyes and opened a small jewelry box that sat on the dresser. She fumbled through a small heap of costume jewelry until she found a white gold ring with a tiny diamond clasped in its mounting. She took it out and lovingly slid it onto her left ring finger. It was time the truth came out. After their latest argument, she didn't care what frame of mind her mother was in. She just wanted to make it clear to her mother that she was not going to be pushed around anymore. With an air of resolution, Leigh opened her bedroom door and set out to find her mother.

She found her busy in the kitchen starting dinner. Her back was to the door, as Leigh took a deep breath and entered the room.

"Mom?" Leigh called out meekly.

"What is it?" Mrs. Ryan said without turning around. Leigh could tell by the tone of her voice that she was still angry.

"I've got something to tell you. I'm sorry that I haven't told you this sooner, but I wasn't sure how you'd take it. I think it's time now." Leigh paused, taking another deep breath as her mother set her paring knife and half-peeled potato on the counter and turned to face her.

"Mom--"

"Yes?"

"Joe and I want to get married." Leigh tried to smile and at the same time held out her left hand to make the small engagement ring visible. "I even have a ring. See?" She watched her mother, who turned quite pale for an instant.

"Oh, Leigh, I'm so disappointed in you. I had no idea that you and Joe had gotten this serious. How can you even think of becoming engaged this soon? Honey, you still have two years of high school ahead of you and it hurts me to think that you would miss out on all the activities because you're waiting to get married. Wouldn't you feel bad about missing them?"

"No, they're boring. And if you're talking about going out with other boys my own age, you can forget it. They're such babies."

"Honey, I just don't want to see you wasting your time waiting--"

"Mom, we want to be married soon. This spring maybe? All you have to do is sign the consent forms and--"

"Absolutely not!" Mrs. Ryan pulled her hand into a fist and slammed it down on top of the counter. At that moment Leigh heard the front door open and shut.

"Hey, anybody home?" Leigh's worst fear had just become a reality. Her step-father was home from work and was walking right in at the worst possible moment.

"Hey, what's all this? You both look like someone just died," Mr. Ryan observed as he strode into the kitchen. "What's up?"

Leigh looked at her mother, daring to pray for help, but her mother just gave her an icy look.

"Leigh has just informed me that she and Joe want to get married this spring. Do you believe that?"

Leigh went to the table and sat down, watching her step-father's eyes widen and his jaw drop slightly.

"Hell of a thing to come home to, isn't it?" Mrs. Ryan continued. "I was just about to tell her about my own misfortune at marrying at such an early age." She, too, went to the table and sat down across from Leigh. "Leigh, you have no idea what you'd be getting into. Oh, I just wish my own mother hadn't given in quite so easily when your father and I got married. I wasn't much older than you are right now, and it proved to be one of the worst mistakes I ever made. Oh, I don't mean that your father and I didn't have some happy times together, but deep down we just weren't right for each other. We were both just too immature--" Her voice trailed off and her eyes grew moist.

"But Mom--"

"Leigh," Mr. Ryan interrupted, "I think you've upset your mother enough for today. As long as you are living under my roof and until you come of age, I don't want to hear another word about marriage to Joe, or anyone else, for that matter. Your mother and I both want to see you get out of high school before you take on that kind of responsibility. Now, I know you're not any kind of genius and we know that you're not planning on going to college, but your education is important!" Mr. Ryan, still standing, paused as if to collect himself. Leigh looked up at his angry reddened face and started to cry. "Oh, you've been asking for this!" Mr. Ryan continued. "Another thing, how in hell do you and Joe think you're going to live? He's going to college. All he has is a part-time job. If you two think you're going to pay the rent with that, then you're both living in a fantasy! Now I don't want to hear any more about it! Do you understand me?"

Leigh buried her face in her hands as the domineering, quick-tempered man left the room in anger. It all seemed so hopeless now. Hopeless.

Leigh was aroused from her memories by a sudden rumble erupting from the baby's rear end. Realizing that he was properly relieved and near sleep, she rose from her chair and started for the bedroom to put him down for his morning nap. On her way to the bedroom she was reminded of the chores that she needed to do that day. Dishes, laundry, dusting, vacuuming, grocery shopping. They were endless, and the last was especially difficult since Joe had put her on the strictest food budget imaginable. It was hard for her to believe sometimes that a year ago she had been struggling through the fundamentals of algebra and now she was having difficulty keeping the checkbook balanced.

Leigh entered the bedroom, and, holding Joey in one arm, pulled back the pale blue comforter with her free hand. She placed him in his bed, the creamy color of his skin making a sharp contrast against the sterile white of the crib sheet underneath him. Hospital white. Leigh shuddered and remembered that other white--just months ago.

"Well, have you made any kind of decision yet?" The rotund, bespectacled social worker had peered over her glasses at Leigh. "These things have to be settled before it's too late, if you know what I mean."

"Yes," Leigh had stammered. "I mean, I know what you mean." She looked from the floor to the woman seated in front of her.

"Well?" the social worker demanded.

"I--I have to talk this over with my hus--" She lowered her eyes to the floor again. "My boyfriend first. I just need more time."

"My dear," the social worker declared, "you don't have much time left. According to your tests you're nine weeks along. Now in this state abortion is legal up to the end of the first trimester, which is twelve weeks and--"

"No!" Leigh shouted, starting to cry. "No, I can't do that."

"If it's a matter of fear of the procedure, I can assure you that here at the Free Clinic, our staff is very competent, and--"

"No, it's not that. I'm Catholic--I mean--I can't kill it."

"Well, have you considered adoption?" the social worker continued flatly. "We have many fine agencies in this area and you can be assured that they would certainly find a suitable home for the baby."

"I--I just don't know." She rose from her chair, sobbing. "I'm sorry--I can't help it." She turned towards the door, opened it, ran tearfully through the outer office and onto the hardness of the city sidewalk, leaving behind the icy white walls of the Free Clinic.

She began to walk briskly, wiping the tears from her face with the back of her hand so that passers-by on the street wouldn't stare. She needed time to think, but the social worker's words kept coming back to her. It was true, she didn't have much time. Suddenly she thought of Joe. How was he going to take this? It was true that when she suspected that she was pregnant she had told him and, in his usual reassuring manner, he had told her that everything would work out for them. But, the fact remained. She was pregnant and Joe would have to know.

Leigh paused momentarily on a street corner where there was a phone booth, then deciding that it was now or never, she stepped inside the booth, closed the door and began fishing through her purse for a couple of dimes. When she found them, she picked up the receiver and deposited the dimes into their slot. She waited for the dial tone and when she heard it, she dialed Joe's phone number and waited for him to answer. She looked at her watch and knew that he would be home from class by now. The ringing finally ceased on the other end when she heard a click and then Joe's familiar voice.

"Hello?" he said.

"Joe! I'm glad I caught you home. I just got out of the clinic." She felt her voice start to quiver just a little.

"Leigh? Is that you? What's wrong? What clinic?"

"Joe, the Free Clinic. I had a test." Her voice shook and tears began to fall. "Joe, it was positive."

There was silence on Joe's end of the line.

"Joe? Are you still there?"

"Yeah, I'm still here, honey. Are you at home?"

"No."

"Leigh, where are you? I'll come and get you. Just tell me where you are."

"Joe, I'm scared!"

"Hey, everything will be all right. I love you. I want to marry you, remember?"

"Yes."

"Okay. Now just tell me where you are and I'll be there in a few minutes."

After telling Joe which intersection the telephone booth was on she hung up the receiver, leaned against the glass walls of the cubicle and waited for the familiar brown station wagon to come and rescue her. . . .

Now the sound of another telephone jangling pulled Leigh from her recollection, as she gave the baby's comforter one final tuck. Quietly, she hurried into the kitchen to stop the ringing before it woke the baby and triggered his incessant crying.

"Hello?" She questioned somewhat breathlessly into the receiver.

"Hi, honey." It was Joe.

"Hi. What's up?"

"Well, I got out of my physics class a little early because I finished the test early and I just called to apologize for the way I acted this morning. I know it wasn't your fault that the baby woke up cranky this morning. It's just really hard sometimes when you're under pressure to keep yourself under control. You still love me?"

"Uh-huh." He never would know how much his early morning anger had upset her. "How'd your exam go?" she said, trying to change the subject.

"Oh, not good, not bad. A lot of the questions came as kind of a shock though, because I wasn't really prepared."

A pang of guilt swept through Leigh. "I'm sorry," she said.

"Hey, it's okay. Really. How's Joey? Did you finally get him quieted down?"

"Yeah, I had just put him down for his nap when you called. I was afraid the phone was going to wake him up but it didn't."

"Oh, that's good. Well, I've gotta go now. My lit class starts in about fifteen minutes and I still have to hike on over to the building. I'll see you tonight. I love you."

"I love you, too." Her words sounded hollow to her. "Bye."

As she replaced the receiver on its cradle she thought about Joe's outburst that morning. Before they were married, Joe had never really shown his temper, not even in the awful confrontation that they had had with Leigh's stepfather.

Leigh found herself back to that early June morning when Joe stopped over at Leigh's home.

They had exchanged a few brief words in the hallway before setting out to the patio to confront Mr. and Mrs. Ryan with the inevitable news.

"Hi, kids," Mrs. Ryan had greeted cheerfully, as she sipped her coffee and turned the page of her morning newspaper.

"Morning, Leigh. Some coffee, Joe?" Mr. Ryan said.

Joe cleared his throat nervously. "No thanks, Mr. Ryan," he said.

"Joe, you're out awfully early this morning. You kids going out for an early game of tennis or something?" Mrs. Ryan asked.

"No, Mom. Joe and I have something to say to you," Leigh started.

"Leigh, I'm warning you, I don't want to hear any more about this marriage thing you've got in your head. I said no and I meant it!" Mr. Ryan said curtly.

"No, Bob. This is something else entirely. I know I've had a hard time accepting you as part of the family, but, well, we really need your help."

"My help! Ha! That really makes my day! Yesterday you wouldn't have taken my help if you had been lying out in the street bleeding to death! My help!" Mr. Ryan chortled.

"Bob, stop it!" Mrs. Ryan begged.

"I'm sorry, dear. Well, if it's that important, pull up a chair and sit." The big man wiped the tears of laughter from his eyes as Joe and Leigh pulled two lawn chairs up to the table.

"Mrs. Ryan, uh--I think I'll have that cup of coffee now," Joe said.

Mrs. Ryan, without saying a word, reached for an extra cup and saucer from the coffee cart and poured a cup for Joe.

"Cream and sugar?" Mrs. Ryan asked.

"No thanks." Joe took the cup into his hands and Leigh watched in amazement as he downed practically the whole cup in one gulp. She knew that Joe was not overly fond of coffee, but how he could drink a hot drink that quickly was beyond her understanding.

"Not thirsty, are you, boy?" Mr. Ryan said, throwing back his head and laughing hard.

Leigh was beginning to get impatient with her step-father's crude sense of humor. "Bob, Mom, Joe and I are getting married," Leigh said, trying to sound assertive.

"Oh, for God's sake, Leigh," her mother said setting down her coffee cup. "We've been through this a hundred times and--"

"Mrs. Ryan--" Joe interrupted.

"No, Joe. Let me," Leigh said, almost whispering. "Mom, this is going to be hard for you, but it's harder for me to tell you." Her eyes filled with tears, and as she looked at her mother, she felt as if her mother already knew what she was going to say. "Mom, I'm pregnant." She wept as she spoke.

"You're what!" Bob Ryan roared.

"I'm going to have a baby." Leigh's weeping turned into sobbing as Joe rose from his chair and put his arm around her.

Mr. Ryan glared at Joe. "You son of a--If I have my way I'll see you locked up for this, you irresponsible son of a--dammit--why? Why?! Why did you let this happen? I want you to get out of this house right now and--"

"Stop it! Stop it right now!" Mrs. Ryan shrieked, picking up her pack of cigarettes and lighting one with her shaking hand. "Bob, there comes a time when I have to handle my children my own way and this is one of them! So if you don't mind I think it would be a good idea if you left us alone for a while!"

Leigh had never seen her normally submissive mother speak to her step-father in this manner before. And conversely, she had never seen her powerful step-father back down either. She actually felt like cheering for her mother.

"Right now I could say 'I told you so' but that wouldn't do anyone a hell of a lot of good!" Mr. Ryan said as he stepped heavily back into the house.

"Now, Leigh, are you sure you're pregnant? Have you been to a doctor?"

"Yes," Leigh answered watching her mother's face sag slightly at her answer. It hurt her to see her mother in so much pain.

"Are you sure you want to get married?" Mrs. Ryan inquired through her tears. "There are so many alternatives nowadays. Oh, I was brought up to be a good Catholic and, God knows I've tried to bring you and your brothers up in the Church but if you want an--"

"No. I couldn't. I can't give my baby up either. I could never live with the feeling of never knowing my own child. I couldn't live with raising my baby alone either. I need Joe to stand by me and give me the strength I need."

"Mrs. Ryan," Joe said, "I love Leigh and I promise you that I will do the best I can to take care of her and make her happy. I don't want anything to happen to this baby either. This little life is as much a part of me as it is of Leigh. I want this baby."

"Leigh." Leigh felt her mother's face searching for hers. "Is this really true now? I'd hate to think you were lying to us just so that I'd give you my permission to be married."

"Mom," Leigh spoke slowly, fumbling through her blue jean pocket and extracting a small white appointment card, "here's the name and phone number of the clinic I went to. If you don't believe us, you can call for yourself and confirm it." She held the card out to her mother.

"Oh, my God--" Mrs. Ryan whispered, her trembling hand accepting the card from Leigh. Leigh watched, feeling the pain of accepting the responsibility of her own actions for the first time, as her mother rested her face in her hands and started to cry.

"I have to think about this," Mrs. Ryan finally said, lighting up another cigarette, seemingly unaware of the one that still lay smoldering in the ashtray in front of her.

"Mom, there isn't much time," Leigh stated, feeling anxious at having to delay a decision any longer. "It's what we both want, Mom. You still seem to think that I'm too young and irresponsible to take care of myself. You're wrong. You're dead wrong. I may have made a mistake, but at least I can accept the responsibility for it." Leigh moved toward her mother's chair, knelt down beside her and with tears in her eyes said, "I'm just damn fortunate, Mom. I'm fortunate enough to have Joe love me enough to stay with me through all of this. A few months ago you doubted that love. But I'm telling you that I believe that if Joe and I can get through this together, we can get through anything."

Mrs. Ryan regained her composure and pulled a napkin off the table and began dabbing at her eyes. She ground her cigarette out in the ashtray in front of her and looked down at her young daughter.

"You remind me of me when I was your age," Mrs. Ryan began slowly. "You're so headstrong, so determined." Leigh noticed that her mother's voice quaked just a little. "Leigh, I just want you to know that I still love you. Sure, I'm hurt and disappointed in you for letting this happen. I want you to know, though, that I've wanted only the best for you." Mrs. Ryan paused again, dabbing at her damp eyes. "I've tried so hard to bring you up to be a good person. I don't know. Maybe I've failed you in some way. Maybe I yelled a little too much, maybe not enough--" her voice trailed off momentarily. "I want to say, though, and it hurts me, that what ever your decision is, I'll support you in it one hundred percent. If you have this baby and it is old enough, I think you'll be able to understand and see for yourself all the things I've been trying so hard to teach you." Mrs. Ryan started to cry again and buried her face in her napkin. "Just remember," she said, almost inaudibly to

Leigh, "if you ever need anything, I will always be here."

Now the salty taste of her tears pulled Leigh from her memories and back to her own kitchen. It wasn't until she recalled her mother's words that she realized how unhappy she was. Here she was, stuck in a tiny apartment with a screaming infant day after day, alone. She couldn't buy anything that she wanted unless it was something that was absolutely necessary. She knew she would need a new swimsuit for summer, a one-piece suit instead of the two-piece suit she owned now, to cover all the ugly marks that childbearing had left on her young body, but she knew deep down that Joe would think she was being frivolous.

Leigh turned toward the kitchen sink and began sorting through last night's dinner dishes waiting to be washed. She turned on the water, plugged up the sink and squirted the dish soap into the sink. She stood, thinking, while she waited for the sink to fill with water.

She thought most of all of Joe's seemingly increasing resentment toward her and the baby. Sure, she thought, he was always big enough to apologize for his outbursts, but they happened all the same and more frequently. She began to think that maybe she really didn't know Joe as well as she thought she had. Maybe she had needed more time before they were married to find out just exactly what she was getting into. She knew she also felt a lot of guilt for demanding so much of Joe's time. She knew that his education was important to him, and although he pretended not to let it bother him, she knew that the responsibility of a full-time job and a family were getting in the way.

As she waited for the sink to fill, she heard little Joey start to scream again. Turning the faucets off so that she could go to her son, she turned from the kitchen and walked quickly into the bedroom. She went to Joey's crib and picked him up, setting him on the changing table again, as she had done so many times before and would continue to do in the future. As she busily removed the soiled diaper from her son, she glanced upward and out the bedroom window. Again she noticed the dark, gloomy weather outside and secretly wondered if the light of spring would ever come again.

## To Look the Other Way

### By Ann Michele Morgan

The fat woman was yelling again. "I worked hard to get where I am. And so did everyone here!" Murmurs of consent were heard around the room. "I don't pay $575 rent to worry about some--some queers fooling around with my kids!" She sat back down among cheers and yells.

Jahna sat back and watched the bickering. This was only her second tenant meeting, and already she hated coming to them. She took a sip of her cocoa. Although it was cooling rapidly, she drank it slowly since she didn't feel like going back to her apartment for more. They only served coffee at these meetings, and she hated coffee. Bitter.

The meeting was getting louder. "I really can't see the harm--" a blonde girl in the back began.

"Can't see the harm!" interrupted the fat woman.

"I REALLY CAN'T SEE THE HARM," the blonde continued loudly, "in some homosexuals moving into the complex. What difference should it make to us? Christ, as much trouble as you all had getting in this place, you'd think you'd be willing to give someone else a break. I mean--"

She was cut off as five people protested. Amidst much shouting, the meeting coordinator stood up. She raised her voice to be heard over the noise. "We obviously," she started, then tried again. "WE OBVIOUSLY AREN'T GETTING ANYWHERE." The room quieted somewhat. "Since I don't know what to tell you all right now, I suggest we adjourn. I'll get in touch with you when I have more information." As she finished talking, several young women came up to ask her questions. The fat woman made her way over to the refreshment table to help yourself to more coffee and doughnuts.

People began to drift off, talking animatedly among themselves. Waiting for the elevator, Jahna heard someone discussing the blond girl who had spoken out. "What does she care unless she's queer too? I'd like to know why anybody would stick their neck out for some lesbos unless they had something at stake, too." Just then the elevator came and the crowd began to push into the small elevator.

Back in her apartment, Jahna went to the kitchen, rinsed her mug out, and placed it in the sink. She went to the couch and lit a cigarette, thinking back to the conversation in front of the elevator. Why WOULD anybody stick their neck out for someone else if they themselves had nothing to gain? She remembered an argument between her parents years ago, when she was fourteen or fifteen. They had been down the hall, but not out of earshot.

Apparently, her father had put his job in jeopardy by organizing the men at work to protest the firing of two Mexican workers.

"Why have *you* always got to be the one?" her mother had asked. "You don't even know any Mexicans, yet you're getting ready to lose your job over some. Have you forgotten we have two daughters--one getting ready to graduate from high school? What're you going to tell Fran when she's all set for college in the fall? Are those Mexicans going to send Fran to school?"

"That's not the point," her father answered. "I've always told the girls *not* to look the other way. Now that I see somebody getting screwed, I can't just go back on that. I have to do what I believe in. I'm sure Fran and Jahna understand, and I want you to understand too,"

"I know." Her mother's voice was much quieter. "I kind of see you have to do what you have to do. It's the way you've always been. It's just that it's hard for me to see such serious action when there's nothing in it for you. Sometimes, it just doesn't seem fair."

Jahna was brought back to the present with a start, seeing that her cigarette had turned to one long ash. The still-burning butt had fallen off the edge of the ashtray and sat smoking on the polished coffee table. She gave a small cry and reached to put it out, briefly remembering the seemingly endless payments on the expensive furniture. After brushing away the ashes, she thought again about what her father had said. "Don't look the other way--you may need someone to be on your side one day." She supposed she really should have spoken up at the meeting. After all, discrimination was illegal, and there wasn't a reason in the world homosexuals or anyone else shouldn't be able to move in if they wanted to.

Just then the doorbell rang, and Jahna looked at her watch. Ten-thirty. She knew it couldn't be Sam, her boyfriend, since he was at work. Looking through the peephole, she saw the slightly convex face of her sister Fran. She opened the door, both pleased and surprised.

Fran stepped through the door with an air of mock indignation. "Some people just aren't part of the family since they've moved into fancy apartment complexes, but I won't mention any names," she chided.

"Hey, Fran, come in and sit down. I'll get you some cocoa--I *know* it's cold outside." Jahna headed for the kitchen. "And if some people were at home at night, instead of out in the streets," she called out, they *might* get a telephone call sometimes."

"Shut up, Jahn," Fran laughed. "And tell me what's going on in your part of the world."

Coming back with two mugs of cocoa, Jahna sat across from Fran. She reached for a cigarette, but refrained at Fran's look of disapproval. Fran hated her smoking. Briefly, she recounted to Fran the earlier meeting, and her guilt for not speaking up.

"C'mon, Jahn, I know you," Fran said across her cocoa. "Something must have kept you from speaking up. What's the deal?"

Jahna winced. Fran knew her too well. "Well, I know this is terrible," she said quickly, "but it's about that promotion I'm up for, the advertising department director. You know, a lot of the people living here work at Merril's too, and I'm afraid they'll think--" she broke off abruptly and slammed her mug to the table. A little cocoa splashed onto the wood, but she didn't even notice. "Oh, Fran, some of the people at Merril's are so damn conservative, it makes me sick. Remember when I told you about the stink there was last year when that guy threatened to sue the company? They fired him when he openly declared himself a homosexual. Of course, they covered it up with red tape, but everyone knew what the deal was."

"I remember," Fran said, finishing her cocoa. "But he never could prove it." She tucked one leg underneath the other. "Why is the company involved in this, though? I mean, what do they care about what you do at home?"

"Well," Jahna said slowly, "a lot of the bigwigs at work live here. As a matter of fact, some of them own a share of the place. Since they want to keep up the apartment's exclusive reputation, they're resisting renting to these two girls." She shifted in her chair. "Besides, a lot of the tenants are complaining, and that's making the management even more uneasy. If I get all mixed up in this, those old stuffed shirts may put me out of the running. I think it's really down to me and Roger Smythe, but there's a couple of other candidates too." Suddenly she sat up straight. "Damnit, Fran, I just don't know what to do. I feel so bad, but I've worked so hard for that promotion. What would you do?"

"That's not fair," Fran countered. "I don't know what I'd do. And that's not the problem anyway; what we need to know is what will *you* do. But don't feel too bad. At least you're being honest with yourself, so you're stepping in the right direction."

"I know," Jahna sighed, "but it's not much comfort." Seeing that Fran was finished, she took the mugs into the kitchen to rinse out. "Remember when Daddy almost got fired over those two Mexicans?" she called from the kitchen.

"Yeah," Fran answered. "But everything turned out all right." She laughed. "I still got to go to school."

"True," Jahna said, coming back in and sitting down, "but he didn't know how it would all end, and that didn't stop him. Maybe I'm just being selfish."

Fran reached across the coffee table and put her hands on Jahna's shoulders. "Lighten up on yourself, Jahn," she said softly. "There's a lot at stake here. I know you'll do what's best."

"I hope so." Jahna leaned her head against the back of the chair, closing her eyes. She was glad Fran had come. Just talking to her made her feel better.

After an hour of talk, Fran stood up. "Well, girl, I gotta run. I have to pick Kevin up at the airport. Let me know about the job, okay?"

After seeing her out, Jahna showered and went to bed, but did not sleep. She thought about the promotion, and the people at the office. There were some really closed minds at Merril's. Maybe she could help the homosexuals in a behind-the-scenes kind of way, sending out letters and whatnot. It would be halfstepping, in a way, but maybe she would feel better. Tomorrow, she would ask the meeting coordinator how she could get in touch with the prospective tenants. With that thought, she drifted off to sleep.

For the next week, Jahna got involved by helping type, send out letters, make telephone calls, and do other odd jobs that didn't call for her to be visibly involved. She advised the girls that it was illegal of the management to have asked them about their sexual preference in the first place, or request extra references in order to delay the renting procedure. She also contacted a lawyer friend and put him in touch with the girls to further inform them of their rights, making it clear that her name was not to be involved. Although she shied away from public commitment, and told the girls so in no uncertain terms, it was her hope that the management would give in to pressure before going to court, where the girls planned to take them if they didn't give in.

Jahna was pleased with the way things were going; she was helping without jeopardizing her chances at becoming the director of the advertising department. Her father would be proud of her.

She was musing over this as she entered the cafeteria at work one day and bumped into someone. "Oh, excuse me," she said automatically, and then recognized the girl. It was the blonde who had spoken out at the tenant meeting, who appeared to be on her way out with coffee. She too was trying to help the girls get into the complex--Jahna had heard her talking about it several times.

"Things are going well, aren't they?" Jahna asked.

"Are you sure you should talk about it here?" the girl said sarcastically. "Or should I meet you in the broom closet?"

Jahna looked at her, puzzled.

"Maybe I should explain," the blonde went on. "I know those girls are grateful for the help you've given them. The lawyer you contacted has given them a lot to go on. But you're so secretive about your involvement that it seems you're ashamed to be helping out. I mean, I understand that you're up for the director and all, but did you ever stop to think that by sneaking around the way you're doing, you're calling more attention to yourself than if you wore a banner? And what if it comes down to the crunch-- where will you be then? Will you still be on their side? I can't help but wonder, and neither can they."

Jahna tossed her head angrily. "Of course, I'll be on their side!" she snapped.

"Will you? Or will it be easier to say that at least you tried? Before you commit yourself, think about what you may not be willing to sacrifice." She brushed past Jahna out of the cafeteria.

Jahna felt as though she were suddenly drained of energy. Where *would* she stand in the crunch? Office politics was so important here, and she really wanted that position. But which decision could she live with? Never look the other way, her father had said. But how far out were you supposed to stick your neck anyway--until someone chopped off your head?

A tray crashed to the floor, startling Jahna out of her reverie. She got into the cafeteria line feeling dazed, and noticed they were serving breaded pork chops. Although she hated pork chops, she got some anyway. Chewing slowly, not really tasting, Jahna thought back to the first time she met one of the girls. She had gone over to their small apartment after getting the address from the meeting coordinator. The girl who answered the door was very small with delicate features, her hair done up intricately in a mass of cornrows. Jahna remembered feeling surprised that the girl was so small and pretty, not at all like she had expected.

"That's silly," she said aloud, then realized that other people in the cafeteria were looking. She finished her food quickly and made her way back to her office deep in thought. She performed her duties mechanically, without concentration, and longed for 5:30. When it came, she was the first one out of the building.

That night, Jahna tossed and turned. What if she openly supported the homosexuals, and lost out on the position? Or what if she didn't support them, and lost the position anyway? What if nobody cared whether she supported them or not? Was she just being selfish? So many things could happen. Damn. She should've called Fran last night. Damn.

The phone rang, startling Jahna so much that at first she didn't know what was happening. Coming to her senses, she reached out and almost knocked the phone off of the nighttable. "Hello," she mumbled sleepily.

"Jahna?" Sam's voice could hardly be heard over the clang of machinery. He was calling from the factory. "I wanted to call earlier, but I didn't get the chance. How're you doing?"

"Well, not too good. I still haven't decided what to do, and it's driving me nuts." Jahna yawned and leaned back in the bed. She had told him a couple of days ago about her dilemma. "And get closer to the phone, I can hardly hear you."

Sam's voice got louder. "You still haven't decided? I told you what I think about it. I really think you'll feel better if you stop hiding. After all, you're usually a pretty straightforward person."

Jahna smiled. He knew her as well as she knew herself. "I'm still thinking about it," she said softly, "but I'll take your advice to heart. I love you."

"I love you too, puddin', but I have to go. I'll come over tomorrow, okay?"

"Okay," Jahna said. "Bye." She hung up the phone and turned over. Sam really was right. There was only one decision she could live with--even if it meant giving up the promotion. The next chance she had to take an open stand on the issue she would. Wondering how her stand would affect her status at work, Jahna fell asleep.

The next morning, the office was buzzing with gossip. The department heads were near a decision for department director; it was down to two candidates. It would be him--no, her. Everyone had heard a different version.

Jahna looked up from her desk to see the blonde girl standing there. She laid a paper on Jahna's desk. "This is a petition," she said slowly, looking directly at Jahna. "We're passing it to people here that we know live in the complex. We need as many signatures as possible." There was no inflection in her voice at all.

Jahna looked at the paper. There were about seven signatures on it. She knew that if she signed it, it would be all over the office in an hour. She didn't care what other people thought, except for the department heads. Remembering the convictions of last night, she reached out and signed the petition. Her hand shook so badly that her signature was a ridiculous scrawl.

"Thank you." The girl smiled, and Jahna could see that she really meant it. She watched her leave the office, stopping someone in the hall. She wondered what would happen now that her name was there for everyone to see. Oh well, she did feel a little better. After all, for better or worse, she had taken a stand. She turned back to her work with a sense of relief and satisfaction. Her father really would be proud of her now.

The rest of the morning was uneventful, and Jahna was glad when lunchtime came to break the monotony. When she came back from lunch, the office seemed strangely quiet. No one looked up as she walked through to her private office in the back. She was just sitting down when the phone rang.

"Jahna Reif?" She recognized the voice of Bill Wruthers, the vice president of the company. "We'd like to see you and Roger Smythe in the conference room as soon as possible please." The line went dead. A decision had been made. Jahna had a pang of regret for a moment, and wished she could rush out and find the petition. But no, it was all right. Because there'd be other causes, and she'd have to take a stand then, too. If they wanted a fence sitter, then she was wrong for the job anyway. Besides, there was always the possibility that she had been chosen. She was really much more qualified than Roger Smythe. Well, there was only one way to find out. For better or worse, she told herself silently. Very conscious of the looks she was getting, but feeling better than she had felt in a long time, Jahna made her way out of the office and headed for the conference room.

## Rites of Passage

### By Linda Decker

Clad only in a slip, Patty paused stilly in the doorway of her closet. She'd taken a shower and unrolled and combed her hair and still the feeling persisted. A vague sense of dread, perhaps even fear rose in her. It began in her stomach and inched to her throat. Patty audibly caught her breath and slightly shook her head. Not something to dwell on now, she thought. Her arm disappeared into the closet and extracted a crisply ironed, Oxford cloth blouse. She slipped her arms into it and buttoned it leisurely, caring little about the time. She walked to the unmade bed and sat on the edge. She pulled on one of the pair of knee socks lying next to her. She picked up the other sock and fingered its rust-colored cable stitching absentmindedly. She recalled the yearly department store buying trips with her mother and sisters. It was always a festive event--they were allowed to each pick out six pairs of socks, six pairs of underwear, four blouses--white only-- and two cardigan sweaters--blue only. So the socks were the fun purchase. Any color was allowed. She envisioned ninety senior high girls lined up to receive Communion--all dressed in identical blue, pleated skirts, matching vests and white blouses. The only distinguishing feature being hair and knee sock color. The image was familiar and comforting, somehow. She had dressed according to this code for twelve years now. The nuns were very strict on dress code--exceptions were rarely made.

Patty wondered about life after high school. Does an office girl wear knee socks and cardigan sweaters? Of course not, she chided herself. She imagined a typical secretary in a typical office. This secretary would be dressed in the latest of fashions. She would be the picture of efficiency and grace in soft pastel suits and pointed, stiletto heels. Clothes are very important to the career girl, she has to look the part.

Patty sighed, she couldn't see herself leaving the uniform behind and adopting a new style. She couldn't see herself leaving high school behind for that matter either.

She flinched as her father shouted from the kitchen that it was getting late and if she wanted a ride she'd better hurry. She slid the matching sock on and raced with the rest of her clothes. Grabbing her stack of books she fled the room and raced down the stairs to the kitchen. She paused briefly at the doorway and braced herself for the normal pandemonium of her family. She placed her books on the nearby chair and turned the corner and made her way into the overcrowded and noisy kitchen.

Her housecoated mother looked up from stirring the steaming oatmeal and said, "Patty, for God's sake, what took you so long this morning? You were the first one up and the last one ready. I could have used your help making lunches. Don't you feel well, honey?"

"I'm okay, Mom, just can't seem to get going today. Sorry about the lunches."

The din overpowered Patty's last words, but her mother didn't seem to notice. She had already turned her attention to the task of washing out extra spoons and bowls for the oatmeal.

Patty's youngest sister, Julie, let out an ear-splitting wail as she hung over the side of the high chair desperately trying to retrieve a square of buttered toast from the littered floor.

"Someone please give the baby some more toast," her mother bellowed louder than the little girl's screams.

Patty picked a still-warm bowl and spoon from the dishrack and hurriedly filled it at the stove. She moved to the mammoth, round kitchen table and was pleased to find an empty chair. She deposited her bowl and saw the toast plate was barren. Patty stooped to pick up the baby's toast from the floor. She tore off the wet, soggy section and returned the ungummed piece to the still-screaming baby. Patty watched as the child quieted immediately, clenched the toast between two tiny hands and jerkily maneuvered it to her mouth. Patty fondled the tight, blond curls and bent to nuzzle the baby's warm and fleshy neck. This baby was the ninth, probably the last. Her mother seemed absolutely sure that Julie was the last. Fifteen years apart, Patty thought. "We're the first and the last," Patty murmured to the two-year-old.

Her brother John shouted, "You're going in first, Tommy, cuz I said so and cuz I went in first last time."

The younger Tommy looked bewildered while choking down a lump of oatmeal. "I'm scared of the dentist," the five-year-old sputtered, seemingly one step away from tears.

"Ohhh, look at the idy, biddy baby gonna start crying?" John began to laugh before mimicking the high-pitched whining of the dentist's drill.

"Leave him alone, Johnny, don't tease him," Patty entreated. Tommy's crying began to escalate along with Johnny's howls of laughter just as Patty's sister Nancy reached for the carton of milk and knocked over a full glass of orange juice.

Everyone squealed and had something negative to say. Nancy apologized and ran to the sink for a sponge. Patty sighed and got up to help clean the mess. "We're not really mad, Nance, don't feel bad. Pour yourself some more and be careful this time," Patty said to her sister.

Patty rinsed the sponge and rejoined the group. She dressed her oatmeal with brown sugar, milk and a generous splat of applesauce and began eating. She concentrated on her food and on spiritually removing herself from the commotion of the others.

Something was wrong this morning, she thought. Free-floating anxiety--she had heard the term in her Psych 101 class. Sr. Joan Therese had said it was a generalized feeling of unease, and it was necessary to get to the root of the anxiousness by a process of elimination. Homework's finished, that's not the problem. Finally got around to making an appointment for her graduation picture--she knew she'd put it off much too long. Patty thought of her father reading the want ads to her the night before--said something about getting a jump on things. It wouldn't hurt to begin looking now, he had said.

The image self-destructed and was replaced with the very real figure of her mother clearing away the used dishes and cooing to her oatmeal-encrusted baby that soon everyone would be gone. Soon it would be bath time for Julie and a cup of coffee for momma.

Entering the kitchen, Patty's father announced the time and jangled his car keys in the air. The final mad dash was on. The table cleared immediately and kids dispersed in every direction. Coats, mittens and books were somehow retrieved from obscure hiding places in the cavernous house. The seven going off to the world grabbed brown lunchbags from the long row on the kitchen counter and planted kisses on their mother's cheek. Their father was in the car by this time and gave a few short toots to speed them up. With much pushing and quarreling they miraculously made it out the door and into the battered blue station wagon.

Patty kept herself a few paces behind the others. She hugged her mother and made a point to say goodbye to the two youngest children left behind. She slid her navy pea coat on, picked up her lunch and books and followed the others.

The ride to their parochial school was quiet. Her brothers and sisters seemed deep in thought. Everyone mulling on the possibilities of the day--possibly silently inventing farfetched excuses for homework uncompleted.

They slowed to a stop at a red light across from the local public school.

It seemed to Patty an ominous, looming structure which rose to become one with the overcast, gray sky. The main building was old, shabby, and of darker colored brick than the new additions. As far as Patty could tell at least three offshoots of lighter colored, newer brick jutted from the main building. One of the newer wings had already been christened by vandals. Giant, white letters boldly slashed the facade, punctuated by windows, heralding the "Class of '67." She watched as the miniature city teemed and swayed to the beat of hundreds of students. She knew she'd never have found her niche in this bellowing, brawling crush of people. Her high school was one-fifth the size of this; she knew everyone and everyone knew her.

A green light released their car and Patty silently thanked her good fortune at being able to avoid the coldness of the real world for as long as she had. Panic welled inside her and she bent her head to her chest feeling very small, very unimportant.

Her sister Kathy nudged her arm. "What's the matter with you?"

"I'm all right," Patty said slowly. "Just thinking about all the things I gotta get done before graduation."

Her father sounded pleased. "Good for you, Patty. Let's think about it before it hits us between the eyes. Make plans. Consider your options."

Patty felt exactly like it was hitting her between the eyes now, pummeling her over and over again.

Kathy, younger by two years, said, "You're so lucky, you could move away to college if you wanted--live in a dorm. I wish it were me graduating instead of you. I can't wait!"

Patty looked at her, then looked away, wishing it was indeed Kathy who was leaving high school behind. Patty wondered why she couldn't muster any enthusiasm of her own. She remembered the conference with the school counselor, Sr. Beatrice Marie, the year before.

"I'm afraid your grades don't reflect college aptitude, Patty. I think you'd be happier in a business curriculum. College isn't for everyone, you know."

Patty had taken the nun's words as more of an absolute pronouncement of the future than a mere opinion. Patty had negat d the question of college instantly, almost as the nun spoke. Patty took it as solid proof that, yes indeed, a university was out of her realm. It made her life simpler, more secure even. It made no difference to Patty that her parents vehemently disagreed with the counselor's point of view.

Patty looked again at her sister who was still extolling the advantages of the college life. "I'll be a cheerleader in college too--it'll be so exciting, much better than the games we have here," Kathy stated with assurance.

"What are you complaining about our football games for? Thought you *loved* them," Patty responded with sarcasm.

"I *do* love them, but Patty, just think of the excitement of college ball. I'm getting goose bumps just thinking about it. Think of all the guys and . . ."

Patty tuned out the trilling, naive words and stared straight ahead. Patty hated being the oldest in the family. She performed first and the others watched, teasing and laughing until she fell. And she always seemed to fall. She had been the first to date--sweating in anticipation, yes, but also sweating because of acute embarrassment. The kids had hidden themselves everywhere that day, waiting to get a look at him--exploding into fits of laughter when they did.

She had timidly introduced the Beatles into her home too. Even something like rock and roll music was not devoid of embarrassment. Her father had made fun of their long hair and their silly lyrics.

My God, she thought--she had even developed breasts and begun to menstruate first. Her many brothers still kidded her about that one. She thought she'd never live down "becoming a woman." She didn't feel like a woman. She was still one of them, just a kid. Graduation was going to hand her over to the world. It couldn't be that a person became an adult after graduation anymore than she became a woman because her breasts grew. She didn't want breasts--didn't want to have anything to do with the swelling additions to her body. She wanted no part of graduation either but that didn't stop it. Time was passing more quickly each day.

Patty put her teeth together and pressed until they hurt. She felt highly irritated--angry even.

They're always gonna laugh at me--no matter what I try. They're just dumb and immature kids. They don't know anything yet. For an instant she felt like one of them again--she didn't know much of anything either. The doubts washed over her and threatened to annihilate the anger. There would be job interviews, she'd have to buy a car, she'd have to deal with adults all day--how was she ever gonna manage that? She knew she'd never do things right. Patty stopped herself. She cancelled her abject fear and reached back for the productive anger.

She looked down at her knee socks and penny loafers. They could stay, she decided--they were part of the image that was herself. And herself was not ready to change--not yet. Good ole comfortable Sacred Heart High may be replaced with an efficiently run office building but the old image of herself would stay. The future seemed somehow kinder.

The car pulled alongside the curb in front of their school. Everyone simultaneously spilled from the opened doors uttering goodbyes and hailing friends. Patty held a door for a few kids then swung it shut and bent to the window to wave to her dad. She straightened and watched as he drove off. She took a deep breath and turned to face her school. She picked her way through the melting snow and mud to the sidewalk. She turned her head noticing some color poking through the snow.

"Crocuses," she said out loud. Patty had just walked through them and realized she had stepped on two. The tiny, purple cups lay temporarily bent, but not crushed. They still signalled the spring, they still made her smile.

Patty walked on, squaring her shoulders and allowing her breasts to protrude through the thin jacket. It might be okay, she thought. It just might be okay . . .

### Acceptance

#### By Kathleen Slayden

Thanksgiving Day. Mama creeps silently through the house, eyes shiny with held-in tears. "How's Daddy?" I ask, with twelve-year-old innocence. Mama stares, then quickly turns away.

"Tell me, mama," I beg her. And she tells me, through convulsive gulps of air, that my father has cancer. He's forty-two years old, and he's dying.

I can't believe it. Don't want to. It must be some mistake. He's so big, so healthy. I think of the dawns when I would awaken, listening for morning sounds. Padding silently on fuzzy slippered feet, I would sneak downstairs to see him at the dining room table, reading the paper and drinking black coffee with lots of sugar. I would kiss him good morning, and we would silently flip through the morning news, content with our roles. Daddy and his little girl. He couldn't die. Not now. Not when I needed him so.

Two weeks pass. The doctors allow him to come home. A hospital bed is rolled into the living room, and mama quickly learns how to give morphine shots. But the pain still exists. Like the cancer greedily devouring his bones, it grows. The morning sounds turn into moans, and false cheerfulness becomes the order of the day. Miracles *do* happen. Of course they do, Mama. Look at the research. Then I see his fingers, wrapped tightly around the beads of a rosary. I am confused. I have tried to talk him into going to church for years. Cheerfully, he always declined. Now he clutches the black rosary beads and shudders as the pain grips him once more.

My sister wants to marry. It is decided that the wedding will be performed in the house, so that Daddy can see it. We pin a white carnation to his pajama top. He loves flowers, that man. Every week he would bring flowers home to Mama--until he got sick.

Their ceremony is short, the priest cheerful. Afterward, he talks to Daddy about paradise and hears his confession. I sit in my room, wondering what he has to confess. He hasn't sinned. He is so good, this man. Why is he dying?

"How much longer?" Mama asks the doctor. It's difficult, he explains. Maybe six months. Maybe a year. Miracles *do* happen.

The days pass by, and schedules are kept. I must go to school every day. I kiss Daddy good-bye each morning, anxious to leave so that I don't have to look at the rosary.

His speech is slurred now. He sounds as if he drank too much beer. The morphine dose increases. I try not to see that he is growing weaker, losing weight every day. Shrinking.

Praying. This isn't my father, this is a dead man.

One day I am leaving for school. Running late, I kiss Daddy good-bye quickly. As I race to the door, he makes a sound; he is trying to speak. I go to him. "What is it, Daddy? Do you want a drink of water?" I hand him a glass of water from his bedstand. He pushes it away, struggling to transform incoherent noises into words. "I can't understand you, Daddy," I say, impatient now. I am certain that I will miss my bus. He smiles warmly, and shakes his head. Never mind, he is saying. He takes my hand and squeezes it tightly. I quickly kiss him. "Good-bye, Daddy," I say, and rush out the door.

We are diagramming sentences. I love it--adjectives, predicates and lines going every which way. I am good at it, and I love it. The classroom door opens. A child with a note enters and hands the note to Sister Mary. She looks for me and calls my name. I am to report to the office. I am perplexed. I don't get into trouble. What would the office want with me?

I walk up the stairs, singing. Maybe someone found the bus card that I lost last week. Of course--that's it! I bound up the rest of the stairs, two at a time, and open the office door. My sister stands there, tears pouring down her cheeks. "I can't tell her," she sobs, and a nun comforts her, arm around her shoulders, leading her to a chair. "Your father has passed away," the nun tells me. I stare at her. Her habit is black and white. She is starched and crisp and I can see that yes, she is efficient. "Cry, dear, you'll feel better." I hear her words through a vacuum. My life is being sucked away. I cannot see clearly. I cannot hear clearly. I certainly cannot cry.

I hear them whispering, the relatives, about what a brave little girl I am. I enter the funeral parlor in a fashionable black dress, gently gripping my mother's arm, silently comforting her as her tears grow into torrents over my father's body. I am silent. I am strong. It's surprising how well I'm taking all of this.

At night the wine and beer flow heavily. The relatives sit at the big dining room table, recounting the good times with my father. My mother joins in. "He would have wanted it this way," she says mistily. I watch through a smokey haze, pretending to read my favorite book. I'll never see him again, I tell myself. What did he want to tell me . . . what?

I go to my room. I lie on the bed and taste the salt streaming down around my trembling lips. The door is closed, and I am crying.

## Pickin' Apples

### By Dan McClory

The college experience is said to linger with individuals through much of their adult lives, and I'm sure the following escapade will be at the forefront of any such thoughts I may recall from time to time.

Back in the fall of 1978, several fellow members of the track team and I were bored and restless. Another balmy, warm Indian summer evening with dinner finished and nothing to do, outside of homework. Dismissing the later alternative immediately, we turned our attentions to conjuring up something constructive to do.

We were a motley group--mostly sophomores, all with some connection to intercollegiate athletics, including several out-of-state students, representing such urban environs as New York, Pittsburgh, and Detroit. Upper and lower-middle-class blacks and whites with an Hispanic or two, we were united in the long-range goal of attaining success on the track, as well as our current aim of salvaging the evening. Strewn about the lounge on our floor in the residence hall, I threw out a suggestion for the group's evaluation.

"Listen, fellas. There's this apple orchard about a mile from here out in the country that I run by all the time," I began, not expecting everyone to be giving me their undivided attention. "There's all kinds of ripe apples just waiting to be picked," I stated matter-of-factly. "The way I see it, we can fit about six or seven people in my car, and we'll bring duffel bags so we can get lots of apples," I predicted.

By now the responses were rolling in, and a near-cheer arose from the twenty-odd members of the throng.

"Sounds cool, Dan," said Tony, a sprinter from New York whose scarred arms revealed more than one encounter with an armed adversary. "Save me a seat," he concluded.

"Count me in," added Darwin, a massively-built javelin thrower from Pittsburgh. "I got me a big bag and I'm gonna get me lots of nice apples."

"Yo Dan, how's about I come along too?" asked David, a mustachioed Puerto Rican from the Bronx.

"Sure thing, fellas," I responded to the now-enthusiastic group. "Let's grab our bags and head for the orchard while it's still light out. We want to see what we're pickin'!" I added with a grin.

The floor was buzzing with conversation as the members of the expedition rushed about to secure sacks and back packs to haul the goods in. Those who weren't going made sure their counterparts were securing an adequate supply for them as well.

Our group numbered six when we met at the elevator to strike out on the mission. Entering the elevator, we drew suspicious stares from the other students. I had to admit, though, it's not every day that you see six smiling eighteen-year-olds draped with empty duffel bags and dressed in dark clothing trying to look inconspicuous in an elevator.

Reaching the parking lot, we piled into my '72 LTD four-door, and I could finally see an advantage to the old gas-guzzler--its size. It would take at least a car that big to hold us and the estimated load of cargo.

I pulled onto Huron River Drive and we made our way towards Superior Road, which would take us to our destination, the Huron Valley Farms Orchard. We were a quieted group as we approached the point of attack, and I smoothly edged the car onto the gravelly dirt shoulder of the road. As we left the auto, I pointed to the prime spots for picking and we agreed to meet at the car in five minutes with as many apples as could be had.

We had to cross a cornfield and a plowed hayfield in order to get to the apples. We would be exposed to oncoming traffic from Superior when we made our dash across the cornfield, and we had to contend with an imposing farm house's view to clear the second obstacle.

Dashing through both fields, we were clear of any visible threats and commenced picking apples at will.

"Check out these fine apples," said Darwin, admiring the growing bulges in his bright pink draw-string laundry bag.

"These delicious ones, they the best," added David, as he chomped down on a healthy-sized piece of fruit.

"Damn, niggers, don't be greedy, let's cruise," said Tony, sharing my sentiments.

"Let's hurry up," I advised, hoping we'd be able to make our exit without incident.

Tossing the bloated bags over our shoulders, we broke into a trot as we crossed the plowed hayfield. Suddenly, without warning, two good-sized German shepherds were at our heels, expelling vicious barks.

"Git away doggie, I got me a big stick!" threatened Darwin to no avail.

"Back!" ordered Tony, and it appeared that his command drew some response as the canines let up for a stride. That's all we need, I thought to myself, envisioning the dogs alerting the farmer across the road, leading to perhaps our possible apprehension by the police. I can see it now, I went on, 'EMU Track Team Jailed.' Coach Parks would have a fit!

We made a break for my car and were glad to find that we'd left the doors unlocked. Jamming into the auto, I fired up the ignition and pulled out, tossing gravel as Tony scrambled to dive into the moving vehicle. The interior was a mass of bodies, bags, and apples.

By now sweating and breathing hard from the near-capture, we looked behind us to see if we'd been followed. Luckily we hadn't, and a relieved sigh was breathed by all when we got within sight of our tower dormitory.

"Man, that was a close call!" said Zac Miller, a fifth member of our entourage.

"You ain't kiddin'!" retorted David, adding, "I wasn't about to let no damn dog catch my ass!"

"Sorry about those dogs, fellas. They never bothered me before," I threw in, hoping to dispel any hostilities I may have rendered.

"It's cool, Dan," said Tony, biting into an apple. "We got the goods and that's all that matters."

Safely back on the home turf of the North Parking Lot, we unloaded our cargo and trudged toward the dorm. We looked like a string of pack mules as we plodded into the elevator.

"What's the deal, brother?" asked one of the elevator occupants to no one in particular. We all chuckled, then Tony finally responded.

"We just got us a good deal on some apples," he stated with a grin, patting the bulging sack sagging over his shoulder. I don't think I could've summed up things any better.

Later in the week my parents came up to watch me in a home cross country meet. As they left I handed them a shopping bag full of golden delicious apples to take home.

"Where'd you get these great apples?" inquired my dad.

"We got this orchard where you pick your own. It's cheaper because we bring our own containers, too," I answered, and my statement bore no falsehoods.

## Come the Moon

### By Cynthia L. Robinson

I trudged slowly up the stairs, halting after each step. I unlocked the door and stepped inside, glad for the unusual silence. The younger ones weren't out of school yet, so I had a little time. I clicked on the radio and plopped down on the bed. Some guy was singing about a girl who had paid her dues, while a guitar strummed thoughtlessly in the background:

She walks in dreams of better days.
A lonely room awaits her in the night.
Dinner for one at an old cafe.
Come the moon, she bows her lonely head and cries.

I flipped the radio off, wondering who had switched the station from Taco Tim, the Disco Dean. I eased my shoes off my feet and let them drop to the floor. I fished in my purse for the now crumpled letter. As I reread it, the same phrases stuck in my mind. "We are happy to inform you . . . due to your high academic performance . . . we would like to award you . . . toward your education at the school of your choice . . . . Taking into consideration your financial situation, you may also be eligible for . . . . Again, congratulations."

I folded the letter and put it on the little night stand. So, it was settled; I could go to college. I could go to school with the best of them. Mama wouldn't have to pay a cent. Of course, it would be rough, but that was nothing new for me. Besides, I would be writing; learning to polish my style. That's all that mattered. I would make it! So why wasn't I happy? Why wasn't I doing flying cartwheels all around the room? I couldn't say exactly, but something was holding me back--keeping me from giggling all over like a silly school girl. I decided it was because I was tired. Anyway, I couldn't really celebrate until Mama came home. I couldn't wait to tell her. She would--

I heard the key click in the lock. Please, I prayed, please let it be Kevin or Randy. Then at least they would go into the boys' room and give me a few more minutes of solitude. Just a few more minutes, that's all I--

The door slammed.

"I just can't satisfy that woman!" Tammy yelled. (So much for a few more minutes of solitude.) She stormed in and threw her books on my bed.

"I can't do it! I try so hard and all I get is 'D-Needs Improvement'. She don't have to tell me that. I can see I need improvement!"

"She *doesn't*," I corrected, lifting her books from my bed and depositing them on the chair.

Tammy just gave an exasperated sigh and went on. "Now she wants to see Mama. I told her Mama works two jobs. She just says, 'Arrangements will have to be made.' So I told her we didn't live in no fancy office where you can just make arrangements. Then she says I'm getting smart-mouth!"

"You were."

"But Toni, you know Mama can't make it. And with the rent coming up, she don't need no extra worries. How could I ask her to come?"

"I guess *I'll* have to do," I said, noticing she was wearing my good blouse.

"But you got classes."

"I can afford to miss one day," I said, rising slowly from the bed. The others would be here soon. "But it's up to you to put forth some effort, kid. We'll go over your paper tonight and see where it needs improvement. If you can do that, Mama doesn't even have to know."

"You're the best big sister in the whole world," Tammy squealed, giving me a big hug.

"Oh yeah, remind me I have something to tell Mama tonight. And take off my blouse before you come to dinner," I said and headed for the kitchen.

. . . . . . . . . . . . *She walks in dreams of better days* . . . . . . . . . . . . . .

I went into the kitchen and tried to think up something for dinner. I remembered Angie saying this morning that she would be eating over at her best friend Rhonda's tonight, so that meant six to feed instead of seven. That helped. I was trying to figure out how to make three potatoes feed six people when Randy burst in. He looked hot and sweaty in his faded blue jean jacket over a dirty, gray-white T-shirt.

"And just where are you popping in from?" I asked harshly in the only tone of voice Randy understood.

"Now don't start on me, Toni! I have enough problems without you putting in your two cents' worth."

"That would be the only money you made today. Don't even try to tell me you went looking for a job wearing that!"

"I didn't look for a job today."

"No kidding!"

"Aw, get off my case!" Randy yelled. "I'll find work soon."

"What's it going to do--walk up and slap you in the face? Look, the only reason Mama let you drop out was because we could use the extra money if you worked. You don't think that was an easy decision for her, do you? She always says she wants to see all of us finish. She already feels like she made a big mistake with you. You going to prove her right?"

"Toni, you know it ain't like that. I'm trying, but it just ain't easy. How many people you think want to hire a 16-year-old high school drop-out with no experience? I'm just not in what you would call popular demand. Don't think I can't see what it's doing to Mama. But I can't make them hire me. It's rough."

His voice had dwindled down to almost nothing. He blinked his eyes, trying to fight on-coming tears. I realized then how very young he was--a boy forced into a man's position. His face was already hard, his jaws set defiantly. Lines of worry had already begun to form around his eyes. Only his eyes showed a faint glimmer of hope that was dimming fast.

"Look, maybe we can work something out," I offered. "There's this teacher at my school who needs a babysitter in the evenings. I could do it. I'm doing it anyway. Two more kids wouldn't make a big difference. It would mean twenty-five more bucks a week. That should be enough to make ends meet. And you could finish school. I'll ask Mama about it tonight when I talk to her. I have something to tell her anyway."

Randy just looked at me for a long time. Then he smiled--his way of saying thanks--and bolted from his room. Mashed potatoes, I decided and turned back to dinner.

. . . . . . . . . . . . *A lonely room awaits her in the night* . . . . . . .

I had just put the last plate on the table when I heard Tammy's scream.

"Toni, come quick!"

I rushed into the hall to see little Nita covered all over with ugly red spots.

"Measles! Oh, my poor little one!"

Kevin, who had entered with her, was looking just as miserable. It was his job to pick Nita up from the After-School Center, and I imagined it had been a big shock for him.

At the tone of my voice, Nita burst into uncontrollable sobs. I hugged her feverish little body to me and carried her into the room.

"Roll the blankets back," I told Tammy. "Get me some aspirin and a cold, wet cloth."

Gently, I laid Nita on the bed, cooing and clucking like a mother hen.

"She--she said I couldn't come back," sobbed Nita, who loved school. "Not until all the spots is gone."

"Well, I guess we have to make them go away fast, huh, angel?"

"She was reading to us about the Sweeping Beauty. I didn't hear the end."

"I'll tell you the end if you promise to go right to sleep when I'm finished."

She smiled and nodded at me, as if I were Sweeping Beauty herself. Well, I could forget school for a few days. It was no problem, though; I could catch up. I always did.

I told the others to go eat while I rendered my version of Sleeping Beauty or what I could remember of it. I waited until Nita was asleep before I went into the kitchen.

I entered just as Kevin was leaving. He stopped and looked at me.

"She's going to be fine," I told his questioning eyes. "So what happened with you today?"

"Where?" he asked innocently, though he knew exactly what I was talking about.

"You know where--in school. What did you do today?"

Kevin shrugged. This line of questioning was a ritual with us, and though he pretended that it disturbed him, he was secretly pleased that I persisted.

"Oh, we just did our regular stuff," he offered.

"Like what?"

"We went over the three times-table again. Some of the kids still didn't under--"

"Three times-table!" I shouted, "I taught you that last year! You're past that." It was true. Kevin was a mathematical wizard. At ten years old, he had already experimented with square roots and was begging me to start him on beginner's algebra. The only thing holding him back was school.

"I know I'm past that. I told the teacher and she said for you to stop teaching me at home."

"Well, I don't care what she says. You do page 34 in our workbook tonight and I'll check it. If she won't help you, I sure will."

Kevin looked pained at this new assignment, but rushed off to begin it. He wasn't fooling me. He loved math. And if I could help him, he was going to excel in it.

I sat down and ate my now cold meal. Mama would be home soon. Then I could rest. Then I could tell her my news.

. . . . . . . . . . . . . *Dinner for one at an old cafe* . . . . . . . . . . . .

Four hours later, Mama was home. The younger ones were asleep. Randy was out somewhere on the streets. Tammy and I were busy toiling over a hot D-grade composition.

"I can't do it," Tammy whined. "I just don't know what she wants from me."

"She wants you to try to express yourself through a series of well-organized paragraphs."

"Girl, you sound more like a teacher each day," Mama laughed from the chair in the corner. "That's enough school for one night. Run, get in the bed now, Tammy, and let your sister come and talk to me."

"Oh yeah, Toni, you said you had something to tell Mama."

"Oh," I said, jumping up.

The letter! In all the excitement, I had forgotten all about it. I tipped in the room and picked up the letter. I checked on Nita, who was sleeping peacefully, and rushed back into the room. Mama had fallen asleep. I looked at Mama, whose strong, broad shoulders now sagged under the weight of the day; who worked hard at her jobs and refused to stay out sick; who hadn't shed a tear when Daddy left; who clung desperately to her faith like a young child clings to his mother's skirt; who fought like a soldier to keep us together; who hadn't seen a new dress in years; who right now was soaking her feet to get the swelling down by morning. I turned away. Mama stirred.

"Antonia, what you got to tell me?" she asked, yawning.

"I made an 'A' on my French test today," I said, balling up the paper in my hand.

. . . . . . . . . . . . . *Come the moon, she bows her lonely head and cries* . . . . . .

## Passing Through

### By Craig Hamann

"We're low on gas, Mike," I said. "I'm going to pull into that gas station."

"That's cool," said Mike. "I want to get out and stretch my legs anyway. I feel like getting a Coke."

I drove into the gas station. It was a small old building with only two gas pumps. It had a garage big enough to fit only one car at a time. A skinny gray-haired man walked out of the station with his eyes downcast. He looked as old as the building. When he finally looked up and saw us, he stopped walking. Pulling a rag out of his pants pocket, he wiped his forehead. Then he grimaced and walked up to my car.

"What'll ya have?" he asked. I thought I noted a trace of petulence in his voice.

"Fill it with regular," I said. He frowned at me and spit on the ground. (He looked as if he might have wanted to spit on my car instead.) He walked over to the gas pump, grabbed the hose, and started to fill my car. I could hear him mumbling something to himself. It didn't sound friendly.

Mike got out of the car. "You got a pop machine?" he asked, walking around to the back of the car. The old man didn't answer but pointed towards the garage without looking up.

I got out of the car, too, and walked back to where the old man was holding the gas hose and concentrating on the spout.

"How far to Clovis?" I asked.

"Not far," he said. He turned his head towards me but looked at the top of my head and not my eyes. "Where you from?"

"Michigan," I said. He still kept looking at the top of my head. I felt uncomfortable, but I didn't know why.

"What ya doin' here?" he asked.

"Just passing through," I said. "I've got an uncle running a dealership in Clovis. We thought we'd stop by and see him."

The old man grunted. "Ya come all the way from Michigan to New Mexico to see your uncle?" he said incredulously.

"No, we're just passing through," I said. "We've never been in the South before. Thought we'd take our vacation here--that's all. My uncle works here. We thought we'd stop by and surprise him." I felt dumb explaining all that to him. Actually, we were running out of money and thought my uncle could get us a loan or a job, but I wasn't about to tell the old man that. "My uncle's name is Fred Parker and he's running Clovis Ford for Ford Motor Company. Maybe you've heard of him."

"Can't say I have," the old man said with an uninterested tone. He pulled the spout out. "That'll be two dollars and thirty cents."

I paid him and got back inside the car where Mike was waiting with a bottle of Coke.

"Want a hit off this, Jesse?" Mike asked. He passed the bottle to me.

"Yeah, sure," I said. I started the car and pulled onto the road. "Man, that guy was weird. He kept looking at the top of my head." I gave the bottle back to Mike after taking a drink.

"Maybe he was looking at your hair, hippie," laughed Mike. Both Mike and I had shoulder-length hair.

"Well, at least my hair doesn't look like some kind of damn sponge," I joked back. Mike's hair was bushy--almost an Afro. Actually, I liked it, but I liked to kid him about it. We drove for about ten minutes in silence.

"I can see a town coming up," Mike said. Sure enough, I could see a couple rows of buildings ahead. We drove a little further and saw a sign saying, "Welcome to Clovis." The first building we saw was an old one story post office. In front of it was an old panel-truck with "U.S. Postal Service" printed on it. There were several other squat, ugly wooden structures, and then what I assumed was their excuse for a supermarket.

"This must be it," I said to Mike. Mike was staring out of his window. "I can't believe how old everything looks."

As we drove on, we saw stores set extremely close together and a lot of people walking on the sidewalks. We passed the "Clovis Barbershop" and saw the barber sitting on a bench in front of the shop. (He looked like he was waiting for some business.)

"How're we gonna find your uncle's dealership?" Mike asked.

"Easy," I said. "It's on Main Street and main streets are always in the middle of the downtown sections in small towns." Within a few minutes I drove into the downtown part of Clovis; there was no problem identifying it. I slowed down almost to a stop in front of a florist's shop.

"Well, here it is," I said. "This must be beautiful downtown Clovis." I was being very sarcastic.

"Yes, this does seem to be the hot-spot," Mike said being equally satirical.

"Main Street should be around here somewhere," I said. I sped up the car and started exploring. We found Main Street without much difficulty. All it had was a lot of old buildings. The town looked ancient. Almost all the people we saw on the sidewalks or leaning against store windows were dressed in old clothes. A lot of men had on cowboy hats and were wearing overalls. From what I could tell, my Capri was about the only sports car in town. Most of them were Chevrolets and Fords, almost none of them late models. I had never before seen so many bumper stickers of the 'America--love it or leave it' or 'I'm proud to be an American' variety.

"There it is, Jesse," Mike shouted, suddenly pointing ahead.

I looked and saw a sign saying, 'Clovis Ford and Mercury.' I parked in front of the building. It was fairly small with a new car showroom capable of displaying only two new cars. The building was made of brick, but it looked old and fit in with the rest of the town. We got out of the car and walked inside the showroom. We stood by the door while I scanned the room for Uncle Fred. I saw Uncle Fred standing next to one of the showroom cars with a man and a woman. The man had overalls on and the woman had an old dress on. Both looked over sixty years of age and were diverting their attention from Uncle Fred to us. At first Uncle Fred looked at us with a blank expression. (I took for granted he didn't recognize me at first.) Then he smiled and walked over to Mike and me.

"Jesse! What a surprise," he said. Uncle Fred stopped and turned around. "Oh, no!" The elderly couple he had been talking to had walked to another exit. Without looking back, they walked outside and left. Uncle Fred's face turned red. "I was so surprised to see you I forgot about my customers," he said. "They didn't like the bucket seats anyway." He shrugged his shoulders and laughed. We shook hands and I introduced him to Mike.

Uncle Fred hadn't changed much from the last time I saw him. His hair was a little thinner, but he still looked younger than most men at fifty-five do. He was perhaps a bit heavier, but certainly not fat. Uncle Fred referred to himself as "pleasantly plump." It was twelve o'clock and Uncle Fred said that he hadn't eaten all day. He offered to buy us lunch at the Clovis Restaurant across the street. We walked over to the restaurant and went inside. The restaurant, like everything else in Clovis, was an old building. There were no customers but us. We sat down at a table by the front window because it was the only table that looked clean. Behind the counter with the cash register was a door that obviously went into their kitchen. The door opened and a bald fat man came out. He stared at us and grunted. The door opened again and a fat woman came out. She, too, was scrutinizing every move we made. I guessed that the man was the cook and the woman was his wife, or waitress, or both. Neither one seemed too interested in waiting on us. Both seemed content just gawking at us.

"How's business?" I asked.

Uncle Fred pulled out a cigarette and lit it. A fly flew in front of his face and he swatted at it, but missed. "I don't really know how business is," he said. He looked for an ashtray, but none of the tables had one, so he used the floor. "I've only been in this town for two days. I was running a dealership in Hobbs, Arizona, when Ford calls me up, and now they got me running this dealership, too. It seems the last owner up and quit, so I'll be running it until Ford finds a new one. I've got to catch a plane back to Hobbs today. I'll be there for a week."

More promptly than I would've expected, the waitress came to our table. "What'll ya have?" she asked. She kept her eyes on Mike and me. She seemed grumpy and probably very unfriendly. Uncle Fred ordered a turkey sandwich, and Mike and I ordered hamburgers and cokes.

The waitress left and our conversation continued. "How far you going on your trip?" Uncle Fred asked.

"Well, we wanted to get to California, but we're running low on money right now," I said.

Uncle Fred leaned back in his chair. "How long you going to stay here?" he asked.

"I don't know," I said. "Why do you ask?"

"Well, you could work at the dealership here in Clovis for a week or two, if you like," Uncle Fred said. "We need a lot of work done in the warehouse. I've got a motel room at the Clovis Motel. It's small, but it has two beds, and Ford is paying for it. You both could stay there while I'm in Hobbs."

We talked it over and decided it was a good idea. After lunch we walked back to the dealership and Uncle Fred took us into the service department. Like the showroom, it was small. There were only four stalls. All of them had cars in them. The mechanics were working, but each one in turn stopped to look at us. The service garage, too, was old, and I noticed cracks in the cement walls. A fat, flabby man of about forty and a thin, small-framed man of about thirty walked over to us.

"Anything I can help you with, Mr. Parker?" the fat man asked my Uncle. He was sloppy. Half his shirt hung out of his pants. His hands were greasy and there were marks all over his clothes where he had wiped them. He had the shortest crewcut I had ever seen. He was smiling, with both hands held casually at his waist. He looked at Mike and me and his smile suddenly disappeared into a smirk.

"You're the service manager, aren't you?" Uncle Fred asked the fat man.

The fat man stepped aside and the thin man spoke. "Uh, no he ain't, sir," the thin man said. He had wavy hair that was combed back into a 1950 "grease-ball" style. I noticed he seemed squeamish. "I'm Henry Folly," he said, "the service manager."

"Hell, where you been?" asked Uncle Fred. "I've been running this place for two days, and this is the first time I recall seeing you. I've never run a place when I don't even know who my damn service manager is."

"Uh, I been here," Henry answered sheepishly. He rubbed his hand through his hair making him look even more like a grease-ball. "Ya see," he continued, "I been darn busy. Right, Guy?" He looked at the floor.

"Yeah, that's right, Mr. Parker," the sloppy fat man said. "I'm Guy. I'm the best mechanic in Clovis." Guy's smile widened.

"Yes, I'm sure you are," Uncle Fred said. He looked at his wristwatch. "Come with me to the warehouse, Henry." We walked to a side garage door which was next to what apparently was Guy's stall because Guy went back to work on a car there. Once outside the garage, we were in an alley about two car-widths wide. The warehouse was across the alley. The warehouse was no bigger than a two-car garage, but it had two floors. It had a garage door that was padlocked. Henry unlocked it and we went inside. It was dusty and as old as every other building Mike and I had seen. We stood by the door.

"Henry, this is my nephew, Jesse," Uncle Fred said. "This is Mike. They're going to work here for a while. You'll be their boss." Uncle Fred looked at his watch again. "I've got to be leaving. You explain to these boys what to do." Mike and I shook hands with Uncle Fred and said good-bye. Before he left he gave us his motel key and told us how to get to the motel. It turned out it was only two blocks down Main Street from the dealership.

After he left Henry began to explain what we were supposed to do. "Ya gotta keep the place clean," he said. He rubbed his hand through his hair. "Now it's a rule that mechanics don't come in here, so you'll have ta get 'em things when they ask ya. Work starts at eight in the mornin'. Ya get off at six. I'm gonna be givin' ya inven--"

Just then a voice broke in calling Henry's name. It was the fat mechanic, Guy.

"Now, Guy," Henry said. "Ya know ya ain't s'posed to come in here." Henry looked at us and then at Guy. Henry looked at the floor.

"Why ya gotta be so bossy, Henry?" Guy asked. "I just come in here to find out what these hippie-boys is doin' in here." Guy smiled and stared at Mike and me. "Besides, Henry, I need to get some rags. Now what's wrong with that?" He definitely needed some rags to wipe some of the filth off of him.

"Nothin', Guy, but it's a rule. Only me and whoever's workin' in the warehouse can come in," Henry said, still looking at the floor. "And these boys are hired by Mr. Parker. They're new help."

Guy's smile broadened. He scratched the top of his burr-head. "Oh, is that what they are?" he said. He pointed to Mike. "Hey, Curly, hand me those rags on that box in back of you." Mike gave them to Guy and Guy left. I looked at Mike and could tell he wasn't exactly flattered by the "Curly" remark.

"Well, start cleanin' the place up, and I'll give ya inventory sheets tomorrow," Henry said. He put his hands in his pockets and walked out of the warehouse.

"There's sure some bizarre people here," I said to Mike.

Mike looked angry. "Yeah, there's strange people here all right," he agreed. "I don't appreciate that fat jerk calling me Curly. You notice how these people stare at us?"

"Well, of course they stare at us," I said. "In a small town everyone knows everyone, and we're from out of town, so they look at us because they know we're strangers."

"Do you really believe that, Jesse?" Mike asked.

"Yeah, course I do," I said. I don't think I really accepted my own explanation, but at least it sounded good. "Forget about Guy and let's get to work and make some money." We started cleaning the place up. We worked until six o'clock when Henry came in and told us we could leave.

After work we ate dinner at the restaurant across the street. When we walked in we were the only customers there. We sat at the same table by the window. This time a young pretty waitress came to our table.

"What'll ya have?" she asked. She had a beautiful face and long, dark hair. She was dressed extremely conservatively. Her face showed no emotion. I doubt that she had any interest in Mike or me.

"I'll have the chicken dinner," I said. Mike ordered the same. When she walked away I noticed the cook was looking at us. Evidently he had come out of the back to gawk at us.

"Did you get a good look at that waitress?" Mike asked.

"Yeah, she wasn't bad," I said. I pushed my chair closer to the table in order to talk to Mike without being heard by the gawking cook. "She's the youngest person I've seen in this town. She must be around our age."

"Too bad her skirt was two inches below her knees," Mike said with a smile. "This is so damn ridiculous. Everyone has 1950 clothes on. The only half-way good-looking girl we see is dressed and ready for the last decade." I laughed and nodded in approval. How inconsistent this town was, I thought.

We couldn't help but regret sitting by the window. We were on view to anyone passing by outside, and it seemed the whole town at one time or another stopped to stare at us through the window. We felt like animals in a zoo. When we got done eating we drove straight to the motel.

The motel was as old as the rest of the town, but by now we were getting used to old-fashioned buildings. Our room, number nine, was small. It was about the size of a regular bedroom except it had a desk, two small beds, a television, and a bathroom all compressed in it. Neither one of us felt like being the center of attraction in Clovis, so we switched on the television and resigned ourselves to staying in the rest of the night. The T.V. had only three channels working. One had an interview with the Clovis Mayor--he reminded me of Walter Brennan. The 'Beverly Hillbillies' was on a channel and 'Farm News' on the other. We fell asleep with the T.V. on.

The next morning we had breakfast at the restaurant across the street from the dealership. After eating bacon and eggs, and receiving our usual stare from the cook, we drove to the warehouse. It was about five minutes before eight. Mike and I decided to wait in front of the warehouse for Henry to open it. But when we got there, we found it was unlocked already. Mike and I went inside.

There was Guy, going through some boxes. He evidently heard us and turned around looking rather startled.

"Did you want something?" I asked, trying to be polite.

Guy's startled expression quickly changed to a smile. "No, thanks, Hairy," he said. Then he abruptly dropped what he was doing and walked in front of Mike. Looking at Mike's hair, he put his hands on his hips. "What type of hair curlers do you use?" He was still smiling. "My, my. They sure do a damn pretty job." Guy started to laugh the nastiest laugh I've ever heard and walked out still laughing. All his disgusting fat shook when he laughed.

After Guy had left, Mike swung his fist, hitting a box quite hard. "How much more of this crap do I have to take?" he asked in an infuriated tone.

I tried to be rational. I knew exactly how he felt. I felt close to the same way, but what could you do? "Mike," I said, "he doesn't like long hair. There's really no reason to get upset. Just laugh it off."

"Oh, I'm laughing," Mike said bitterly. He grabbed a broom and started sweeping the floor violently. I didn't know what else to say to Mike. We needed this job. Without money we could never make it to California.

It was about ten o'clock when Henry came inside the warehouse. He gave inventory sheets to Mike and me, and told us to start listing all the parts inside the warehouse. We started checking the parts. Most of them were there, but a few were missing. I noticed the missing parts were all for Capris. I knew this because my car was a Capri. One particular part that was missing was an Abarth exhaust muffler.

Around twelve noon Henry came back in the warehouse to tell us we could take a lunch break. We told Henry about the Abarth and the other missing parts.

"Dammit," Henry said. "Y'know, that Abarth was important. It only fits Capris. It don't fit Fords or Mercurys. Are ya sure ya didn't miss somethin'?" Henry was double-checking behind us when Guy walked in.

"What's the trouble, Henry?" Guy asked.

"Who said there was any trouble?" Mike said. I stepped in front of Mike. I didn't want any friction between Mike and Guy.

"An Abarth's missin'," Henry said. I noticed Henry didn't berate Guy for coming in the warehouse this time.

"Abarths are hot items," Guy said. "Someone might've swiped it to sell it and get some good money for it."

Henry rubbed his hand through his hair and looked at the floor. He lifted his head. "Yeah, that's what happen all right," he said. "Sure ain't no misagreement there." I noticed Henry was acting squeamish again. He pulled a cigarette out of his shirt pocket and dropped it on the floor. Then he picked it up and lit it, turning towards Mike and me. "Ya got half a hour for yer lunch," he said. The cigarette was shaking in his hand. "Don't waste it." Henry turned around and left.

Guy stood with his hands on his hips. "By the way, hippies," he said, "what type of car do you drive? Wouldn't be a Capri by any chance, would it?" He smiled and walked out. Mike and I stood in the warehouse looking at each other, but not saying anything. Yet, I could tell we were both thinking about the same thing.

Mike was first to speak. "You know, Jesse, I think Henry thinks we ripped off that Abarth," he said. He started to look angry. "And fat Guy practically said we did."

I was way ahead of him. I began to see what the score was as soon as Guy had walked in when we were talking to Henry. "Aw, don't worry about it," I said. "Nobody came right out and accused us, and besides, we're innocent. Quit jumping to conclusions." Mike was always kind of quick-tempered. In the three years I'd known him, I'd always have to be the one to calm him down.

"Look, why don't you run over to the restaurant and get us two carry-out hamburgers," I said. "I'll keep taking inventory." I gave Mike a dollar for my food and he left. Then I walked upstairs to start checking parts on the second floor.

I had been there for about two minutes when I thought I heard someone shuffling around in the boxes on the first floor. At first I thought it was Mike, but he couldn't be back from the restaurant that soon. I ran down the stairs to see what was going on. When I got to the first floor I saw Guy leaning over and inspecting the inside of one of the boxes. I didn't know whether to sneak up on him or not. I decided to play it by ear since I wasn't even sure what he was looking for.

"What are you doing?" I asked. I couldn't think of anything better to say.

Guy quickly stood up and turned around. He looked stunned, and his face was pale white. But in a split second his color returned to his face and so did the typical smirk. "What did you say, hippie?" he asked.

"I asked you what you're doing," I said. I tried to be unemotional. "Henry said we should get whatever the mechanics want and you're not supposed to be in here." I tried to be even polite. "If there's anything you want I'll be glad to get it for you."

Guy stood still and just smiled. "Ain't you s'posed to be out eatin' lunch?" he asked. "Or maybe hippies don't eat."

I knew he was evading my question. "Did you come in here for something or not?" I asked trying to sound more stern this time. "If you didn't, then you'll have to get out."

Guy put his hands on his hips. "Well, now. You've been here for two whole days and you're already givin' me orders." His smirk broadened into a full, insulting grin. I began feeling frightened. He walked up to me and grabbed my shirt collar with one hand and made a threatening gesture with his fist. "Don't give me no orders, hippie. I don't take no orders, hippie," he said. "Ya know, I'm a wrassler." He started breathing his words. "I don't take kindly to hippies givin' me orders and I'm liable to get real mean." He pushed me away and laughed. He walked out laughing. He stopped in the alley and turned around only to laugh harder. Then he walked back in the direction of the service department.

I was embarrassed. I felt horrible. I had tried to be stern and ended up being humiliated. I heard someone walking in the alley. It was Mike. He was back from the restaurant.

"I got us a couple of hamburgers, two orders of fries, and two cokes," Mike said. He stopped. He must have noticed by my expression that I was upset. "What's wrong?" he asked. "You look really bummed out. Did something happen while I was gone?"

I didn't know how to phrase it. "I just caught Guy snooping around in the boxes and I tried to bitch him out," I said. I could barely talk right. My embarrassment was turning into anger.

Mike gave me a hamburger and bit into his. He sat down on a box. He looked very concerned. "So, what happened after that?" he asked.

"That fat-ass grabbed me and told me he didn't want me giving him orders," I explained. I was getting more and more angry the more I talked about it. "He told me he was a wrestler or something." I paused, and then looked Mike in the eyes. "The fat slob laughed in my face." I took a bite out of my hamburger, but it tasted like cardboard. I suddenly realized I wasn't hungry any more.

Mike got up from the box and put his hand on my shoulder. "We could tell Henry," he said. "Listen, Guy is twice your size, Jesse. There's no use getting upset. Besides, I think I can take him. Just 'cause he's fat doesn't mean he's rough."

Mike was a damn good fighter, but I was afraid of trouble. "You can't do that," I said. "Nobody likes us around here to begin with. If I say anything to Henry, or you tangle with Guy, we'll get fired for sure. Or what's worse, we'll get my uncle in trouble." The whole situation was hopeless. Guy could do as he damn well pleased and we couldn't stop him because we were outsiders--long-haired outsiders, at that.

"Why don't we just leave?" Mike asked.

"Do you want to go to California?" I said.

"Yeah, really bad," Mike said.

"Then we've got to make money and there's no one around here who'll hire us except my uncle," I said. "Of course, we could always get our hair cut." I knew what Mike's reaction would be to that.

"No way, man. I don't want to do that. That's giving in too much," Mike said. He sighed out of frustration. "Well, we might as well get back to work."

As we continued taking inventory we found a tachometer for a Capri was missing as was a pair of Capri back-up lights. Around two o'clock Henry came in the warehouse to see how we were doing. We were about to tell him about the missing parts when Guy just happened to walk in.

"What ya need?" Henry asked Guy.

"I need a pair of back-up lights for a Capri I'm workin' on, Henry," Guy said. He was talking like he was rehearsing for a play. He looked at me and made a sly grin. "Ya wanna get 'em for me?" he asked.

I turned to Henry. "They're missing," I said. "Mike and I couldn't find them when we took inventory. I think they might have been stolen." As soon as I said that, I couldn't help but wish I hadn't.

Henry looked at the floor. "A lot a parts been missin' lately," he said. "A hell of a lot." Henry gritted his teeth and acted like he wanted to say something, but turned around instead and walked out.

Naturally, Guy had enjoyed all of what had just happened. I could see the overwhelming delight on his fat face. He smiled and then laughed. Obviously he was proud, and I knew exactly why. He waddled out of the warehouse laughing up a storm. Mike started after him.

"Mike, you'll get us in trouble," I said, grabbing him by the arm. Mike pushed me away and, for the first time since we had been friends, gave me a look of contempt.

"Just what in the hell is the matter with you, Jesse?" Mike asked. He had a look of total disbelief on his face. "You know damn well Guy stole those parts just to make us look bad.

What are you--stupid or something? I mean, you're the one who's supposed to be so damn logical and have his shit together. Why the hell can't you see through an idiot like Guy?"

I tried to be calm and reasonable. "What do you propose we do?" I asked.

"Kick the living hell out of him!" Mike yelled.

"Where does that get us?" I asked. I was trying to keep my cool. Mike sat down on a box and took a deep breath. "We need money to get to California and we have to have this job. If we fight Guy we'll just get fired or something. Besides I think--"

"Forget it, Jesse," Mike butted in. "Stay on your intellectual ego-trip. Go ahead and keep getting pushed around. Hell, if you're content to let Guy walk on us, then I guess it's okay by me." Mike got up off the box and walked up the stairs to the second floor. I felt like a spineless fool. I knew Mike was gravely disappointed in me. In the past he had always admired the way I could talk, con, or trick our way out of anything. Now I wasn't coming through for him. I couldn't help but feel that Mike may have wanted to call me a coward. We didn't talk to each other for most of the day.

Shortly before closing time, Henry asked me to come into the service garage and empty a pan of old oil they had drained out of a truck. As I walked into the garage, I got the expected stares of customers and mechanics alike. For some reason they seemed more unbearable than before. Is another three days of pay worth another three days of stares, I thought?

I picked up the pan of oil which, by coincidence, was in Guy's working stall. As I started to the alley to dump the oil in a barrel, Guy started walking towards me. I got ready to receive the usual verbal abuse. He stood by the garage exit next to the barrel. As I walked next to Guy, I turned my head away hoping he wouldn't say anything. He didn't, but instead tripped me. I fell down and the oil splattered everywhere. My hands and clothes were drenched in oil. Guy was laughing and I was boiling. Without saying a word I got up and walked into the warehouse. I got some rags and cleaned up the mess in the alley the best I could. California cannot be worth all this, I thought.

It took me until closing time to clean the mess up. After work Mike ran inside the Clovis Restaurant and got us two carry-out dinners. I was just too dirty from all the oil to go in. Besides, we knew we'd get stared at enough even if we were completely clean. I never guessed anything like that would ever bother me, but I was sick to death of stares. After dinner I cleaned up and Mike and I lay on our beds watching a boring movie on television. We still were not talking to each other much and it was bothering both of us.

"I'm really sorry about yelling at you today," Mike said. The tone of his voice was emotional. I knew he meant it.

"That's okay," I said. "You have a right to your opinion. Anyway you had every right to yell at me."

Mike sat up quickly. He looked at me curiously. "I did?" he said. His eyes were opened wide. He looked as if someone had just told him his clothes were on fire. "Why did I have a right to?" he asked.

I almost had to laugh at Mike's surprise. "Because I really don't want Guy to walk on us," I said. I sat up on my bed. "Listen, man. I don't think I can stand any more humiliation. I don't think I can bear much more of this shit Guy has dealt us." I was surprised to hear myself say that.

"What can we do?" Mike asked. "I mean, you don't want to get your uncle in trouble." Mike looked at me anxiously. I could tell he was eagerly waiting for my answer.

"Mike, I don't know what to do," I said. Mike sighed and lay back down on his bed. "I'm sorry I can't come up with a solution." I got up and turned off the television and the lights.

Mike fell asleep fast, but I couldn't. My mind was working overtime. My thoughts were on the events that had happened the last two days. Why couldn't I act? What was preventing me from taking action against Guy? Maybe I could talk to Henry. I could wait until Uncle Fred got back, but how was I going to be able to cope with Guy until then? Why couldn't Henry see what Guy was doing to Mike and me?

I couldn't let this go on. I was losing my best friend's respect and respect for myself.

I knew that Guy had stolen those parts to make us look bad. Yet, I wondered what made Henry so blind to it all? I couldn't help but wonder how Guy had gotten inside the warehouse in the morning if only Henry had the key. I wondered why Henry had taken Guy's word that the Abarth had been stolen. It seemed odd that Guy would always walk in the warehouse just when something was missing and Henry couldn't notice it. Also why did I have to take out the oil that just happened to be in Guy's stall? Who was our worst enemy, after all? It was now apparent that there was more than one. Guy was open with his hatred, and Henry was too afraid to do anything. Was I afraid, too? Was I like Henry? The thought appalled me. I closed my eyes and tried to sleep.

The next morning we went to the restaurant as usual to have our breakfast. While waiting for our food, Mike was talking about cars. I wasn't listening closely because I was still pondering over the thoughts I had had during the night.

Obviously noticing my inattentiveness, Mike stopped what he was saying. "What's wrong, Jesse?"

"Nothing, Mike," I said. "I just didn't get much sleep last night."

"Why's that?" Mike asked looking concerned.

"Let's talk about it later," I said. "I've got some things to figure out." Mike said okay and went back to talking whatever he was saying about cars before.

After we were done eating we drove to the warehouse. Once again we were early. We didn't see anyone around, but the warehouse garage door was open. This time the lock was smashed. Mike and I walked inside and saw a rear stabilizer bar for a Capri lying on the floor. Nobody was inside the warehouse but us.

"Wow! Someone tried to rip that off," Mike said examining the stabilizer bar. The torn box for the bar was beside it.

"I think everything is in just the right order," I said. "At least in the order they want it to be."

Mike looked at me. "They?" Mike said. "What the hell do you mean by that? If this is a set-up to make us look bad, I can tell you right now it was fat-ass Guy who did it."

"Not just Guy," I said. I was feeling like Sherlock Holmes. Before, I was like I thought Henry was. I had been blind. "Come on, Mike. I'm sure they're waiting." We walked outside into the alley only to be greeted by Guy and Henry.

"There they are," Guy said. He had a big smile on his plump face. "See, just like I told ya. Ya can't trust hippies. They've been stealin' parts." I could tell this was Guy's final attempt to get rid of us.

"Uh, I'll, uh," Henry was stammering. He was simply disgusting. He was like an actor forgetting his lines. Henry looked at Guy.

"Don't ya think ya should check the evidence, Henry?" Guy asked. The absolute absurdity of the situation was damn near amusing.

"Yeah, I'm checkin' it right now," Henry said, trying hard to act with authority. He walked past us and inside the warehouse. I walked inside behind him, and Mike and Guy followed me. Henry looked at the stabilizer bar. He brushed his hand through his hair.

"Henry," I said, "you know damn well we had nothing to do with this."

Henry looked at the floor. "I gotta fire ya for this," he said.

"For what!" I screamed. I pointed to Guy. "That fat animal planted all this. Henry, for the love of God, believe me. This is ridiculous. There's a damn stabilizer bar on the floor, the lock is broken, and that makes you think we broke in? Hell, that's ridiculous!" I couldn't help shouting. I started pacing the floor.

Henry shrugged his shoulders. "I saw ya runnin' out of here," he said. He kept looking at the floor.

"Shit! We were walking, not running," I said. "We weren't even carrying the damn stabilizer bar." I stopped pacing and waited for Henry's reply, but he wasn't saying anything.

Guy spoke up instead. "They probably dropped it when they heard us comin'," he said. Henry nodded his head in agreement. Henry walked out of the warehouse with his hands in his pockets and his eyes glued to the ground. Guy smiled and held his hands at his hips. I could tell he was real proud of himself.

"You bastard," I said staring straight at Guy's fat face. "Well, you did a good job. I hope you're proud of yourself." I was shaking with anger. I could no longer keep any self-control.

"I must admit, I sure am proud," Guy said. He took his hands off his hips a little and curved his arms like he was carrying something under them. He crouched over a little. I took for granted this was his "wrasslin' " form. "I'm a wrassler so don't try nothin'," he said. I'm sure he was daring us more than warning us. "Now you hippies clear out before I wip both of ya," he said with a big grin.

I looked at Mike. His fists were clenched and his face was red. This was it. It was time to defeat Guy the only way we possibly could. "So, you're going to wip the both of us, huh?" I said. I was nervous as hell, but mad enough to go through with this.

"That's right, hippie," Guy said advancing towards me.

"Try it," I said. Guy rushed me and tried to grab me around the waist, but I managed to knee him quite hard in the groin. He let out a cry of pain and dropped to his knees. Mike ran over and kicked him in the face, knocking him over on his back. I saw blood running out of his nose and down into his mouth. I felt pure hatred for Guy and pleasure because of his pain.

Guy got up and wiped his nose with the back of his hand. He was breathing hard and his face was flush red. "So, ya wanna fight, do ya?" he said. He seemed to have forgotten he had been the instigator. "You damn hippies. I can wip any of you." He struck Mike and they started to fight. Mike was kicking the shit out of him. I heard someone come in behind me. I turned around and saw Henry with two other mechanics. The mechanics ran over to the fight between Mike and Guy.

This gave me a chance to get some truth. I walked up to Henry and grabbed his shirt collar like Guy had grabbed mine. "You little miserable son-of-a-bitch," I said to Henry. He was shaking like hell. "You were in on this all the time, weren't you?"

"Who said?" Henry was falling to pieces. "D-Did Guy tell ya? He planned it." That was all I had to hear. I let Henry go. In the meantime, the mechanics had broken up the fight between Mike and Guy.

"Call the police, Henry," Guy said. He was panting like a dog. "Call 'em up, Henry. These hippies attacked me when my back was turned." Guy wiped his nose with his hand again.

Henry pointed his finger at me. "Now ya get outa here," he said. His voice was shaky and he was acting terribly excited. "I'll call the cops! I just fired ya; didn't I fire 'em, Guy?"

"You sure did, Henry," Guy said. "You're the boss and ya fired 'em. Call the damn police if they don't leave." Guy and the other two mechanics started to walk towards us. Henry stood in back of them.

I realized that all the fighting that needed to be done had been done already. "Okay, we're leaving," I said. I was still angry and I could tell by Mike's expression that he was, too. Guy and the two other mechanics followed us menacingly to my car. Henry walked in back of them. Mike and I got into my car and I started the engine. Before we left I rolled down my window. "Yeah, you're the boss, Henry!" I yelled. "If you don't believe me, then ask Guy." We drove away.

As we drove to the motel I noticed Mike kept looking at me. "All right," I said. "What's on your mind?" He shrugged his shoulders. "Come on, man, let's have it. What are you thinking about?"

"You were great," he said. Mike shook his head in amazement and halfway laughed. "You were really great. I mean, I never thought you were going to stand up to Guy like that." Mike smiled sinisterly. "We really gave those guys hell," he said. "That was great the way you told them off. You really put the shits to Henry, too." Mike laughed. I had his respect.

"Do you care about California?" I asked.

"The hell with California," Mike said. We pulled into the motel parking lot. "We could drive into another state. Maybe we could get a job there."

"Yeah, maybe," I said. We got out of the car and walked into the motel room. We gathered our clothes together and cleaned the place up a little. I left a note for my uncle telling him I would explain everything later. We left the room and got inside my car.

As we left Clovis I felt a hatred surging through my body. I wasn't sure what type of hatred it was because I hadn't had one like it before. When we passed the post office, on the outskirts of Clovis, we saw a man with a crew-cut wearing overalls. We watched him walk out. It was odd, but Mike and I were staring at him as we drove down the highway.

# A STUDENT'S GUIDE
# TO CREATIVE WRITING

Part Two
POETRY

# Naomi Long Madgett

Eastern Michigan University

Penway Books
Detroit

Library of Congress Catalog Number: 79-93055
ISBN: 0-916418-24-3

PENWAY BOOKS
*(The instructional division of Lotus Press)*

Post Office Box 21607
Detroit, Michigan 48221

Part Two
POETRY

## Chapter 8

## A Rhyme Does Not a Poem Make

For centuries poets and critics have sought to define poetry. That their definitions are stated so differently and so uninclusively is indication that no one yet has come up with the ultimate definition that will satisfy the majority of discerning readers and writers. Without adding to the confusion by still another vague or incomplete definition, we may make several observations concerning a few of the qualities of poetry which help to distinguish it from prose.

It would be naive to assume that forcing ideas into a regular pattern of rhythm and rhyme (versifying) is the same thing as creating a poem. Many readers are more familiar with verses written in traditional form than with poems that do not rhyme, although unrhymed poetry is thousands of years old. Perhaps because our acquaintance with rhythmic poems often begins in our infancy and carries into later years, our expectation of rhyme and regularity is not hard to explain. The nursery rhymes we learned in childhood, the textbook anthologies containing a wealth of material by older poets which we used in school, and the lyrics of popular songs have all strengthened our association of poetry with a recognizable form.

But styles change in poetry, as they do in general language, clothing, and other aspects of life, and many of today's poets have broken with some of the traditions which many expect to find in poetry. Confronted with a poem written in free verse, many readers are baffled and want to know, "If it doesn't rhyme, what makes it poetry?"

We might well turn that question around and ask, "Is a piece of composition poetry simply because it rhymes?" If we were to arrange a grocery list in such a way that reading the items together would produce a repeated rhythm and the words coming at regular intervals rhymed, would the result be a poem? Hardly. We would still have no more than a rhymed market list. There must, then, be some other distinguishing factors that permit us to tell the difference between poetry and prose. Let us try to identify some of them.

### IMPLICIT QUALITY

Students are sometimes disappointed in their first reading of a poem because they have only a vague idea — or none at all — of what the poet is trying to say. "Why doesn't he say what he means?" they may ask. "Why does he 'beat around the bush' and try to confuse the reader instead of enlightening him?"

This is an understandable reaction for the reader who is accustomed to reading through a short piece of prose and, with little effort, being able to summarize the main points. He expects a poem to be just as lucid, just as direct, just as explicit as the prose he normally reads and writes, and he may well feel cheated when he finds this is not so. After all, haven't English teachers always taught the virtues of a good topic sentence, followed by explanations or examples to support his main points? Hasn't he always been directed to write with clarity and coherence?

Yes, but the poet is about a different kind of business. While the prose writer is explicit, the poet is inclined to be implicit — to entice the reader to search beneath surfaces, to read between the lines.

One day a psychiatrist reportedly found himself approaching a young colleague on the street. As they met, the young man pleasantly greeted the older man by saying, "Good morning, Doctor." After they had passed each other, the older psychiatrist turned around to stare after the receding figure, scratched his head in puzzlement, and mumbled to himself, "Now I wonder what he meant by that?"

The reader of a poem should always ask himself, "I wonder what the poet meant by that," understanding that the words on the page are only the surface manifestation of moods and meanings hidden between the lines. The poet does not intend to be difficult; he only wishes to involve the reader in the experience of the poem. He tosses out a suggestion of a meaning — a possibility — and hopes that the reader will reach out from his own experience to catch and share it. If the student is willing to do this, reading the poem not once but several times, he will discover that the poem belongs to him; his own experience and emotions will be bound intricately and permanently with the poet's. We should not think, then, in terms of *the meaning* of a poem but of many possible interpretations. Since each reader will bring something of himself to the poem, and the two selves will merge somewhere — the poet-self and the reader-self — no poem will mean exactly the same thing to everyone who reads and understands it.

This is not to say that any interpretation of a poem is as valid as any other. Any interpretation should be able to stand being held up to the poem itself for comparison. If an interpretation cannot be backed up with internal proof from the poem, it is not sound. One should be able to point out certain words, phrases, or statements within the poem to lend credibility to the assumed meaning. The poem may contain a central idea on which there is general agreement, but the unspecified details may provoke disagreement. It is seldom possible to ask the poet what he or she meant (and even if it were, the explanation might not be reliable), so the poem must stand on its own, and the reader, in bringing his own experience to it, must decide what those details mean for *him*. As strange as it may seem, a poet does not always know exactly what he means himself because of the important role that the subconscious mind plays in the creation. Some years ago, the poetry editor of a national magazine wrote an analysis of Robert Frost's famous poem, "Stopping By Woods on a Snowy Evening," in which he interpreted the closing lines as a death wish. The poet responded by saying, in effect, "That is not what I meant at all." The editor responded in turn, "Yes, it was; you just didn't know it." It is indeed possible for the poet not to recognize his deeper meanings, as is true of all of us at times.

The poem, finally, will mean what it will mean to each reader, but each interpretation, to be valid, must draw its veracity from the poem itself. That a poem may contain a central idea on which agreement can be reached, while at the same time implying something that is open to interpretation can be demonstrated by my poem, "Tree of Heaven." This tree, properly called *ailanthus altissima*, is city-wise and hardy, thriving in the most adverse circumstances. It is a weed tree which is troublesome to many because it grows wherever it pleases, multiplies rapidly, and has leaves that produce a foul odor, giving it the nickname of "stinkweed."

I will live.
The ax's angry edge against my trunk
Cannot deny me.  Though I thunder down
To lie prostrate among exalted grasses
That do not mourn me,
I will rise.

I will grow:
Persistent roots deep-burrowed in the earth
Avenge my fall.  Tentacles will shoot out swiftly
In all directions, stubborn leaves explode their force
Into the sun.
I will thrive.

Curse of the orchard,
Blemish on the land's fair countenance,
I have grown strong for strength denied, for struggle
In hostile woods.  I keep alive by being the troublesome,
Indestructible
Stinkweed of truth.

I often read this poem to groups of students and ask them what they think I was saying. On the most obvious level, they are able to identify the "I" in the poem as the tree; beyond that, there is disagreement on who or what else might be speaking through the poem, if indeed there is another voice. There is little difficulty, however, deciding that whoever the poem is about, he, she, or it exists in a hostile atmosphere and is determined to survive. References to "the ax's angry edge," "exalted grasses / That do not mourn me," "Blemish on the land's fair countenance," "strength denied," and "hostile woods" all validate the hostility of the environment. The repetitions of determination in such phrases as "I will live," "I will rise," "I will grow," "I will thrive," and the "persistent roots" that will avenge and the "stubborn leaves" that will "explode their force" all testify to the determination of the speaker. Beyond that, each reader is left on his own to grasp the meaning. I know what I meant when I wrote the poem, but it is interesting to hear other meanings that are possible. I have heard at least five interpretations which, though they did not coincide with what I had in mind, were every bit as valid. This range of possible meaning exists because the poem is implicit rather than explicit.

## COMPRESSION

Another difference between poetry and prose is the amount of space given to the expression of an idea. While an essayist takes one or several main ideas and expands them, bringing in subordinate points for clarification, the poet takes one large idea and compresses it into only a few lines. His task might be compared to removing the water from whole milk and collecting the powdered residue in a small capsule. It is up to the reader to mix the substance — the essence — with the fluid of his own imagination and experience in order to restore the poem whole and make it meaningful on a personal and individual level. A good poet knows how to suggest a great deal in the minimum amount of space, selecting words and details with such care that each one conveys the message as precisely and as economically as possible. Often a very short poem tells more than a longer one, and with greater force and impact. A good poet knows when to stop once the point has been made.

If you have ever thought about the ways in which certain ethnic and racial groups are sometimes stereotyped, you will appreciate the following concise poem, "The Negro," by James A. Emanuel:

> Never saw him.
> Never can.
> Hypothetical,
> Haunting man:
>
> Eyes a-saucer,
> Yessir bossir,
> Dice a-clicking,
> Razor flicking.
>
> *The*-ness froze him
> In a dance.
> *A*-ness never
> Had a chance.

## IMAGERY

While figurative language is not the exclusive property of the poet, he is likely to make more extensive use of it than the writer of prose. Much of what a poet writes is not to be taken on the literal level. Those who wish to increase the emotional power of their writing will do well to explore the unlimited possibilities of figurative language, such as the simile, the metaphor, and other figures of speech, which will be discussed in Chapter Ten.

Figures of speech are useful in the creation of vivid images and the compression of ideas. It is not enough for the poet to tell the reader how a particular person, object, or scene impressed him. If description is to be effective, the reader must be invited to participate in the experience for himself. The poet can help the reader conjure up in his own imagination an image of sight, sound, smell, or touch so real and vivid that the reader will no longer have to take the poet's word for the way things are, but will know as if from first-hand experience. It is this image-making aspect of a poet's work that makes him an artist as surely as if he had created life-like scenes or figures on a canvas. One never tires of reading and rereading many times poems with such vivid imagery that the experience remains fresh and interesting each time he returns to it.

In the two of my own poems which follow, I believe that I was reasonably successful in the creation of vivid and consistent imagery:

## WASHERWOMAN

Time is
an old washerwoman
who scrubs away
the grit of memory
rinsing    wringing
hanging in the sun
to dry    till the garment
of experience becomes
soft and wearable.

## CONQUEST

If it comes on like a cave man
I'll write it.

If it kicks down the door
I'll let it overcome me.

No polite knocking, no pleading, no
waiting to see if I'll let it in.  I won't.

Unless it clubs me, subdues me,
drags me by my hair,

the poem
will never get written.

## SYMBOLISM

Closely related to imagery is the symbol, which may occur in fiction as well as poetry. Often a writer can present an idea more effectively through symbolism than by direct means. Symbols surround us in our everyday lives, and they are the things of which dreams are made.

Some symbols are universally understood, while others are personal, growing out of the uniqueness of an individual's experience and perception. *Water* is generally accepted as a symbol of life, as well as of purification. The *green years* symbolize youth, while *sunset* represents old age or death. Everywhere around us are symbols, objects or signs which have seemingly unrelated meanings, in addition to the obvious ones. There is nothing about the color red which means *stop*, but throughout the world people recognize the danger of proceeding in traffic against a red light. Red may symbolize danger, valor, or anger, among other things; we are aware of the feelings of a person who informs us that he "sees red." Notice the symbolism in the following poem:

## VIRTUE

Sweet day, so cool, so calm, so bright,
  The bridal of the earth and sky:
The dew shall weep thy fall tonight;
  For thou must die.

Sweet rose, whose hue, angry and brave,
  Bids the rash gazer wipe his eye:
Thy root is ever in its grave,
  And thou must die.

Sweet spring, full of sweet days and roses,
   A box where sweets compacted lie;
My music shows ye have your closes,
   And all must die.

Only a sweet and virtuous soul,
   Like seasoned timber, never gives;
But though the whole world turn to coal,
   Then chiefly lives.

George Herbert

Many of us wear as jewelry gold or silver symbols of our religious faith or some movement in which we believe. Organizations often select symbols for their causes, and whenever we see them displayed, we are reminded of certain ideals for which they stand. Even the naming of many of our collegiate sports teams involves symbolism.

In addition to generally understood symbols, a writer may use symbols which have a personal meaning which he wishes to share with the reader. I know a poet whose childhood was harsh and deprived of ordinary security, but beauty shone like the sun for him, and he kept his face turned toward it. One of his personal symbols is the sunflower, to which he has made several references in his work. (Some knowledge of a poet's life can be helpful in an understanding and interpretation of his writing.)

While symbol-hunting may become an end in itself, depriving a reader of a deeper enjoyment of the whole poem, it is helpful to recognize the role that symbolism plays in poetry. Symbolism should not be forced into everything we read where perhaps none was intended, but an awareness of the possibility of its presence should be kept in mind.

## APPEARANCE

One of the most obvious differences between poetry and prose is the way it is set up on a printed page — or perhaps that statement should be qualified to say that some contemporary poets choose to classify as poetry writing that has almost none of the characteristics of this art form, in which case we can only take their word that it is poetry because they intend it to be. If you are confused by this, you are not alone.

Poetry is centered on the page and printed in lines, with each line often beginning with a capital letter. (See Chapter Nine for further discussion.) It is written in stanzas (or strophes, in the case of free verse), which are separated from each other by a space. Nevertheless, the basic unit is still the sentence, not the line, and even though a stanza somewhat resembles a paragraph in prose, it does not have the same function as a paragraph and should not be confused with it. In general, we do not even have to read a poem to know that it is not prose.

Some poets have enjoyed creating shapes with printed words as a means of reinforcing meaning. Such **concrete poems**, as they are called, have tested the imagination of a number of modern poets, but they are by no means a recent invention. The following concrete poem, written in the seventeenth century, illustrates the early popularity of this kind of form.

## EASTER WINGS

Lord, who createdst man in wealth and store,
Though  foolishly  he  lost  the  same,
Decaying    more    and    more
Till     he      became
Most  poor;
With   thee
Oh,  let   me   rise
As      larks,       harmoniously,
And   sing   this   day   thy   victories;
Then shall the fall further the flight in me.

My  tender  age  in  sorrow  did  begin;
And  still  with  sicknesses  and  shame
Thou   didst   so   punish   sin,
That    I      became
Most  thin.
With  thee
Let   me   combine,
And  feel  this  day  thy  victory;
For  if  I  imp  my  wing  on  thine,
Affliction  shall  advance  the  flight  in  me.

George Herbert

However, appearance is the least significant difference between poetry and prose, and as we have pointed out, not even the absence or presence of rhyme can be counted on to provide an answer. While there are other differences that may be considered, the implicit quality, the compression, and the dependence upon image and symbol are a good beginning point in helping us to determine what a poem is.

## Chapter 9

## Practicing the Scales

When we think of poetry, it is natural to associate with it a kind of literature which is rhythmical and musical. The earliest literature possessed this quality, and children at an early age are still exposed to the song-like qualities of traditional verse. While much modern poetry is not rhythmical in the same way or to the same extent as the poems of the past, many adults, as well as children, continue to prefer the lyricism to which they were first exposed to the more prosaic flow of much of today's poetry.

Whether a poet chooses to write in traditional form or not is a matter of personal taste, but because it is the foundation for later developments, a beginning poet will do well to learn the mechanics and the way they work. Learning to **scan** a poem can be compared to learning the notes on a piano and becoming proficient in practicing the scales. While exceptions can be found in some notable instrumentalists who do not read music at all, many of the most innovative jazz musicians have mastered the techniques of classical music, so that when they choose to break the rules of tradition, they are able to do so knowingly, creating effects that do not just happen but can be predicted to appeal to the senses in the way that they intend. Let us therefore consider three basic kinds of poetry according to form.

### TRADITIONAL VERSE

All spoken language possesses rhythm. When we look up a word in the dictionary, one of the things we learn is the rhythm of that word. That rhythm depends upon where the accent falls. In every word of more than one syllable, the dictionary indicates with an accent mark (') which syllable or syllables are pronounced with the greatest stress. We learn, for example, that *wonderful* is pronounced *WON-der-ful* (with the accent on the first syllable), that *forgetful* is pronounced *for-GET-ful* (with the accent on the second syllable), and that *understand* is pronounced *un-der-STAND* (with the heaviest accent on the last syllable. There is a lighter accent on the first syllable as well, so that the word may also be pronounced *UN-der-STAND*.)

In traditional verse, the poet writes in one of several basic rhythms, producing a recognizable pattern. Such a rhythm (called the **beat** in music) is referred to as the **meter**.

#### Meter

To **scan** a poem (indicate its form), it is customary to mark an accented syllable with the same kind of mark that the dictionary uses, except that it is placed *above* the accented syllable rather than after it. An unaccented syllable is marked with a loop that resembles the letter *U*. When an unaccented syllable is followed by an accented syllable repeatedly, the meter is called **iambic**. (This is the most frequently used meter in poetry in the English language, as well as the basic rhythm of our spoken language.) For example:

$$\cup \; / \; \cup \; / \; \cup \; / \; \cup \; / \; \cup \; /$$
The cur-few tolls the knell of part-ing day

When an accented syllable is followed by an unaccented syllable repeatedly, the meter is called **trochaic**. For example:

$$/ \; \cup \; / \; \cup \; / \; \cup \; / \; \cup \; /$$
Nev-er, nev-er shall her glo-ry fade

Less frequently found are the three-syllable meters, one of which is one accented syllable followed by two unaccented syllables; this is called **dactylic**. For example:

$$/ \quad \cup \; \cup \; / \; \cup \; \cup$$
One more un-for-tu-nate

The reverse of dactylic meter is **anapestic**, in which two unaccented syllables are followed by one accented syllable. This produces a tripping rhythm which obviously is not suitable for many poems. For example:

$$\cup \; \cup \; / \; \cup \; \cup \; / \; \cup \; \cup \; / \; \cup \; \cup \; /$$
They are gone like the green of the heath and the hill

Still another meter, rarely used because of its galloping effect, is the **amphibrach**, in which one unaccented syllable is followed by an accented syllable and then another unaccented syllable. For example:

$$\cup \quad / \quad \cup \; \cup \quad / \quad \cup \quad \cup \quad / \quad \cup \; \cup \quad /$$
I sprang to the stir-rup, and Jor-is, and he

When two accented syllables come together, the resulting meter is **spondaic**. This meter rarely makes up an entire line of poetry but is used in combination with another meter. For example:

$$/ \quad / \quad \cup \; / \quad \cup \quad /$$
Tom, Tom, the pi-per's son

**Spondaic     Iambic**

Unimportant words, such as articles (*a, an, the*), short prepositions (*to, for, by*), and short conjunctions (*but, and, or*) are not accented in poetry, just as they are not accented in ordinary speech.

If you can recognize the basic meter of a poem, you have mastered the first step in scanning it. Let us hasten to say, however, that a good poet seldom sticks slavishly to the meter he has chosen. Such regularity would be as boring as the ticking of a metronome, unless the very regularity is important to the idea being conveyed. Notice the monotonous meter of the following excerpt from *The Song of Hiawatha*, by Henry Wadsworth Longfellow, which forces it to be read in a sing-songy manner.

> Then the little Hiawatha
> Learned of every bird its language,
> Learned their names and all their secrets,
> How they built their nests in Summer,
> Where they hid themselves in Winter,
> Talked with them whene'er he met them,
> Called them "Hiawatha's Chickens."

Most poets today prefer occasional irregularities so that the meter is not so predictable, and therefore more interesting.

### Length of Line

In each of the meters we have examined, let us call each unit a **foot**. If the meter is iambic, each pair of unstressed-stressed syllables makes a foot. If the meter is dactylic, each set of three syllables in the stressed-unstressed-unstressed combination makes a foot. In the following line, then, there are five feet:

$$\cup \; / \; | \; \cup \; / \; | \; \cup \; / \; | \; \cup \; / \; | \; \cup \; /$$
The cur-|few tolls |the knell |of part-|ing day          5

In the next line there are two feet.

$$/ \quad \cup \; \cup \; | \; / \; \cup \; \cup$$
One more un-|for-tu-nate          2

And in the following line there are four feet:

$$\cup \; \cup \; / \; | \; \cup \; \cup \; / \; | \; \cup \; \cup \; / \; | \; \cup \; \cup \; /$$
They are gone|like the green|of the heath |and the hill          4

In the next line, there are 4½ feet.

$$/ \; \cup \; | \; / \; \cup \; | \; / \; \cup \; | \; / \; \cup \; | \; /$$
Nev-er |nev-er |shall her |glo-ry |fade          4½

The count begins anew at the beginning of each line; it does not continue from line to line. Notice that the feet are separated by a long diagonal mark. Not all the lines are identical in length, but each stanza as a whole indicates a pattern. There are names for the number of feet as well as the kind of meter, such as **tetrameter** for four feet, **pentameter** for five, **hexameter** for six, and so on. Therefore, if the dominant meter of a poem is an unaccented syllable followed by an accented syllable and there are five feet to the line, the poem is written in **iambic pentameter**. Indicating the length of line by feet is the second step to scanning.

### Rhyme Scheme

Words rhyme with each other when the initial consonants of two words are different but the accented vowel and final consonant sounds are the same, as in *done/won*, *seven/heaven*, and *listen/glisten*. Rhyme depends upon the sounds of the words, not their spelling. While *through* and *rough* have similar spellings, they are not pronounced alike and do not rhyme, while *through* and *true* do rhyme even though their spellings are not similar.

The poet who chooses to write in traditional form creates a pattern of rhyme that is repeated from stanza to stanza and is called the **rhyme scheme**. Recognizing this is the third and last step in scanning a poem. Let us examine one stanza of my poem, "When I Was Young," to see which words rhyme.

When I was young and loved life's laughter     A
I climbed tall hills and touched the sun.     B
I never learned till long years after     A
That ecstasy and pain are one.     B

Obviously, the first and third lines rhyme, as do the second and fourth. Using the first letter of the alphabet to indicate the ending word of the first line, we will call it *A*. Any other word in that stanza which rhymes with that line will be given the same letter. Since the second line does not rhyme with the first letter, let us move to the next letter of the alphabet, *B*. Since the third line rhymes with the first, we will call that *A* also, and since the fourth line rhymes with the second, we will call that *B*. This pattern is referred to as an **A-B-A-B** rhyme scheme. If we had a six-line stanza with lines ending *together / mean / whether / unseen / sever / forever*, we would have an **A-B-A-B-C-C** rhyme scheme. Or if a four-line stanza ended with *power / blink / suffer / think*, the rhyme scheme would be **A-B-C-B**.

Let us look at the entire two-stanza poem, "When I Was Young," and scan it, remembering to (1) identify the dominant rhythm, (2) indicate the length of line, and (3) recognize the rhyme scheme.

When I | was young | and loved | life's laugh- | ter,     A   4½
I climbed | tall hills | and touched | the sun     B   4
I nev- | er learned | till long | years af- | ter     A   4½
That ec- | sta-sy | and pain | are one.     B   4

But now | that I | have ceased | pur-su- | ing     A   4½
My laugh- | ter has | been hushed | by Time     B   4
For pain | is all | left for | re-new- | ing     A   4½
There are | no more | tall hills | to climb.     B   4

We can see that the second stanza follows the same pattern as the first. If this poem were to continue for several more stanzas, each would be in the same form. Notice that almost every line contains some variation in meter, but the dominant meter throughout is iambic.

While rhymes most often appear at the ends of lines (**end rhyme**), they may also appear within a line (**internal rhyme**). Edgar Allan Poe, in "Annabel Lee," used internal rhyme to produce a musical quality.

> For the moon never BEAMS without bringing me DREAMS . . . .
> And the stars never RISE but I see the bright EYES . . . .

In other instances, especially in modern poetry, one can often find words rhyming in a kind of hit-and-miss fashion, appearing in no particular place within the poem but merely at random. Such **occasional rhyme** may be found even in **free verse**, which will be discussed in another chapter.

### Alternatives to Perfect Rhyme

Sometimes words in rhyming positions do not rhyme exactly but are very close. **Near rhyme** occurs when the final consonant sound is the same but the preceding vowel sound and the initial consonant sound are different. *June/tone, real/fall, place/farce,* and *night/sweet* are examples of near rhyme, while *bone/tone, fall/call, place/face* and *light/night* are examples of perfect or exact rhyme. The use of near-rhyme is not an indication of sloppy writing; it usually is an indication that the poet has practiced his scales well and is straying from the expected pattern knowingly. An experienced reader can tell the difference between near rhymes which are intentional and approximate rhymes that are the result of ignorance.

**Assonance** is the repetition of the same vowel sound between different consonant sounds. *Stir/word* and *moon/wooed* are examples of assonance.

**Consonance** refers to words whose beginning and ending consonant sounds are the same, but the vowel sound in between is different. *Food/freed, tone/teen,* and *soak/seek* are examples of consonance.

**Alliteration**, which is quite similar to consonance and often confused with it, is the repetition of the same consonant sound, often within words rather than at the beginning or end. Its popular appeal is apparent in its frequent use in advertising.

### EXERCISE:

Scan the following poem, "Because I Could Not Stop for Death," by Emily Dickinson, determining whether the poem possesses perfect rhyme, near-rhyme, assonance, consonance, or a combination of these.

> Because I could not stop for Death
> He kindly stopped for me;
> The carriage held but just ourselves
> And Immortality.
>
> We slowly drove — he knew no haste,
> And I had put away
> My labor and my leisure too
> For his civility.
>
> We passed the school, where children strove
> At recess in the ring;
> We passed the fields of gazing grain;
> We passed the setting Sun,

Or rather, he passed us.  The dews
Drew quivering and chill,
For only gossamer my gown,
My tippet, only tulle.

We paused before a house that seemed
A swelling of the ground.
The roof was scarcely visible,
The cornice, in the ground.

Since then, 'tis centuries, and yet
Feels shorter than the day
I first surmised the horses' heads
Were toward Eternity.

### Alternatives to Traditional Meter

*Accentual Meter.* Poets who write in traditional verse usually vary the chosen dominant meter, as we have said, for interest and to add texture and emphasis. There are two alternatives to regular meter which serve the same purpose on a larger scale. One is called **accentual meter.** Instead of writing in the iambic, trochaic, or other traditional meters, the poet may prefer to write lines in which there is a fixed number of accents per line, without regard to their order or the number of unaccented syllables which precede or follow them. To tell where the accents fall, one need only listen to his own voice, or someone else's, as the poem is read aloud; the accents fall in no particular pattern but approximate everyday speech.

Read the selection below aloud and notice where the accents fall. Notice, too, that this example has regularity in form in that each line contains the same number of accents.

```
 /  ∪  /  ∪  /  ∪
Still it hung suspended                    3 accents per line throughout
 ∪  ∪  /  ∪∪ ∪   /   ∪ ∪    /
on the air as if the wind had ordained
 ∪  ∪ / ∪∪  /  ∪  ∪∪ ∪   /
its precarious balance, as if the dark
  /   ∪  ∪  ∪  / ∪ ∪  /
hour had not predicted its fall
  ∪  ∪  /   /   ∪  /   ∪
with the first streak of dawnlight —
  ∪   /    /    /  ∪ ∪
one frail branch, ice-coated,
 / ∪  ∪  ∪   /  ∪  /
heavy with the weight of doom.
```

*Syllabic Verse.* A second alternative to traditional meter is **syllabic verse.** In this kind of poem, it does not matter how many syllables in a line are accented, or how the unaccented syllables are arranged in relation to the accented ones. The thing to pay attention to is simply the number of syllables per line. In other words, each line may have the same number of syllables, or the number of syllables in some other way falls into a pattern when all the lines of a stanza are taken together. For example:

With what hurt dismay                    5 syllables per line throughout
This nothing-sphere that
Could have been the world
(Bright, round enough to
Circle all my strength)
Totters on the edge
Of certain doom now.

## BLANK VERSE

Blank verse has two of the characteristics of traditional verse, but not the third. It has a regular meter, which is iambic, and a definite length of line — five feet (pentameter) — but does not rhyme. Shakespeare's plays are an example of blank verse.

## FREE VERSE

Free verse has few of the elements of traditional verse; it does not flow in any one meter, the length of lines is irregular, and it does not rhyme. It must not be assumed, however, that it is therefore not poetry at all. Neither can we assume that it is easier to write than traditional verse because of its freedom from the restraints of form. More will be said about free verse in Chapter Eleven. At this point, let us simply note the differences between free verse, blank verse, and traditional verse. Examine the following passages for their differences in form:

## COMPARISON OF FORMS

|  |  |  |
|---|---|---|
| I must give back to each the borrowed dreams | 5 A | Traditional Verse |
| I worshipped with intensity and fire — | 5 B | |
| Back to the river, all its silver streams | 5 A | |
| That never flowed except in my desire . . . . | 5 B | |
| Beneath the dome of star-infested sky | 5 A | Blank Verse |
| I rode the wind through autumn's stubbled fields | 5 B | |
| And if it howled I did not choose to know | 5 C | |
| And if it wailed I could not bear to hear. | 5 D | |
| The tiny lights were ornaments alone, | 5 E | |
| No beacons for the blind to guess their way. | 5 F | |
| The doves are flap-ping im-pa-tient wings — | 4 accents, 9 syllables  A | Free Verse |
| The late birds fly-ing a-lone | 4 accents, 7 syllables  B | |
| And coo-ing a fare-well | 2 accents, 6 syllables  C | |
| That is for-ev-er good-bye. | 2 accents, 7 syllables  D | |
| Oh, pi-ty the last, still lat-er birds | 5 accents, 9 syllables  E | |
| Who have no wings — | 2 accents, 4 syllables  F | |
| Who may on-ly walk in the cold shad-ows | 4 accents, 10 syllables  G | |
| A-lone, a-lone in the night. | 3 accents, 7 syllables  H | |

## FIXED FORMS

In traditional poetry, the various parts are divided into **stanzas**, groups of lines separated from the next group (stanza) by a space. These divisions are by form only, not necessarily by units of thought, unlike paragraphs in prose. The poet may select or invent whatever stanza form he wishes, and the reader can usually expect that, once that form is established, each ensuing stanza will follow the same form or pattern. If the poem begins with a six-line stanza (**sestet**) with an A-B-C-A-B-C rhyme scheme, the reader anticipates a continuation of that pattern. (There are several exceptions to this, such as the **refrain** and the **envoy** in certain kinds of poems, but we need not consider them here.)

There are a number of fixed forms with which a beginning poet might wish to experiment. These forms have been used effectively over long periods, and many readers have found them aesthetically satisfying. They present a real challenge to an aspiring poet, and there is much to be learned through a practice of writing in these forms. Let us consider a few.

### Ballad

A **ballad** is a narrative poem which lends itself to being sung. The early ballads of Scotland and England are called **popular** or **folk ballads** because they originated with the common people, were anonymous, and, being passed along by word of mouth, were subject to change. Troubadours or minstrels would pass from village to village singing these songs of heroic deeds, battles, supernatural occurrences, unfortunate love affairs, or sensational murders. A number of folk ballads, such as "John Henry," later originated in this country among black people, and there are other examples of American folk ballads as well, especially those of the West, but because this nation was founded after the invention of the printing press, there was little reason for the development of orally preserved literature in the United States, except for that wealth of folk material produced and preserved by unlettered slaves and their progeny. The folk ballad has often been imitated by poets whose names are well known; these re-creations are known as **literary ballads**.

Folk ballads frequently depended upon dialogue, though not complete, and the story was told in a way that moved rather abruptly from one event to another with little or no transition; perhaps transitional stanzas, being weaker in interest than those depicting action, were eventually forgotten or dropped during numerous retellings. The speaker often showed a lack of emotion even in the most violent circumstances and seemed somewhat outside the events even when the story was told in first person. These poems most often told stories of the common folk, although the nobility were sometimes the subject. A frequently used rhyme scheme for folk ballads was A-B-C-B and the lines often consisted of 8, 6, 8, and 6 syllables each, in that order.

The modern poet who imitates the folk ballad seldom follows it in every respect. He selects whatever characteristics he chooses for the purpose of his own creation and ignores the others. The following literary ballad, "The Ballad of Birmingham," by Dudley Randall, may be compared with any of the folk ballads with which you may be familiar for form and content.

"Mother dear, may I go downtown
instead of out to play,
and march the streets of Birmingham
in a freedom march today?"

"No, baby, no, you may not go,
for the dogs are fierce and wild,
and clubs and hoses, guns and jails
ain't good for a little child."

"But, mother, I won't be alone.
Other children will go with me,
and march the streets of Birmingham
to make our country free."

She has combed and brushed her nightdark hair,
and bathed rose petal sweet,
and drawn white gloves on her small brown hands,
and white shoes on her feet.

The mother smiled to know her child
was in the sacred place,
but that smile was the last smile
to come upon her face.

For when she heard the explosion,
her eyes grew wet and wild.
She raced through the streets of Birmingham
calling for her child.

She clawed through bits of glass and brick,
then lifted out a shoe.
"O, here's the shoe my baby wore,
but, baby, where are you?"

### Haiku (pronounced HIGH-koo) or hokku (pronounced HOE-koo)

This is a little poem which originated in Japan, consisting of only seventeen syllables, usually (but not always) arranged with the first line having five syllables, the second line seven, and the third line five. It is written in the present tense and presents a vivid image which appeals to the sense of sound, sight, or touch. It is a form of syllabic verse, in that only the syllables are counted, not the number of accents, and it does not matter where the accents fall. The following example is from my poem, "Refuge":

| | |
|---|---|
| Shaggy brows brooding, | 5 |
| A deserted house keeps watch | 7 |
| With its blinded eyes. | 5 |

### Cinquain (pronounced sing-CANE)

Originated by Adelaide Crapsey (1878-1914), the cinquain consists of a five-line stanza, the first line having two syllables; the second line, four; the third line, six; the fourth line, eight; and the fifth line, two syllables. Like the haiku, this is a form of syllabic verse but without the necessity of a strong image. For example:

| | |
|---|---|
| Somewhere | 2 |
| above the clouds | 4 |
| I left my heart winging | 6 |
| its way like a swallow across | 8 |
| the sun. | 2 |

### Sonnet

The sonnet is a fourteen-line poem written in iambic pentameter (unstressed-stressed syllables, five feet to a line). There are several varieties, but the rhyme scheme of the most popular sonnets in English is A-B-A-B-C-D-C-D-E-F-E-F-G-G. The first eight lines (octave) usually make one statement, and the final six lines (sestet) show a turn of thought. (Sometimes the last six lines are in the form of a quatrain — four lines — and a concluding couplet — two lines.) The following sonnet is #18 of Shakespeare's famous sonnet sequence.

Shall I compare thee to a summer's day?
Thou art more lovely and more temperate.
Rough winds do shake the darling buds of May,
And summer's lease hath all too short a date.

Sometimes too hot the eye of heaven shines,
And often is his gold complexion dimmed;
And every fair from fair sometime declines,
By chance, or nature's changing course, untrimmed.
But thy eternal summer shall not fade,
Nor lose possession of that fair thou ow'st;
Nor shall death brag thou wand'rest in his shade,
When in eternal lines to time thou grow'st.
So long as men can breathe or eyes can see,
So long lives this, and this gives life to thee.

### Rondeau (pronounced RAHN-DOE)

Of French origin, this poem has three stanzas divided into thirteen lines and uses only two rhymes throughout. It has a refrain, usually unrhymed, which is made up from the first part of the first line. This refrain comes at the end of the second stanza and at the end of the poem. The rhyme scheme (with $R$ representing the unrhymed refrain) is: A-A-B-B-A A-A-B-R A-A-B-B-A-R.

"In After Days" by Austin Dobson is an example of the rondeau.

In after days when grasses high
O'ertop the stone where I shall lie,
    Though ill or well the world adjust
    My slender claim to honored dust,
I shall not question or reply.

I shall not see the morning sky;
I shall not hear the night-wind's sigh;
    I shall be mute, as all men must
        In after days!

But yet, now living, fain were I
That someone then should testify,
    Saying — "He held his pen in trust
    To Art, not serving shame or lust."
Will none? — Then let my memory die
        In after days!

### Villanelle (pronounced VILL-uh-NELL)

Perhaps the most challenging of all fixed forms of poetry to write is the villanelle, a nineteen-line poem consisting of five three-line stanzas and ending with one four-line stanza. Like the rondeau, only two rhymes are permitted throughout the entire poem. In addition, certain lines are repeated in specified places. With $X$ and $Y$ denoting repeated lines, let us examine the rhyme scheme of the villanelle. It is: **AX-B-AY A-B-AX A-B-AY A-B-AX A-B-AY A-B-AX-AY.** The following poem, "The Villanelle," by William Ernest Henley, illustrates this form:

A dainty thing's the Villanelle.
    Sly, musical, a jewel in rhyme,
It serves its purpose passing well.

A double-clappered silver bell
    That must be made to clink in chime,
A dainty thing's the Villanelle;

And if you wish to flute a spell,
   Or ask a meeting 'neath the lime,
It serves its purpose passing well.

You must not ask of it the swell
   Of organs grandiose and sublime —
A dainty thing's the Villanelle;

And, filled with sweetness, as a shell
   Is filled with sound, and launched in time,
It serves its purpose passing well.

Still fair to see and good to smell
   As in the quaintness of its prime,
A dainty thing's the Villanelle,
It serves its purpose passing well.

It must be added that, in spite of Henley's description of this verse form and its possible uses, the villanelle, with longer and more flowing lines, has been used successfully for more serious expressions, as in "Do Not Go Gentle Into That Good Night," a famous villanelle by Dylan Thomas.

### Terza rima (pronounced TER-zuh REE-muh)

This poem, perhaps of Italian origin, consists of three-line stanzas, usually eleven syllables to a line, with rhymes that interlock from one stanza to the next, and ends with a couplet rhyming with the word carried over. The rhyme scheme is: A-B-A B-C-B C-D-C D-D. The beginning of "Ode to the West Wind," by Percy Bysshe Shelley, is an example of terza rima.

O wild West Wind, thou breath of Autumn's being,
   Thou from whose unseen presence the leaves dead
Are driven, like ghosts from an enchanter fleeing,

   Yellow, and black, and pale, and hectic red,
Pestilence-stricken multitudes!  O thou
   Who chariotest to their dark wintry bed

The winged seeds, where they lie cold and low,
   Each like a corpse within its grave, until
Thine azure sister of the Spring shall blow

   Her clarion o'er the dreaming earth, and fill
(Driving sweet buds like flocks to feed in air)
   With living hues and odors plain and hill;

Wild Spirit, which art moving everywhere;
Destroyer and preserver; hear, O hear!

## A FINAL WORD

### Punctuation and Capitalization

At one time it was customary for poets to capitalize the first word of each line of poetry. Many of today's poets have freed themselves from this tradition, which is not only meaningless but also can stand in the way of understanding. We are accustomed to seeing capital letters at the beginnings of sentences, signalling that a new thought is being introduced. Since the first word in a line of poetry often is not the beginning of a new idea, the capitalization of such a word tends to set up an expectation that is not fulfilled. It seems more practical, then, to capitalize poetry in the same way that we do prose. Wherever a sentence begins, whether at the beginning of a line, somewhere in the middle, or near the end, the first word is then capitalized, and other rules of capitalization observed in prose are also observed, such as proper nouns and the pronoun *I*.

Some poets have gone a step further by discarding capital letters altogether. It is our opinion that, unless there is a reason for doing so, the poet is better off not calling unnecessary attention to form by straying too far from the expected. The use of all lower case letters seems just as distracting and unnatural as the meaningless use of capital letters at the beginning of each line and, except for some specific effect, should be avoided. (A speaker may effectively refer to himself as *i* rather than *I* if it is his intention to call attention to his insignificance or inadequacy.)

Another common practice among modern poets is to eliminate punctuation. While this new freedom may open ways to broader interpretation, we must caution against novelty for its own sake. In free verse, which will be discussed later, the poet may create a sense of punctuation, without the marks themselves, by his arrangement of words within a line and his choice of where a line should break, as well as with indentation, but in traditional verse, the absence of punctuation is likely to create problems in communication and understanding. Unless there is some justification for eliminating the help that conventional punctuation provides, it is probably better to use it the same way that it is used in prose.

### Enjambment (pronounced en-JAM-ment)

At one time, it was popular for poets to make the end of a line coincide with the end of a thought, or at least a pause in thought, such as would be represented by a comma, semi-colon, dash, or period. Such lines are referred to as **end-stopped**. Today's poets, however, are more inclined to carry over a sentence or clause from one line to another, or even from one stanza to another. This carry-over is called **enjambment** or an **enjambed line**. This technique causes a poem to flow more freely and makes end rhyme, if there is any, less conspicuous than it would be if the rhyming word were also the end of a clause or sentence. In a great deal of modern poetry written more or less traditionally, it is difficult to tell that a poem rhymes at all, because the rhyme is not noticeable, although it contributes in a subtle way to the overall texture of the poem and its musicality. Modern poets tend to avoid the monotonous, sing-songy effect created by rhythm that is too regular and rhymes that are too obvious and expected; enjambment is one way to keep the form of a poem subordinate to the totality of the poetic experience.

### Caesura (pronounced seh-ZHEE-ruh)

We have already discussed the irregularities that often occur in metered verse. Through such irregularities, which include the dropping of a syllable or the addition of an extra one, the poet may slow down or speed up the reading of a line, create a pause which would not normally be there, and place emphasis in important places. These irregularities add interest and a special musical quality through the unexpected rhythms created. A caesura is a pause at the end of a line or within a line of poetry, a break made to accentuate the beat of the rhythm. Such a break can come through punctuation, of course; it can also be achieved through an irregularity of the dominant rhythm, such as by placing two or more accented syllables together or mixing meters as in the following lines from "Break, Break, Break," by Alfred, Lord Tennyson:

<pre>
      /      /      /
Break, break, break,
     U  U  /   U   /    U /
On thy cold  gray stones,  O Sea!
   U U  /    U  U   /     U  /  U
And I would  that my tongue  could ut- ter
     U     /      U U /  U /
The thoughts  that a-rise  in me.
</pre>

CONCLUSION

It is not our intention here to include a complete discussion of form but only to provide some exposure to various possibilities. There are a number of excellent books on versification available, which the interested student may study for more detailed information. While many students prefer not to write in traditional form, it is helpful, nevertheless, to understand and master it well enough to make an intelligent choice and to avoid the careless, slipshod qualities that reveal ignorance on the part of many amateurs. Imitating some of the fixed verse forms is an excellent way of "practicing scales" in preparation for a freer and more original kind of expression.

Chapter 10

## "Shall I Compare Thee to . . . ?"

In the last chapter, we discussed the more frequent use of figures of speech as one way to distinguish poetry from prose. Let us go into more detail. Webster's Collegiate Dictionary defines *figurative* as "expressing one thing in terms normally denoting another with which it may be regarded as analogous" — that is, similar in some aspect. A figure of speech is a means by which one thing may be suggested by another.

A literal statement is one that means exactly what it says and is to be taken at face value. It is clearly understood on its most obvious level. A figurative statement, on the other hand, is not meant to be believed in the same way, and yet the idea being conveyed is understood. Through figurative language it is possible to add color, vigor, and a picturesque quality that is mentally stimulating and aesthetically appealing. Many slang expressions owe their popularity to the vividness of figures of speech. Descriptions such as "cool," "wild," or "far out" are clearly understood although they have nothing to do with temperature, jungles, or distance. But the purpose of slang — to save thought for both speaker and listener — and its ready-made phrases, which lack any specific expression, make it inappropriate and ineffective in most poetry. To call someone a "pig," "a doll," or a "rock" is using language in a figurative way. If one is interested in only providing information, he might say simply, "Night came" — a literal statement. Another person might use the common expression, "Night fell" — a figure of speech which has become an idiom. A more imaginative person might say, "Nature pulled her curtain down" — a figurative statement. All three of these statements provide the same information, but it is the third that suggests a comparison, and in so doing, permits the listener to *see*. It brings his imagination into play by surprising him into a fresh awareness. Figurative language is essential to the imaginative and emotional impact that good poetry has upon the sensitive reader.

### SIMILE

One of the most common figures of speech is the simile (pronounced SIM-ill-lee), which compares one thing to another by using the word *like* or *as*.

*Examples:*

> When you came, you were like red wine and honey,
> And the taste of you burnt my mouth with its sweetness. (Amy Lowell)

> What happens to a dream deferred?
>
>> Does it dry up
>> like a raisin in the sun?
>> Or fester like a sore —
>> And then run? (Langston Hughes)

> He comes, and probably for years
>   Will he be coming yet, —
> Familiar as an old mistake,
>   And futile as regret. (Edwin Arlington Robinson)

> the wind is like a blade
> Brandished upward, unafraid. (Helen Woodbury)

> If we must die — let it not be like hogs
> Hunted and penned in an inglorious spot. (Claude McKay)

### METAPHOR

A metaphor is similar to a simile, except that it compares one thing to another directly without the use of *like* or *as*; instead of saying that the wind is *like* a blade, it says that the wind *is* a blade.

*Examples:*

All the world's a stage,
And all the men and women merely players.        (William Shakespeare)

An aged man is but a paltry thing,
A tattered coat upon a stick, unless
Soul clap its hands and sing . . . .        (William Butler Yeats)

A boy not beautiful, nor good, nor clever,
A black cloud full of storms too hot for keeping,
A sword beneath his mother's heart . . . .        (John Crowe Ransom)

The crowds upon the pavement
Were fields of harvest wheat.        (W. H. Auden)

Work is love made visible.        (Kahlil Gibran)

The fog comes
on little cat feet.        (Carl Sandburg)

The power of both simile and metaphor comes from the linking of two things that are not normally associated with each other. In using these figures of speech, the poet should not fall into the trap of mixing his metaphors — that is, setting up two images that are incompatible. (For example: "Following in the footsteps of Pride, he was too blind to see that each step was gnawing away at his integrity.) In addition, he should be aware of the ease with which clichés can sneak into use without our realizing that these expressions have lost their freshness and impact through overuse. To compare rain with tears, the ocean with depth, and the snow with a blanket is to rob one's writing of vitality and originality. Avoid comparisons that you have heard or read before.

## PERSONIFICATION

A third figure of speech is **personification** in which an inanimate object, an animal, or something abstract is given human or animate qualities.

*Examples:*

Life's but a walking shadow, a poor player
That struts and frets his hour upon the stage
And then is heard no more.        (William Shakespeare)

I'm living now with Pride —
A cold bedmate.        (Dorothy Parker)

. . . over me bright April
Shakes out her rain-drenched hair . . . .        (Sara Teasdale)

So silent I when Love was by
He yawned, and turned away;
But Sorrow clings to my apron strings,
I have so much to say.        (Dorothy Parker)

And Death heard the summons,
And he leaped on his fastest horse,
Pale as a sheet in the moonlight.        (James Weldon Johnson)

Nobody but Misfortune visits me or telephones.        (Naomi Long Madgett)

Notice that when *life, pride, sorrow, death, misfortune,* and similar words are personified, they are usually capitalized. The capitalization of a common noun in poetry is a signal that personification is intended.

## APOSTROPHE

Another figure of speech, which is often used in conjunction with personification, is **apostrophe** (which has no connection with the mark of punctuation of the same name). This is a way of directly addressing something or someone who is not present or is incapable of answering. It may be a person or an abstract thing.

*Examples:*

O Death! where is thy sting?                                   (The Bible)

Time, you old gypsy man,
Will you not stay?                                             (Ralph Hodgson)

Milton! thou shouldst be living at this hour.                  (William Wordsworth)

To what purpose, April, do you return again?                   (Edna St. Vincent Millay)

Roll on, thou deep and dark blue ocean, roll.                  (George Gordon, Lord Byron)

Build thee more stately mansions, O my soul.                   (Oliver Wendell Holmes)

When the speaker in a poem addresses someone or something directly, the apostrophe is often preceded by *O*, which is capitalized. It has no meaning except to announce that an apostrophe follows, and is not to be confused with the other interjection, *oh*, which is not capitalized except at the beginning of a sentence.

## HYPERBOLE

Still another figure of speech is **hyperbole** (pronounced high-PURR-buh-lee), another term for **overstatement**. It is a means of exaggeration for special effect. The student who says, "I had a million pages of history to read last night," is using hyperbole.

*Examples:*

Swifter than the wind he ran, and twice as silently.

Her heart was bigger than the ocean's span.

Of all the mountains in the world, he stands the tallest.

Her smile was brighter than ten thousand suns.

## METONYMY (pronounced met-TONN-uh-MEE)

Metonymy is the substitution of one thing for another with which it is closely associated. If someone were to ask, "Have you read Anne Sexton?" he would be asking about the *poetry* of Anne Sexton, not the person herself. If one says, "The kettle is boiling," it is understood that the kettle itself is not boiling but the water in it. To say that "the desk called an hour ago" means that someone at the desk did the calling.

## SYNECDOCHE

This figure of speech (pronounced sin-NECK-doe-kee) is very similar to metonymy, using a part to represent the whole. A sailor may call for "all hands on deck," when he obviously means the complete persons.

## CONTROL OF IMAGES

In some poems, one or more separate images are created through the use of figurative language. These images may appeal to sight, to sound, to smell, to taste, or to touch. While the reader does not actually see, hear, smell, taste, or feel what the poet is describing, his imagination is led to conjure up sensory perceptions that are vivid and memorable.

Other poems develop one sustained image throughout, each word and phrase carefully chosen to add to the unified, total effect of that image. A good poet tries to eliminate any possibility of his images running wild — that is, contradicting each other or detracting from the single impression he wishes to make. If too many different images appear too close together within the same poem, the reader may find himself doing mental gymnastics to try to adjust his perception with each change. (A comparison of "Trees," by Joyce Kilmer, and "Fog," by Carl Sandburg, will illustrate the uncontrolled and controlled use of imagery, respectively.) In writing a poem, when we discover that we have created a vivid and appropriate image, it is often wiser to build upon that single image than to introduce others that may not be compatible.

## EXERCISES

1. (Oral) Read the following poems aloud; then read them again silently, paying special attention to the figurative language and the images evoked. Then, as a class, discuss how effective the images are and whether each poem contains one central image or several different ones. If several different images are created, are they controlled in such a way that they work together to create unity, or are they at odds with each other? If one central image is created, how does the word choice reinforce it? Are the images appropriate for what the poet has to say, or would some other kind of descriptive phrases be more effective? How successful is each poem as a whole?

### THE SCREAM

I am a woman controlled.
Remember this: I never scream.
Yet I stood a form apart
Watching my other frenzied self
Beaten by words and wounds
Make in silence a mighty scream —
A scream that the wind took up
And thrust through the bars of night
Beyond all reason's final rim.

Out where the sea's last murmur dies
And the gull's cry has no sound,
Out where city voices fade,
Stilled in a lyric sleep,
Where silence is its own design,
My scream hovered a ghost denied
Wanting the shape of lips.

May Miller

### OFFSPRING

I tried to tell her:
    This way the twig is bent.
    Born of my trunk and strengthened by my roots,
    You must stretch newgrown branches
    Closer to the sun
    Than I can reach.
I wanted to say:
    Extend my self to that far atmosphere
    Only my dreams allow.

But the twig broke,
And yesterday I saw her
Walking down an unfamiliar street,
    Feet confident,
    Face slanted upward toward a threatening sky
And
    She was smiling

And she was
Her very free,
Her very individual,
Unpliable
Own.

Naomi Long Madgett

## JUNE HAS GONE

Illegible the signature
June scrawled on a young sky,
Her image lost except
To those of double sight.
Brilliant wings are reduced
By jewellers' craft
To brooches worn on black.
The morning song is stilled
In the unaccented void
Of cold throats.
Dead things are dead
In the definitive wind.
The once-insurgent leaves lie
Quiet in the gullies
And green rebuttal of the firs
Does not deny petals falling
On a brass tea tray.

May Miller

2. (Written) Select two words from the list below and write five sentences for each one, using figures of speech (a total of ten sentences). Try to avoid **clichés**, phrases that have become trite through overuse. Be as original as possible, aiming for fresh description that is not commonly used, and remembering that an image may appeal to senses other than sight.

| rain | stars | men | sleep |
| snow | the moon | women | promises |
| darkness | dreams | cat | grass |
| morning | hope | dog | clock |
| winter | love | books | time |
| spring | life | alcohol | work |
| autumn | truth | hair | marriage |
| travel | death | eyes | beauty |

3. (Written) After you have completed Exercise 2, and perhaps shared your efforts with other members of the class, select one of your images that you feel is successful and expand it into a little poem of four to eight lines. Do not make it rhyme or give it any particular kind of rhythm; feel free to let your imagination work without restrictions.

4. (Written) If you are pleased with your effort in Exercise 3, try writing a haiku (See Chapter Nine), using the same idea or working with a new one.

## CONCLUSION

It is not important that you remember the names of the various figures of speech discussed in this chapter, but it is important that you know how to recognize them, experiment with them, and understand how they work. They are the very essence of poetry, and without the images that they create, it is difficult to go beyond the less demanding, less imaginative, and less memorable experience of a great deal of prose.

## Chapter 11

## Playing Tennis Without a Net

In Chapter Nine, we discussed traditional poetry and its characteristics: regularity of meter, a definite length of line, and a rhyme scheme. Those who are accustomed to reading contemporary poetry, however, are aware that most of it does not follow this pattern. Unless they are accustomed to the kind of regularity apparent in traditional verse, they may prefer to write **free verse**.

Free verse goes all the way back to the Hebrew poetry of the Old Testament. Thousands of years ago, The Psalms, the Song of Solomon, and the Book of Job prepared the way for the much later work of Walt Whitman, whose *Leaves of Grass* in 1860 caused traditionalists to declare with shock that this wasn't poetry at all because it didn't rhyme! Since then it has become a favorite kind of poetic expression.

While free verse is, in one sense, freer than traditional verse, it is also, in another sense, more demanding. The writer of a sonnet, for example, understands the rules of the game and knows that he is expected to abide by them. The guidelines are clear and predetermined. The task may not be easy, but he knows, at least, what the limitations and requirements are. The writer of free verse, on the other hand, is not restricted in form, but at the same time, he is not assisted by it either. He must not only create the poem, but he must also determine its shape. If he cannot depend upon meter, length of line, and rhyme to produce the special effects of poetry, then he must devise some other methods. Robert Frost once said, "Writing free verse is like playing tennis without a net." If there is no net, then one must use his imagination to erect something else that will serve the same purpose. To use another comparison, imagine that you are snowbound for days with nothing to eat except a can of beans, but there is no available can opener. You will have to find some other means of getting the beans out of the can. This is the problem facing the writer of free verse. Although he is indeed free to pursue any path (to mix a metaphor) that might lead him to his destination, he has first to *clear* the path before he may proceed.

Many beginning poets mistake the freedom of free verse for license to discard order and discipline entirely and to express themselves in any way that comes to mind, feeling perhaps that there is something sacrosanct about inspiration and spontaneity. As a result, there is a great deal of bad poetry being written, and sometimes even published. While it is helpful to experiment with free verse as well as traditional verse, we must not for a moment deceive ourselves that free verse is easier to write. It isn't, if it is well written. Let us consider some ways of creating imaginary but functional tennis nets.

## PAUSE AND EMPHASIS

### Line Breaks

One of the most puzzling questions to many beginning writers of free verse is where a line should end. It might seem logical to keep lines more or less uniform in length, ending each at a natural point, such as at the end of a grammatical unit like a prepositional phrase or a subject-verb combination. Some poets do break their lines in just such an orderly way, and there is nothing wrong with doing that. However, since readers *expect* grammatical units to be kept intact, there is no element of surprise or challenge in such an arrangement. There are more effective ways to use the line break than that.

The first and last words in a line are in positions of greatest emphasis, with the last word receiving slightly more emphasis than the first. One may consider, then, which words he wishes to emphasize and place them accordingly, even though (or perhaps *because*) such an arrangement may mean carrying over the completion of meaning of that unit to the next line (enjambment). The last word in a line, even when unpunctuated, calls for a pause, however brief, and this pause contributes to the emphasis placed upon it.

Line breaks can also substitute for punctuation, a point to remember for those who wish to break away from dependence upon periods and commas.

## Use of Space

Blank space on a page is useful in creating emphasis and dramatic pauses. To set one word or a group of words alone on a line is to call attention to it. Indenting or centering can serve the same purpose, as can extra space between words or groups of words within the same line. Indentation can also indicate, as in an outline, points that are intended to be subordinate to other points.

## Punctuation

Pauses (or stops) and emphasis can, of course, be achieved by conventional punctuation, either within a line or at the end of it. If such a pause or stop comes within a line, enjambment is brought into play, creating more suspense and surprise than if a comma or period came at the end of the line in its more expected position. Emphasis falls naturally on the words just preceding and just following punctuation. Punctuation at the end of a line, therefore, serves to intensify the emphasis that is already given by the end position of the last word.

## Rhyme

While most free verse does not rhyme, there is no rule that says it cannot. If true rhyme, near-rhyme, consonance, assonance, or **alliteration** (the repetition of the same consonant sound coming close together) is used in free verse, especially at the ends of lines or in approximately the same position within several lines, it has the effect of creating a subtle symmetry as well as emphasis, and a special kind of unity. But wherever rhyme may appear, even without any kind of regularity, the fact that it is there at all has a tendency to emphasize and at the same time to bind together.

## Rhythm

We have said that free verse does not have the same regularity of meter that traditional verse has. However, the degree of regularity — or approximate regularity — within that freedom contributes to the emphasis and the pauses suggested in the reading of the lines. If a line flows along more or less smoothly and then runs into an unexpected irregularity, emphasis is given to that part of the line whose regularity is violated. A caesura achieved by the placing of two or more accented syllables together creates a pause and thereby slows down the line in which it occurs.

The length of line also contributes to the rhythm of the poem. Long lines help to produce an harmonious flow, a rhythm of expectation, especially if a pause occurs in about the same place in every one. Shorter lines may suggest a quicker, more clipped movement.

## Strophe Break

The term **strophe** (pronounced STROH-fee) comes from that part of the Greek ode of ancient times in which dancers moved from left to right on the stage while chanting, eventually making a complete circle. Writers of free verse have adopted this term to indicate a unit — a group of lines in which a cycle of thought, rhythm, or emotion is completed. While the stanza in traditional verse may have little if anything to do with the development of thought or a unit of meaning, the strophe in free verse, also separated from the next by space, does serve somewhat the same purpose as a paragraph. Emphasis is achieved when a new strophe is introduced, and the entire strophe stands out apart from any that might precede or follow it. While free verse is usually written in sentences just as traditional verse is, the strophe makes a complete circle as a stanza does not. A poem may be complete in only one strophe, but whether it has one or several, there is a kind of unity in each one.

## Repetition

Repetition, especially at the beginning or end of a line of free verse, serves to emphasize. Sometimes the repetition is exact; sometimes it is slightly changed, with a build-up effect (**incremental repetition**). Notice the effect of repetition in the following examples. Notice also the rhythm in The King James Bible and in *Leaves of Grass* by Walt Whitman.

Give unto the Lord, O ye mighty,
give unto the Lord glory and strength.

Give unto the Lord the glory due unto his name;
worship the Lord in the beauty of holiness.
The voice of the Lord is upon the waters:
the God of glory thundereth: the Lord is upon many waters.
The voice of the Lord is powerful;
the voice of the Lord is full of majesty.
The voice of the Lord breaketh the cedars;
yea, the Lord breaketh the cedars of Lebanon.                    (Psalm 29:1-5)

Then the waters had overwhelmed us, the stream had gone over our soul:
Then the proud waters had gone over our soul.                    (Psalm 124:4-5)

I cried unto the Lord with my voice;
with my voice unto the Lord did I make my supplication.          (Psalm 142:1)

I have compared thee, O my love, to a company of horses in Pharoah's chariots.
Thy cheeks are comely with jewels, thy neck with chains of gold.
We will make thee borders of gold with studs of silver.
While the king sitteth at his table, my spikenard sendeth forth the smell thereof.
A bundle of myrrh is my well-beloved unto me; he shall lie all night betwixt my breasts.
My beloved is unto me as a cluster of camphor in the vineyards of Engedi.
Behold, thou art fair, my love, behold, thou art fair; thou hast doves' eyes.
Behold thou art fair, my beloved, yea, pleasant: also our bed is green.
The beams of our house are cedar, and our rafters fir.     (The Song of Solomon, 1:9-17)

By the rivers of Babylon, there we sat down, yea, we wept, when we remembered Zion.
We hanged our harps upon the willows in the midst thereof.
For they that carried us away captive required of us a song;
and they that wasted us required of us mirth, saying, Sing us one of the songs of Zion.
How shall we sing the Lord's song in a strange land?             (Psalm 137:1-4)

Press close bare-bosom'd night — press close magnetic nourishing night!
Night of south winds — night of the large few stars!
Still nodding night — mad naked summer night.

Smile O voluptuous cool-breath'd earth!
Earth of the slumbering and liquid trees!
Earth of departed sunset — earth of the mountains misty-topt!
Earth of the vitreous pour of the full moon just tinged with blue!
Earth of shine and dark mottling the tide of the river!
Earth of the limpid gray of clouds brighter and clearer for my sake!
Far-swooping elbow'd earth — rich apple-blossom'd earth!
Smile, for your lover comes.

Prodigal, you have given me love — therefore I to you give love!
O unspeakable passionate love. (Walt Whitman, "Song of Myself," #21, *Leaves of Grass*)

Coffin that passes through lanes and streets,
Through day and night with the great cloud darkening the land,
With the pomp of the inloop'd flags with the cities draped in black,
With the snow of the States themselves as of crape-veil'd women standing,
With processions long and winding and the flambeaus of the night,
With the countless torches lit, with the silent sea of faces and the unbared heads,
With the waiting depot, the arriving coffin, and the sombre faces,
With dirges through the night, with the thousand voices rising strong and solemn,
With all the mournful voices of the dirges pour'd around the coffin,
The dim-lit churches and the shuddering organs — where amid these you journey,
With the tolling tolling bells' perpetual clang,

Here, coffin that slowly passes,
I give you my sprig of lilac.
(Walt Whitman, "When Lilacs Last in the Dooryard Bloom'd," #6, *Leaves of Grass*)


O how shall I warble myself for the dead one there I loved?
And how shall I deck my song for the large sweet soul that has gone?
And what shall my perfume be for the grave of him I love?

Sea-winds blown from east and west,
Blown from the Eastern sea and blown from the Western sea, till there on the prairies meeting,
These and with these and the breath of my chant,
I'll perfume the grave of him I love.
(Walt Whitman, "When Lilacs Last in the Dooryard Bloom'd," #10, *Leaves of Grass*)

## CONCLUSION

Good free verse is poetry in its truest sense. It challenges the writer to discover subtle ways by which its essence can be distilled — to be more selective and to make more critical choices that are not always required to the same extent of a traditional poet.

Even though free verse is, in some ways, more difficult to write than metered verse, it is probably a good starting place for many beginners, especially those who are likely to become enslaved by rhyme. It has the advantage of freeing them to say what they wish without having to force their thoughts into a predetermined conformity.

## Chapter 12

## Making the Workers Work

Keeping in mind that a poem is more compressed than prose (a point made in Chapter Eight), let us now concentrate on getting the most mileage out of the fewest words possible for the greatest effect. An effective poem is economical; nothing superfluous is allowed to remain in it. Unless a word or phrase adds significantly to the unity of the poem, unless it has a need to be there, unless it carries more than its own weight, it probably ought to be omitted in the process of revising — or at least restated for as much tightness as possible.

To paraphrase an observation made in the novel, *Animal Farm*, some words are more equal than others. There are hard workers, and there are hangers-on. There are bare bones, without which the body of an idea cannot move, and there is excess fat that can be trimmed without any noticeable damage. A good poem moves on its most "equal," most hard-working words, its nouns and verbs.

### SUBJECT AND VERB

A sentence is made up of several parts, some more essential than others. Every student of English composition learns how to identify the subject and predicate of a sentence. In addition to these parts, sentences with transitive verbs also require direct objects, just as sentences with intransitive verbs sometimes call for complements (completers). If only these necessary parts of a sentence are given, a reader will have all the basic knowledge that the sentence contains, even though that sentence is not fully fleshed out. "Babies cry" is a complete sentence with nothing else added. "Baby cried" also makes sense, but only a small child would say this; it is obvious that something more is expected. We know that this is a particular baby, perhaps "the newborn baby in the third crib from the end." Having this additional information is helpful, but it is not necessary to tell who is performing the action. The noun *baby* may also be modified by such adjectives as *frail, tiny, chubby,* or *round-faced,* or such a prepositional phrase as "with a deep voice." The noun *baby* serves the function of identifying, but by itself it does not tell anything about the baby.

A writer may choose between sentences that need many words to convey complete meaning and more economical sentences that make the basic words do a large share of the job, thereby eliminating the need for additional words and phrases. Consider the alternative of choosing another word or grammatical unit to refer to the baby. Notice how much more is implied if, instead of calling the baby simply what it is, we referred to it as "a little angel," "a brat," or "a crumb-snatcher." Such words not only identify the child but also suggest something about the speaker's attitude toward it. Whenever it is possible, eliminate adjectives and prepositional phrases by using nouns that provide the same kinds of information.

The verb is probably the most important word in a sentence; a sentence cannot be complete without it, for one thing, but more importantly, it has the power of providing, through suggestion, helpful information regarding not only the action itself but also the performer as well. The verb *cried* is useful in identifying action, but it does not reveal how, when, or where this action occurred. It might have been "loudly for ten minutes," "weakly," "shrilly," or "in a frustrated manner." Every mother understands the language of her baby's various cries and reacts to it accordingly. Added information is more descriptive than the simple act of crying. A more thoughtfully chosen verb can often eliminate the need for extra words and phrases. To say that the baby *screamed* suggests that it was in severe pain or was perhaps angry. To say that it *whimpered* implies something altogether different.

*Walk* or *enter* and *sit* are other verbs that only identify actions; they tell nothing about the walker or his manner of entering a room and taking a seat. Notice what different mental pictures are conjured up from the following sentences:

He *shuffled* into the room and *slumped* into the nearest chair.

She *waddled* into the room and *flopped* into the nearest chair.

She *floated* into the room and *perched* upon the nearest chair.

He *staggered* into the room and *collapsed* in the nearest chair.

## EXERCISE

1. (Written) Make a list of (a) twenty additional verbs that can be substituted for *walked* or *entered*, (b) ten words that can be substituted for *cried*, and (c) a separate list of five verbs that can be substituted for *sat*.
2. (Oral) Share your three lists with other members of the class and discuss what each verb suggests to you about the performer of the action and the action itself. Decide which are the most descriptive.

## ADJECTIVES

Adjectives tend to weaken poetry when they are superfluous. However, there are times when a well-chosen adjective is the best possible way of describing. When they are necessary, it is best to avoid those that have been overused, as well as those which involve value judgments. It has been said that "beauty is in the eye of the beholder." To describe a person or thing as beautiful informs the reader that the speaker considers this to be true, but he is asking the reader to take his word for it; he does not give the reader an opportunity to judge for himself. It is not enough for the poet to see; he must invite the reader to see, too, and to share the joy of his discovery. A good rule to follow, however, when *any* adjective is used is to ask yourself if it is absolutely necessary, if it is the *best* word to use, not merely the easiest.

## WORD ORDER

We have said earlier (Chapter Eleven) that the first and last words in a line of poetry are in the most emphatic positions. The poet needs therefore to choose with care the words that begin new lines, especially those that appear at the beginning of the poem. Sentences that begin with "There is" or "Here are" draw attention to their lack of power, since these are merely introductory words which add nothing to the meaning of the sentence. Rather than beginning a poem with "There were two men sitting at the bar," one might consider "Two men sat at the bar" or, if the location is of more concern to the poem than the men, "At the bar sat two men." Better still, one might also think of substitutes for *sat* that would serve a more important purpose than simply to identify.

In general, sentences that follow their natural word order are preferable to those that are inverted, although in some instances a sentence is deliberately inverted to place a word of primary importance as close to the beginning of a line as possible. Unless such a reason justifies turning the sentence around, the order of subject-verb-direct object (or complement) is probably best. Poets of the past inverted their sentences with some frequency, often, no doubt, because of the conformity to regular patterns of rhyme, but modern poets prefer the more natural order. One is more likely to say, "The woman worked at her desk" than "At her desk worked the woman."

## STRONG VERBS

The active voice is generally preferred (in all writing, not just poetry) to the passive voice. Unless the performer of an action is unknown or of no importance, the active voice is considered to be more effective. "David played a new song" is preferable to "A new song was played by David."

The regular present and past tense verbs tend to be stronger than the progressive verb forms. "He stares" is more direct than "He is staring," giving the impression of greater immediacy.

While *be* and its various forms are necessary to language, they are nevertheless passive. *Be* is called a state-of-being verb because it indicates merely that something or someone exists; it does not indicate action. An action verb is therefore stronger than *be*, *am*, *is*, *are*, *was* or *were* because it can provide information more concisely. "She is in the room now" indicates someone's whereabouts only. Sentences like "She dozes by the window in her room" or "She stares at the clock on the wall" go beyond physical presence to action and provide better visibility for the reader.

## UNIMPORTANT WORDS

Greater economy and force can sometimes be obtained by the judicious elimination of articles, such as *the*, *a*, and *an*, as well as conjunctions, especially the much overused *and*. This is not to suggest that all such words should be avoided. Since the poet does not wish to place unnecessary stumbling blocks in the way of the reader's understanding, he should not omit words that are necessary for effective communication. At times, however, these little words become superfluous, diverting attention from the stronger words and thereby detracting from the directness and power that a poem might otherwise possess.

## THE SPECIFIC AND CONCRETE

In selecting descriptive material, a good poet strives to present as clear and vivid an image as possible. A reader cannot visualize broad generalities or relate to abstractions as well as he can to the specific and concrete. A poem that seeks to discuss love or faith or despair in general terms is headed for almost certain trouble. While the subject may have meaning for the poet, his treatment of it has little chance of involving the reader in the experience of the poem. The Bible says, "God is love" and states also that "the Word became Flesh" through Christ. Humankind needed a specific example of love and truth in order to comprehend and experience it. The poet who is willing to shape a generality into something more specific, to work with concrete rather than abstract material, is likely to succeed in a way that he cannot do with only the intangible mists of broad concepts. A poem about failure may best be illustrated through a particular character who experiences failure. (We are not referring to the poet's attempts to express his own personal sense of failure, which may not make it past the point of self-expression and into the world of effective literary communication.) The poet who wishes to describe the glories of springtime might better concentrate on the concrete details of a particular spring day in a specific time and place, perhaps even reporting the observation through the eyes of a fictional character.

"The dying branches of elms" evokes a more vivid image than "trees." "Star-silvered wings of gulls" is more effective than simply "birds." The *illustration* of theme can be counted on to make a more lasting impression than the mere *statement* of theme. The advice given concerning short fiction applies equally to poetry: Don't tell; show!

## CONCLUSION

Finding the best possible words and arranging them in their most effective order is one of the primary concerns of a serious poet. It is not an easy task and requires a great deal of open-minded self-criticism and revision, which accounts for the fact that there are few truly great poets. But the creation of a good poem is a challenge that can bring a great deal of satisfaction to the effort, even when the finished product is less perfect than we wish it to be. And what a sense of victory we thrill to when we do come close to what we hope to achieve!

## Chapter 13

## To Do and Not to Do

From the foregoing chapters it should be obvious that a good poem does not just happen. If the finished product gives the impression of being spontaneous and yet completely right, so much the better; the reader does not need to be aware of the inner struggle which went into its making. By way of summary now, let us repeat briefly some points that have already been discussed and introduce some new ones, all of which are intended to lead to unity. It is improbable that you will sit down in advance and plan how every single ingredient of a good poem will be added. You will probably want to get down on paper, as fast as possible, the impressions and ideas that first come to mind. It is only after you have jotted down this first rough draft that you will consider what is working well in the poem, what parts of it are not successful, and what changes might be made for a better, more unified, more aesthetically satisfying piece of art.

### LITERAL VS. ARTISTIC TRUTH

In "One's-Self I Sing," Walt Whitman wrote: "One's self I sing, a simple separate person . . . ." Again in "Song of Myself" he wrote:

> I celebrate myself, and sing myself,
> And what I assume you shall assume,
> And every atom belonging to me as good belongs to you."

Each of us is entirely unique as an individual, and the details of a particular experience naturally have a great deal of personal meaning. However, if this experience is the basis of a poem, it must be related in such a way that it evokes an emotional response from others and permits them to share that part of the experience that is basically human and universal. The poet may experience sadness or joy over a special occurrence in his life which the reader may not share, but the reader is capable of feeling the same emotions if the inclusion of personal details do not prevent him from doing so. The raw and literal truth is not art, but it can be refined and altered to whatever extent is necessary so that it is possible for art to emerge from it.

Poems are usually born of emotional experiences rather than ideas. That experience may be first-hand, vicarious, or based on an observation. A poet may react to a newspaper article or advertisement, a movie or television program, or to a fragment of conversation overheard on the street. But he must identify with it — participate in it on an emotional level — before he can convert it into an effective poem. It is therefore the poet's "self" that he sings, not in the narrow, egocentric sense, but in the human and universal sense which all may share.

If a poem that begins with personal experience remains personal and private, it may have little value for anyone else. Writing such a poem, as a means of self-expression, may be good mental therapy, but it will seldom be good art.

### PURPOSE

One is often tempted to try to do too many things in a single poem. It is a good idea to stop at some point and decide what your purpose is in writing it, what you hope to accomplish. A good poem may accomplish several purposes and still be unified, but without some care taken in the matter, it is likely that it will do too many things and not any of them well. If you are aware of your primary purpose, you will have some idea of when that has been accomplished and therefore where the poem ought to stop. Frequently beginning poets let their material become unwieldy because they are not decided on their purpose for writing it.

A poem may have as its primary purpose to tell a story, but we are not mainly interested here in narrative poems, some of which tend to be quite long. Some shorter narrative poems have as a secondary purpose to teach a lesson. (Didactic poetry today, however, is not popular.) The purpose may be to paint a word picture describing a scene or an object; or it may be to portray a character. It may be to create an awareness in the reader of some social condition; or to express an emotion; or to simply make a statement of observation or truth.

If the poet's purpose is to make a statement, either directly or indirectly through suggestion or illustration, that statement (the central idea or theme) can usually be summed up in one sentence. The poem is unified in thought if everything within it leads to that central idea and if there is nothing within it that leads off in another direction. If the poet recognizes his purpose, he will find it easier to limit the poem accordingly.

## DICTION

The poet should be careful to use diction appropriate to the mood, message, and purpose of each poem. *Diction* refers to the choice of words, their multiple meanings, and the levels of usage which they represent. Modern poets steer clear of the kinds of language that were popular and acceptable in days gone by. They are more inclined toward the natural language of speech — that is, the *best* of natural speech — which can be just as precise as the most formal language. One common failing of beginning poets is their tendency to imitate the diction of the poetry on which they were schooled, forgetting that much of it was written in a different century. Another mistake is to assume that certain words are more poetic than others. Try to avoid unnatural ways of saying things — words no longer in common use, archaic spellings and contractions, inverted sentences, pretentious words, and "arty" words and expressions. Be a poet of your own generation, not of the past.

Avoid clichés. Your message may be old, but your way of conveying it should be fresh and original.

It is important to select the most precise word available for what you wish to say, remembering that one word may have only a single intended meaning while another may suggest two possible meanings which are both applicable. Remember, too, that there are no true synonymns; while two or three words may mean the same thing in one context, in another context they cannot be interchanged. Words should be selected, then, not only for their precise meanings, but also for other possible meanings which they may suggest. For a disciplined poet who strives for excellence, the approximate meaning just is not good enough; only the best possible word will do. (The sounds of words may help to determine which of two words meaning approximately the same thing is most effective.)

## SOUND

Poetry is meant to be heard. Although much of our acquaintance with it comes from reading, sound is too important to be neglected. An inner music goes on even when the ear does not actually hear the words. The texture created by words working harmoniously with each other, as well as in harmony with the mood of the poem, should be considered. A factually stated poem with no regard for sound may successfully get across the central idea that a poet intends, but then, so may a piece of prose. Lyric poetry may be thought of as song, although without music, and as such, its effectiveness in oral rendition should not be overlooked. If a poet wishes to create a unified impression of discord or harshness, on the other hand, the choice of word sounds is likely to be quite different. The sounds of some words are suggestive of their meanings. (These are called **onomatopoetic** words.) Notice the closeness of sound and meaning in such words as *swish*, *screech*, *splash*, *crackle*, *moan*, *shriek*, *boom*, and *tinkle*. The sound of a poem should contribute to its unity.

Unfortunately, there is no magic recipe by which the ingredient of sound can be added to a batter of meaning, blended smoothly, and baked into tasty poetic fare. Much has been written about the suggestive qualities of certain vowel and consonant combinations, and there is merit in some of these observations. It *is* helpful to understand what is happening to our vocal equipment when speech occurs. But it would be a mistake to assume that all that is needed to simulate anger, joy, grief, or calm is to string together a series of the right letter combinations and all will turn out well.

Keeping in mind that sound is an integral part of meaning and not an element that can be isolated from it, you might find the following suggestions helpful when you have completed your first draft:

1. Read what you have written aloud — several times — using a tape recorder whenever possible. Have someone else read, too, and listen — carefully.

2. Pay close attention to determine how easily — or with what difficulty — the lines flow over and through the nasal passages, the lips, the tongue, and the teeth.
3. Judge whether what you hear is what you mean.
4. If any parts of the poem bother you, try to determine why they are not working well. Analyze the sounds of individual words in combination with each other; consider what impression you intended to create. When you have located the problem, rework those lines or phrases to eliminate it.
5. Repeat the process with your revisions incorporated — as many times as necessary — until you are satisfied that you have done your best.

### MOOD AND TONE

Consistency of mood and tone is something else a poet needs to remember. Whether the speaker gives the impression of anger, bitterness, light-heartedness, seriousness, joy, or some other feeling, it should be identifiable to the reader and consistent throughout the poem.

The way the speaker feels about his subject should also be consistent. If he is writing about a person, for example, does he treat him with sympathy and understanding? Does he poke gentle fun at him? Is he critical of him in a destructive way? Does he hold him up to bitter ridicule? Whatever the speaker's attitude may be, the reader should not be confused by inconsistencies in it.

### POINT OF VIEW

Poems, like stories, are told by one person. In poetry, that one person may be the poet himself, or it may be someone — or even some*thing* — else. It is easiest for the poet to speak directly out of his own experience, but there are times when a different speaker is preferable. The *persona* (or speaker) in a poem is the voice we hear, either the poet's own, or that fictional person or thing which he pretends to be. (In Gilbert K. Chesterton's poem, "The Donkey," the persona is the donkey itself; in "Caliban in the Coal Mines" by Louis Untermeyer, the speaker is a coal miner; the "I" in Langston Hughes's "The Negro Speaks of Rivers" is a black person who speaks for the entire race; and in "The Builders" by Sarah Henderson Hay, the speaker is one of the three little pigs of the fairy tale.)

Be alert to the possibility of some other point of view than your own when you are writing a poem. Ask yourself if the experience can be related best from your own personal point of view or through the eyes of someone else.

### AUDIENCE

Most poems are addressed to a general audience — that is, whoever happens to read it. Some poems, however, have a particular audience in mind. It might be an individual or a group. Most love poetry is addressed to the beloved, who is often referred to as "you." Sometimes the "you" is a particular segment of the population. If there is a "you" in a poem, it should be carried through the poem with some consistency. Ask yourself as you write each poem what particular audience, if any, you are addressing. Then be consistent throughout so that you do not talk *about* someone in one place and *to* him in another — or worse still, to several someones.

### COMMUNICATION

All language is intended to be communication. Some poems may be so private that the poet hides them away in some secret place and never shares them with anyone, but in most instances, the first thing we want to do when we have completed a poem is to share it with someone else. Even though the primary reason for writing may not be for communication, eventually we hope that someone will read and understand what we felt and were trying to say. In order for this sharing to occur, the poet must communicate well.

This is not to say that a poet needs to clarify every detail in the poem, for a good poem is left open for interpretation, but there should be enough clues to permit an intelligent, sensitive reader to get at least the central idea. If he cannot, the poem fails to communicate effectively.

Don't go out of your way to be difficult. Don't try to impress the reader with your wide vocabulary or your ability to write impressive-sounding description. If you do, your poem may fool some easily-impressed readers who may think what you have written is "just beautiful," but on closer scrutiny, you may find that they don't have the slightest idea what you are talking about. (And maybe you don't either!)

Remember that, like prose, poetry is based on the sentence unit. An intelligent reader should be able to read your poem, sentence by sentence, and get a sense of logic in the construction of each one. He may not understand each sentence thoroughly on the first reading, but at least he will have the satisfaction of knowing that, except for special effects, each sentence unit is complete.

## RHYME

If you choose to use rhyme, keep it unobtrusive. Use it sometimes irregularly within the line (especially in free verse) instead of always at the end.

Avoid placing rhyming words too close together, as in every two lines, where attention will be drawn to them.

Avoid the easy, expected rhymes. (A good rhyming dictionary can be quite helpful when all else fails.)

Don't sacrifice thought for rhyme; don't let the necessity for finding a rhyming word change what you really want to say.

Experiment with near-rhyme, assonance, and consonance as alternatives for perfect rhyme.

## SELECTIVITY

Resist the temptation to "tell it all." Select only those details that will contribute to the theme of a particular poem; save other details and other thoughts on that subject for later poems.

Through selective word choice, be content to suggest or imply your full meaning; give the reader a chance to "get it" on his own. Write for the intelligent reader, one who is willing to meet you halfway, rather than the lazy reader who wants all the work done for him in advance.

Be careful to select the best positions in a line for the most important words.

## PREPARATION

Read. Read a great deal. Read the best poetry available. (Textbook anthologies can often serve as a useful guide to what critics consider *good* poetry. After you discover which poets you like best, you can gradually move to entire collections of their work.)

Read poetry produced in various periods of time, not just contemporary poetry. Learn what the good poets of all times have done with both traditional form and free verse.

Practice your scales. Study and experiment with the styles of individual poets; try imitating them, illustrating how three different poets might have handled the same subject.

After you have done this, concentrate on developing your own style. Dare to innovate; dare to be your own individual self.

## UNITY

With good luck, self-discipline, and hard work, a poet may produce a gem in which all facets glowing together achieve a marvelous unity. The reader may not be consciously aware of form or the effectiveness of diction, sound, and tone as separate entities but will be pleased, perhaps even dazzled, by the harmonious whole. The vocabulary will give the impression of being the *only* words that could have been used; the point of view will seem to be the only possible one.

Let all parts of your poem work together toward a common goal, not pull in separate directions.

Make every word carry its own weight; eliminate unnecessary ones. Tighten up your language so that the idea, impression, or emotion you intend can be conveyed as concisely and economically as possible.

Remember that the silence between sounds can be as dramatic as the sounds themselves — sometimes even more so.

Show, don't tell.

Control your images. Rely heavily on figures of speech, but keep them consistent with each other. Experiment with images of sound and touch (and sometimes even smell), as well as sight.

Let the rhythm of the poem reinforce its mood, rather than work against it.

Avoid novelty for its own sake. Examine your reasons for discarding conventional punctuation and capitalization; be sure that you can justify the special attention called to the parts of the poem that are treated in an exceptional way.

Avoid grand generalizations; try to zero in on the particular, the concrete and the specific.

And finally, feel free to disregard all advice if what you are doing works!

## REVISION

Be willing to revise a poem once you have completed the first draft. Occasionally a good poem springs into existence full blown, but the chances that this will happen are very small. Most poems need to be worked and reworked. The willingness to revise — to work toward perfection — is one of the marks of a good poet. After the inspiration comes the perspiration of revision.

When the poem is at last completed, the hard work will not be apparent to the reader; it will seem that this is the way the poem had to be. But that sense of inevitability does not come easily. Only the poet will know what dissatisfaction, self-criticism, and disciplined labor went into the finished product.

## A POEM IN THE MAKING

Let me share with you the process of revision of one of my own poems, "Grand Circus Park (Twenty Years Later)." I do not often have as much trouble with a poem as I had with this one, nor do I have to work as long on it as I did in this instance. Nevertheless, it will illustrate the value of revision.

Grand Circus Park is a square in downtown Detroit which at one time was a focal point for me. In the days before I could afford even the cheapest car, I used to take the Cadillac-Harper bus from my modest eastside home to the shopping area. When there was a babysitter available — and that was not often — my stopping-off place downtown became synonymous with freedom, hope, joy, and a sense of life.

Many years passed, and I moved to another part of town, another busline, my own car, a new marriage, a new job — and Grand Circus Park became a thing of the past.

Suddenly one day, the baby was grown up, the marriage had fizzled, and I was bluntly reminded of all this past when for the first time in years I had to pass again the same corner where my downtown Detroit adventure had once begun. The beginning of a poem buzzed around in my brain. But what I wanted to say was not clear; there were too many things happening at once, and I knew that. Although the words I wrote had some kind of vague possibility, I was having problems. The first version of my poem read:

> The old men still sit on the benches
> Watching a dubious sun slant through new trees.
> It is hard to remember that they are not
> The same old men.
> They are grizzled and bleary-eyed.
> (Even the memories are distant now.)
> But the young men are also grizzly
> And bleary-eyed,
> And they do not even have the memories to blur.
> It is hard to tell the difference.
> The old men are new old men.
> The others have rotted in their graves
> Since I first walked among them here.
> It is hard to see the grass growing and know the difference.
> Wives and husbands have loved and cursed each other and been unfaithful
> And died and mourned awhile
> And children who stumbled on uncertain feet
> Have erred and strayed and then come home again,
> And all has been lost and all forgiven;

> They walk upright now and brush their infants' hair in curls.
> And the men grow older.
> The Cadillac-Harper bus still stops in the same place
> But the destination is no longer home
> And it is hard to remember what was and understand what is.

Well, the poem just wasn't right; it was going out in too many directions at once. I wasn't sure what I wanted to comment about — the men, the city, the despair of today's youth, my own unfortunate marriage, my college-age daughter's problems. What? All of it was there. The poem could have taken any direction; that was the problem. It didn't know where it wanted to go.

In the second version, I had the old men "dozing" instead of just sitting, and they were "welcoming May's dubious warmth" instead of just watching. There were other minor changes, not necessarily for the better. The single line that originally only hinted at the youth as "new old men" was expanded into four lines that further complicated my problem.

The third version, written a number of months after the second, still lacked a sense of direction the poem needed. A word was changed, deleted, or transferred here and there, but this version presented the same problems as the first.

The fourth version was still faltering. The benches changed from "the" to "same" to "city" to "green," and they still weren't right. Then somewhere along the line, the branches became specifically elm trees. They became not new branches, but branches that were dying. Somehow, mysteriously, I discovered that I wanted to talk about a dying city — not myself — and that the old men were important as symbols, as were the trees dying of Dutch Elm disease.

About the same time, a bit of music started gnawing in the back of my memory. When I was a teenager just out of high school and waiting for the fall semester at college to begin, I had my first job — singing in an NYA choir which was directed by Ken Billups, himself a college student. He would either write or arrange almost everything we sang, and I appreciated the spirit of the old black spirituals through his arrangements better than I had ever done through the more sophisticated arrangements of Hall Johnson and R. Nathaniel Dett. One of the arrangements we had sung in Ken Billups' choir was based on the Biblical pronouncement that "the axe is laid unto the root of the trees; therefore every tree which bringeth not forth good fruit is hewn down, and cast into the fire." This music came back to me, in combination with my other thoughts, and I recognized the men as unproductive figures of the past, discarded by society. I now knew that the park benches had to be, not green, but gray.

Then a photo-essay came out in one of the Detroit papers of several old men in Grand Circus Park feeding pigeons. The old men feeding pigeons and the gray benches and the dying elm trees now all symbolized the same things. Young mothers sensed this death and were embarrassed by it. They did not want to be reminded of what the hopeful youth of their children would eventually come to. The bus riders no longer reached their *destination* when they left the Cadillac bus, but their *point of exit* because they were not *arriving at*; they were *leaving*. The wind, the old men, the young mothers (confused, disturbed by their hope because of what they saw in the despair of age), the dying trees, the suburbanites: all of them knew and understood that the city of Detroit was no place of hope or life.

The following expresses the meaning at which the poem finally arrived:

### Grand Circus Park
*(Twenty Years Later)*

> Old men still drowse on gray park benches
> Watching a dubious sun leak through
> The dying branches of elms.
> > "The axe shall be laid (Hew, hew!)
> > To the root of the trees . . ."
> It is hard to realize
> They are not the same old men,
> Grizzled and bleary-eyed as memories.

Bold, raucous pigeons flaunt themselves
Before the glazed, glaucomic stares.
Young mothers quickly look away, caress
With special tenderness their infants' proper curls.
    "And every tree that bringeth not forth
    Good fruit . . ."

The Cadillac bus still stops at the same spot,
But the passengers are not the same
And the point of exit is no longer home.
Even the wind is dying, and an autumn fog
Settles like a shroud upon the old men's shoulders.
Do they dream of sputtering logs
In open fireplaces —
Or do they shake with the impotent rage of trees
    "Hewn down and cast into the fire"?

## WRITTEN EXERCISES

1. Write a poem from the point of view of a fairy tale character, a character from the Bible, or a character from some other well-known piece of literature. Select a particular moment of that character's experience and relate his or her thoughts at that time. (For example: Cinderella at one minute before midnight or Little Red Riding Hood when she first suspects that her grandmother doesn't look just right.)

2. Write a poem based on an old photograph of yourself and other members of your family. Recall how you felt or what was going on in your life at the time, and try to recapture those thoughts.

3. Listen to a recording of mood-music and write a poem that captures the impressions conveyed by the song.

4. Find an illustration in a magazine story in which one of the characters is showing some kind of emotion. Imagine that you are that character. Write a poem expressing your thoughts and feelings at the time of the picture.

5. Write a poem based on a person's name. (Be sure to select a name or nickname that suggests something to you, such as Grace, Joy, Felicia, "Spike," "Rock," or "Dizzy." In the section containing students' poems, you will find a poem, "Dawn," based on a girl's name.)

6. Write a cinquain, sonnet, villanelle, or one of the other fixed forms that were discussed earlier.

7. If you have access to a large sea shell, write a poem describing it. Be sure to use figures of speech to tell what it reminds you of when you look at it, how it feels when you run your fingers over it, and what it sounds like when you hold it up to your ear.

8. Write a trio, a poem of only three lines which (a) is in present tense, (b) presents two impressions or observations, and (c) ends with a summary observation that relates to the other two.

    *Example:*         A frozen branch snaps under the weight of ice.
                         Black windows frost in cold and empty rooms.
                         How I wish for your warm laughter!

9. Write a poem of approximately eight or ten lines in which no adjectives are used.

10. Write a poem of at least eight lines in which the personal pronouns *I*, *you*, or *we* are not used at all.

# Evaluation Guidelines

## FORM

Is the form recognizable as free, blank, or traditional verse? Is the poem more effective in this form than it might have been in another?

If the poem is in traditional form, do the meter, rhyme, and length of line follow consistently throughout the poem?

Is the rhyme (if any) well-chosen and unobtrusive? Does it avoid being monotonous?

Does it matter whether the poem rhymes or not? What effect does the rhyme have upon the overall effect?

Is the rhythm varied enough to avoid a sing-songy quality? Is the dominant rhythm appropriate? Are the variations interesting without a complete breakdown of order? What, if anything, does the rhythm contribute to the poem?

If the poem is written in free verse, do the lengths of the lines, the line breaks, the use of space, and the placement of words within the lines contribute to effective pauses and emphases?

Does each strophe contain a logical unity?

If there are short and choppy lines, is there a logical explanation for them? If the lines are long and smooth-flowing, is their effect in keeping with the poem as a whole?

Is the content of the poem reinforced by the form? Does the shape of the poem on the page contribute to its overall unity?

## POINT OF VIEW

Is the point of view clear? Is it clear whether the speaker is the poet himself or someone (or something) else? Can that speaker be identified?

Does the speaker remain constant throughout the poem?

Has the poet used the most effective point of view for this particular poem?

## AUDIENCE

Is it clear whether the audience is general or someone in particular?

If the intended audience is other than general, does the person addressed remain constant throughout?

Would the poem be more effective addressed to an identifiable audience or to nobody in particular? Why?

## DICTION

Is the level of usage appropriate for the persona of the poem?

Is the vocabulary precise and well chosen? Is each word the best word possible within that context?

Where a word has more than one possible meaning, are the general meanings equally valid and consistent with the rest of the poem?

Does the diction contribute to a consistent mood and tone?

Is the word order natural to contemporary speech? If not, does the unusual arrangement contribute any special effect that the poet might have intended?

Are the sounds produced in the poem pleasant to the ear and harmonious, or are they harsh and grating? What effect results? Is this effect in keeping with what the poet seems to be trying to do?

## IMAGE AND SYMBOL

Are appropriate figures of speech used to create sensory impressions?

Are the images within the poem controlled and unified?

Are these images (or a single sustained image) appropriate for what the poet is trying to describe?

Are any identifiable symbols used? If so, are they appropriate for this particular poem?

How much more effective is symbolism here than a simple, non-symbolic statement?

UNITY

Is it clear what the poet's purpose is — what he intends to accomplish in the poem? Is the purpose (or are the purposes) consistent throughout the poem? Has the poet refrained from trying to do too many things at once? How well has he succeeded in accomplishing his purpose(s)?

Is there a single recognizable theme? Has the poet confined himself to a single unified statement? Has he refrained from trying to say too much on the subject of the poem?

Is it clear what the subject of the poem is?

Does the poet communicate his ideas well without being too explicit? Is the poem implicit enough to invite a variety of interpretations, while at the same time providing enough clues to the central idea so that a thoughtful, intelligent reader can "get the point" after several careful readings?

Is the poem tightly constructed and compressed, without superfluous words and phrases? Does it rely heavily on strong verbs and nouns, avoiding unnecessary adjectives and other modifiers? Do whatever adjectives may be used avoid value judgments?

Is the presence or absence of conventional punctuation and capitalization helpful to the poem? In what way, and to what extent, does it affect your understanding?

Does the poem rely upon the concrete and specific rather than abstractions and generalizations?

Is the poem (except for special effects) written in complete sentences so that an orderly communication of ideas is possible?

Does the poem challenge you on an intellectual level and at the same time involve you on an emotional level?

If there are any **allusions** (references) within the poem to persons or events in history or literature, do these allusions help to unify the poem?

If an **epigraph** (a direct quotation from other literature or some other inscription) follows the title, is it helpful in enlightening the reader on the poet's theme, thus unifying the poem?

Is the title appropriate? Is it more than just a handle? Does it add significance to the poem itself and therefore contribute to unity?

Do all parts of the poem work together for one meaningful whole?

## Untitled Poems

Hope knocks on my door
I am frightened to let her enter
for she has been a fair-weather friend
But I will welcome her
for she is all I have.

Lori Schaefer


Sunlight sears barren desert . . .
Black buckets of cool rain
    hiss on hot sand . . .
I wait thirstly
For love to quench my soul.

Lori Schaefer


I blush with pleasure
As death clutches me close
And murmurs passionate oaths
    of release from torment
As I abandon life
And succumb to his desires.

Lori Schaefer


it may be a cliché
but, to you, i want
my life to be an open book.

take me.
read me.
study me carefully.
read between my lines if you have to.

but, whatever you do,
don't slam shut
my covers
and throw me
upon a shelf in the
back of your mind.

my bindings are not secure
and i may fall apart.

Renée Walton Schwall


he stands
in a green field
with grass still damp from dew.
he stands alone, very quiet,
aloof.

Renée Walton Schwall


your absence
is the nativity of my solitude.
my days are heavy with
december's frozen isolation,
and just as
december's enceinte clouds
give life to
an undefiled veil of snow,
i am in painful labor with
tears
as pure.

Renée Walton Schwall


kids singing
bells ringing
ice pinging
time winging,
    what a season!

snow falling
trees talling
deck-the-halling
cars stalling,
    winter's colder!

kids toying
folks joying
santa ploying
how annoying!
    what's the reason?

snow bunny
nose runny
spend money
not funny,
    i am older.

Renée Walton Schwall

## Dawn

Dawn,
your cool gray eyes
cloud with the mist of morning,
reluctant to open to the sudden day.

Dreams
of the closed, unalterable past
haze your consciousness of present being,
admit no possibility of either pain or joy.

Wake.
It is not the mornings, after all,
that tell a lifetime.
It is not beginnings alone
that mean.

Let the sun
fan back the flame into your smoky eyes
and let your sunflower face
follow with gladness this day's new gold.

**Cornelia Withers**

## Trios
*(An anonymous classroom exercise)*

A lone star winks through the murk of a March fog.
A yellow blossom pushes through the dirty snow.
I think I am going to fall in love again.

The soft gray cat lounges in the corner chair.
The love seat fades in the sunlight from the open window.
We grow old together.

The clatter of milk running over my cereal.
A clock banging away the minutes on the wall.
Last night I turned eighteen at Bimbo's.

A mouse tiptoes across a lion's cage.
The quiet calm after the summer storm.
How I dread your uncontrollable anger!

Snow falls on the little house.
The furnace operates to bring the heat.
Enough of this; let summer come.

### Spying on a Woman Swimming Nude in Lake Superior

*She moves as water moves, and comes to me*
*Stayed by what was, and pulled by what will be.*
— Theodore Roethke, from "She"

Nipples break the water.
Breasts leap like river salmon.

If you walk for twenty minutes
east across the sand
you will see children
chancing ankles to the quickest waves.

She rises.
Water pearls cling to her vulva.

The children call the dry ones
"Chicken"
until everyone is wet to the knee,
then they dry themselves and
hopping feet to rough stones
they race for the shelters.

She falls gracefully to spray.
From thigh to neck to wake
in a turn.

I wait,
watching from behind a shoreline birch,
and hope for her resurfacing.

**John Reinhard**

### Before the Snow

The honor of it all is insignificant.
You want what you want.

I know

that somewhere a good man's favorite daughter
is running away with an Indiana teamster
who will abuse her for her pleasure.

And that somewhere else a good woman's favorite son
is wide smiling and about to sin
with an unclean Episcopalian.

And that in some nearby highway rut
two maggots, Easter lily white,
dance and steal kisses on the groin of a dead cat.

I know these things.

So forgive me, if
when I see dark Martha sleeping
on outside straw before the snow,
her hair upon her
like the brown river boughs
of an autumn willow,
I ignore all the honor I can hold
and cautious to the frost
I take her mouth inside my own
to stay the cold.

**John Reinhard**


### Dark Martha Works in a Greasy Spoon

I have not told you that.

She works in a greasy spoon
right where they're trying to rebuild the town.
I walk her there.  The first morning.
At the bridge a duck is sticking to the river.

I walk as close as I dare to her.

"You are so mysterious," she tells me.

She is afraid of my shoulder, of my wrapping arm.
Choose me, I want to say to her.

She works for tips and the minimum wage.
Most of her customers come for eggs.
Some only come to drink water
for hours.  Never pay.

"Romance just isn't the way it's written," she says.

**John Reinhard**


### Oh, Could Cheryl Ferguson Dangle

Oh, could Cheryl Ferguson dangle:
In the Lincoln School playground in 1963
she was a vision hanging from the monkey bars
and making faces at me as I watched
while a perverse wind
played with her skirt;

to show my affection for her,
I threw small pebbles at her open mouth.
She swallowed one
and then she dribbled down her chin
with uncommon grace for 1963
and the fifth grade.

Most people,
who sew the past together with rough thread,
stick a needle into 1963
and run the thread through the fragments
of Kennedy and November,
wrapping the days in black sheets
and laying them perfumed into the ground.

But for me,
1963 is white-socked and red-cheeked
as Cheryl Ferguson dangles
in the Lincoln School playground,
sticking out her tongue like candy,
as a slick,
nasty wind
plays strange, wonderful games
with the pleats in her skirt.

**John Reinhard**

## Walking the River

*A little girl who belonged to somebody else,*
*A face thin and haunted appeared*
*Over my left shoulder, and whispered, Take care now,*
*Be patient, and live.*
— James Wright, from
"The Old WPA Swimming Pool in Martins Ferry, Ohio"

1.
I made love to you again last night
in the cricket shed, where the water
drops and levels off beside the half-eyed moon.

I am drunk this afternoon
on cheap white wine from the corner store
the Turks run.
I take my pleasure in not quite
avoiding mud along the path.
Beneath the mourning shrill of black
and piercing wing
my steps are slow, uncertain,
but continuing.
I am drunk and humming,
walking the river from the hill.

2.
Chemical suds on the Huron stir
like white water building in a hard crevice
of the sea.

The clear centers of the river swallow leaves.

An unbreakable, red-haired girl
has been tied-up by a wicked little boy
to a tall, straight tree.

And I see your brown eyes descending in the shoulder-high falls.

I could die almost happily
with your long, clean hair
tickling my thighs.

But I am more concerned these days with straight lines,

as I hear, above the crows,
our hopeful children
drowning in the shallows.

And on a beach of quiet fern the flies are sleeping . . .

Our spot is there.
I pass, humming Irving Berlin
like a tongueless, happy fool,

walking the river from the hill.

John Reinhard

## Boa

I do not wish to eat you,
    Chewing each morsel slowly,
But to swallow you whole, as a boa does her prey.
You will not lie quietly in my maw, awaiting
    Slow annihilation.

You will gather power —
Press back
Retaliate
    until belly slacks,
    fangs imbed, and
    jugular pulses red pins.

I'll bury you gently under fertile soil.

Saulte Declercq

134

### Touch-Clear — The Shaking Off
*(for my Lemonade Prince)*

Last winter,
    when even the day dove under her comforter and stayed
    till noon,
We met in the bar, after three, to drink secrets.
And I stayed touch-clear of you,
Remember that.

Before I ever knew you,
    I brushed you in rose colors, and wore you on my lips,
    in expectation.
And all my lovers had left me to you,
Thinking you'd want me when the time came.
I never told you that, you found it in your beer that afternoon.
Remember that.

You drink your secrets alone now,
    in New York
Making love to dark women from behind the wheel of a 56 Checker.
And sealing your whispers in brown envelopes — mailed late.
You left angry.
Remember that.

This winter,
    when only pale stars brave the cruel visit longer than
    the sun,
We'll meet in the bar, after three, to drink secrets.
And I'll stay touch-clear  Again.
Remember that.

### Touch-Clear — The Taking Hold
*(for Fleshtone)*

This summer,
    when vapours rising up from concrete walks gave way to brave
    night-air,
We met in the dark, after the bar, to drink wine.
And I drew sterling-sight of you,
And took hold of that.

I never dreamed you,
    in fanciful colors.
        I wear you in fleshtones warmer than any red; carry you in
        tunes hummed under breath — off key.
And my Lemonade Prince gives way to your touch,
Clears the path for your tracks.
I've never told you that, you found it in the wine last night.
Take hold of that.

I make myself poor of secrets
    with you, now,
Hugging like freshly laid tar to the soles of careful steppers
And loving the assurances of the flesh more than even the dreams — just a bit.
The die is quick.
Take hold of that.

Next summer,
      when June flies dazzle their time away in streetlights,
We'll meet in the dark, after the bar, to drink wine.
And we'll cast silver-visioned advents,
And take hold of them.

                                         **Saulte Declercq**

## Our Children

You all want children.

And I give them to you,
      though you'll never know it.

Away from you I cry round, soft babes
      who mirror my eyes,
      who wave my nose,
      who trace my lips,
And though there is nothing of you in them,
They are your children.

Sometimes I share them with you.
From two inches away
There is all of you in them.

And though you do not lay claim,
And I do not lay suit,
      They are your children —
      every one.

I rock them late in my room —
      night nursery,
And nestle them to my breast —
      warm stains,
And tell them stories,of the fathers
      who will never see them in my eyes.

Though your flesh babes will seem more real,
      and you will wear them as the first

I will carry and birth daughters over and over
      for you.

                                      **Saulte Declercq**

## Pocket Girl

In Daddy's wallet's a pixie girl,
      riding on Daddy's knees,
      dimpling around Daddy's neck,
      charming to Daddy, spoonfeeder.

There's a party girl,
        gliding on Daddy's arm,
        teasing miss under his watchful eye.

There's a prancing girl,
        on stage in leotard.

There is no poet,
        no scholar,
        no dreamer,
        no lover,
        no woman,
        no me.
    For,
Though he wears "his girl" in his pocket,
There is nothing of Me in her smile.

**Saulte Declercq**


## Moon-Child

*And I carry you like the crescent child that carries*
*its own full mother in its belly . . .*
        (Walt Whitman — "Song of Myself")

There is more of you in me everyday,

Though I keep it hidden
        in winter fashions,
        shielded from the wind.
Sky-hung now,
        that tender-something would be a tasty morsel
        for the winds.
Gobbled up in the dark like the last firefly of the night.

But it gains strength in me.
Give it time.

I am scratchy as a Hudson Bay blanket.
Repellent as a storm window against the wind.
For now.

But when that thing is full
        and strong
It will glow warmer than snow in January sun,
Guide me gently against the gusts of dark.
There'll be no need for sharp protection.

From behind this eclipse,
A crescent moon waits in me,
        Mother.
Give it time.

**Saulte Declercq**

## Selected Bibliography

Brooks, Cleanth, and Robert Penn Warren, *Understanding Poetry*. Fourth edition. New York: Rinehart and Winston, 1976.

Ciardi, John, *How Does a Poem Mean?* Boston: The Riverside Press, 1959.

Clayes, Stanley A., and John Gerrietts, *Ways to Poetry*. New York: Harcourt Brace Jovanovich, Inc., 1975.

Cotter, Janet M., *Invitation to Poetry*. Cambridge: Winthrop Publishers, Inc., 1971.

Dessner, Lawrence Jay, *How to Write a Poem*. New York: New York University Press, 1979.

Dickson, Frank A., and Sandra Smythe, eds., *Handbook of Short Story Writing*. Cincinnati: Writer's Digest, 1970.

Henderson, Stephen, *Understanding the New Black Poetry*. New York: William Morrow and Company, Inc., 1972.

Jerome, Judson, *The Poet and the Poem*. Cincinnati: Writer's Digest, 1974.

Kennedy, X. J., *An Introduction to Poetry*. Fourth edition. Boston: Little Brown and Company, 1978.

Mirrielees, Edith Ronald, *Story Writing*. Boston: The Writer, Inc., 1966.

Perkins, George, ed., *American Poetic Theory*. New York: Holt, Rinehart and Winston, Inc., 1972.

Raffel, Burton, *Introduction to Poetry*. New York: New American Library, 1971.

Stewart, Vincent, *Three Dimensions of Poetry*. New York: Charles Scribner's Sons, 1969.

Taylor, Henry, *Poetry — Points of Departure*. Cambridge: Winthrop Publishers, Inc., 1974.